IMAGES
of America

DUNMORE

I0806300

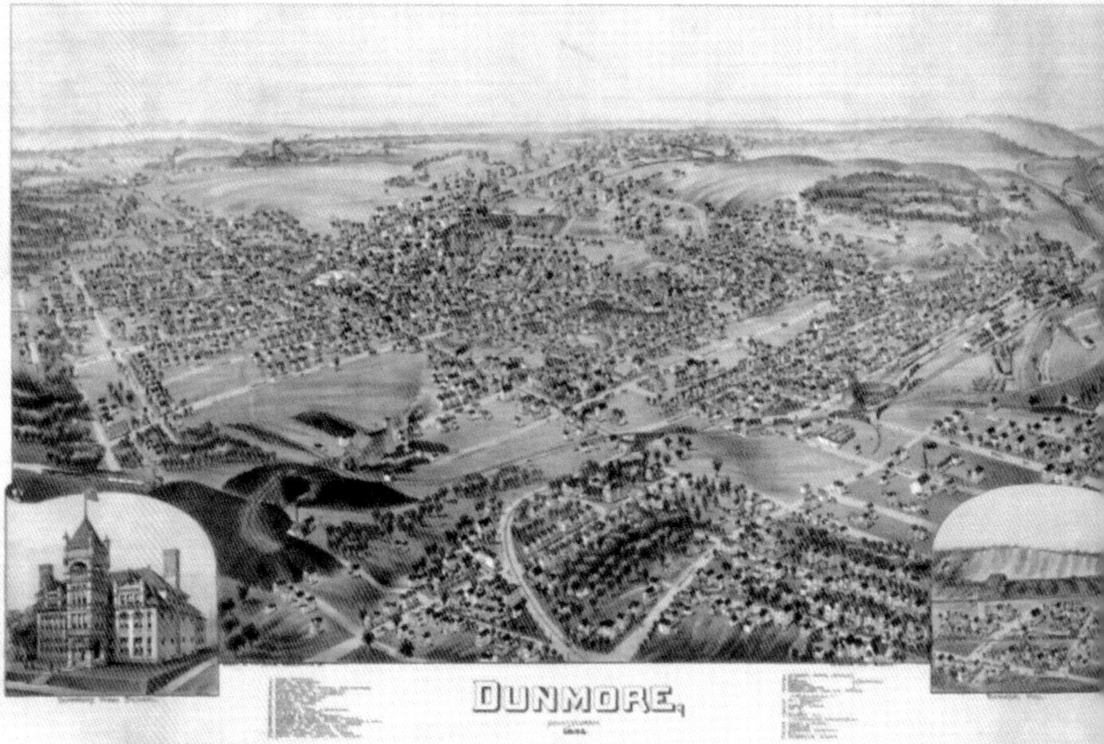

This 1894 map shows how rapidly Dunmore grew following its incorporation as a borough in 1862. Collieries, railroads, and mines belonging to the Pennsylvania Coal Company can be seen dotting the town's landscape as well as a heavy concentration of buildings in the Dunmore Corners district. In the inset can be seen Dunmore High School's "Central School," which opened in 1891 and was destroyed by a fire in 1908. The inset at right shows the Bunker Hill neighborhood. (Courtesy of the Dunmore Historical Society.)

ON THE COVER: Returning World War II veterans march down Dunmore's Drinker Street during the town's World War II victory parade in 1945. (Courtesy of Mary Riccardo)

IMAGES
of America

DUNMORE

Stephanie Longo

ARCADIA
PUBLISHING

ISBN 978-0-7385-9228-2

Published by Arcadia Publishing
Charleston, South Carolina

Printed in the United States of America

Library of Congress Control Number: 2011939537

For all general information, please contact Arcadia Publishing:
Telephone 843-853-2070
Fax 843-853-0044
E-mail sales@arcadiapublishing.com
For customer service and orders:
Toll-Free 1-888-313-2665

Visit us on the Internet at www.arcadiapublishing.com

This book is lovingly dedicated to my mother, Ann Marie Longo. Thank you for raising me with the courage to always follow my dreams and for always believing in me, even when I didn't believe in myself. I am proud to be your daughter.

Contents

Acknowledgments		6
Introduction		7
1.	The Birth of a Borough	9
2.	Bucktown	27
3.	School Pride	65
4.	The All-American Town	93
5.	100 Years and Beyond	107

Acknowledgments

This book was born thanks to what most journalists would call the "dreaded" municipal beat that, instead, for me turned into one of the most fulfilling beats of my career. For the past year, I have been the Dunmore municipal beat reporter for *Go Lackawanna*, and it is thanks to that beat that I was able to learn more about the town my family called home upon arriving from Italy in 1927. I would like to thank the staff of *Go Lackawanna* not only for introducing me to this beat but also for their help in acquiring photographs and publicizing this book in print as well as online and for allowing me to pursue my passion for writing every week by publishing my articles.

I would also like to thank the current and past members of the Dunmore Borough Council for their help with discovering the history of their town and for publicizing this book, which will coincide with the borough's 150th anniversary in 2012. I am most grateful to the Dunmore Historical Society, the Dunmore School District, the Diocese of Scranton, and the various churches and businesses in Dunmore for delving into their archives to find the "right" images for this book. To the Scranton Chapter of UNICO National, I say a heartfelt *grazie mille* for helping this book become a reality.

I am especially grateful to the Main Branch of Fidelity Deposit and Discount Bank in Dunmore, in particular the tellers, customer service representatives, and branch staff for sponsoring this book as the main drop-off point in Dunmore for pictures, many of which I never would have been able to include if it wasn't for their dedication to seeing this project succeed.

To my editor, Darcy Mahan, thank you for your patience and encouragement over the last few months. It has been a pleasure to work with you, and I am proud that both you and Arcadia Publishing decided to take on this project.

To everyone who donated photographs to this book, words cannot express how grateful I am that you took the time to dig through your albums to help me record the history of your town. I would also like to thank everyone who will read this book; I hope that it brings back cherished, happy memories for you of your hometown. It was my honor to be the person to record this history for you, and it is my sincere hope that you enjoy reading it as much as I enjoyed writing it.

Introduction

What is now known as the borough of Dunmore was originally inhabited by an offshoot of the Delaware tribe of the Iroquois called the Monsey whose chief was named Capoose. Capoose chose the area that now includes Dunmore Corners up to the Moosic Mountains as his hunting grounds. Then, in 1742, a missionary named Count Zinzendorf of Saxony arrived in America and began preaching to Capoose and his tribe, naming the area "Saint Anthony's Wilderness."

By 1754, the area that now comprises Dunmore was purchased from the Delaware tribe by the Susquehanna Company of Connecticut. Then, in 1770, the Lackawanna Valley was divided into two townships named Providence and Pittston. Dunmore was originally a part of Providence Township.

The year 1783 saw the birth of the Dunmore that we know today with the arrival of William Allsworth of Connecticut. Allsworth was a shoemaker by trade and one night decided to set up camp in present-day Dunmore while en route to the Wyoming Valley from Connecticut. Allsworth originally planned to settle in the Wyoming Valley but liked the location of Dunmore so much that he decided to bring his family to the area and settle there instead. His log cabin at present-day Dunmore Corners was the first building in what was to become the borough of Dunmore.

Allsworth eventually decided to open his home to guests who were traveling from Connecticut to the Wyoming Valley. By 1795, other settlers, including John West, Charles Dolph, and John Cary, built their own homes around Allsworth's Inn.

Because of the abundance of deer in the woods surrounding Allsworth's Inn, roast venison was a permanent fixture on his menu. Since the area around Allsworth's Inn did not have a name, travelers and settlers began to call the area "Bucktown," a name that is used to this day as a nickname for Dunmore.

In the early 1800s, when the first footpath from Blakely to Roaring Brook crossed the Wyoming Road (present-day Blakely Street) or Connecticut Road (present-day Drinker Street) at Allsworth's Inn, the area became known as the "Corners," marking the birth of today's Dunmore Corners business district, which is considered by many to be the heart of Dunmore.

Between 1799 and 1805, more settlers began to make their home in Bucktown, including Edward Lunnon, Isaac Dolph, Levi Depuy, and John Brown. Dr. Orlo Hamlin, for whom the village of Hamlin in Salem Township, Wayne County, is named, was the first physician to live in Bucktown, settling about a mile north of the Corners. He left after a year because there was not a large enough population in Bucktown to keep his business afloat and settled in Salem Township.

Bucktown continued to grow from a small outpost in the woods to a settled town thanks to the building of the Philadelphia and Great Bend Turnpike, also known as the Drinker Turnpike, between 1825 and 1826. During this time, Henry Drinker, the chief promoter of the turnpike, opened a store and tavern at the Corners.

Drinker is the person responsible for convincing the residents of Bucktown to change the name of their settlement to Dunmore. He had interested an English nobleman, Sir Charles

Augustus Murray, the son of the Earl of Dunmore, in his plan for developing the Lackawanna Valley, in particular the construction of a railroad over the Moosic Mountains to the Delaware River. Sir Charles Murray promised Drinker financial assistance. Drinker, wishing to express his gratitude to him, urged the residents of Bucktown to consider renaming their village "Dunmore" in his honor.

Whether or not Sir Charles Murray ever set foot in Dunmore is not known, but records do show that he visited Drinker at his family's home in present-day Clifton Township, Lackawanna County, on a hunting trip. Sir Charles Murray's promise of financial assistance to Drinker also never materialized as when he returned home to England he wrote Drinker saying that he was unable to raise the necessary funding. Present-day Drinker Street, which was once the Philadelphia and Great Bend Turnpike, was named in Henry Drinker's honor.

By 1862, Dunmore had grown so much that it was named a borough on April 10 of that year. Its area at the time of its incorporation as a borough was somewhat larger than present-day Dunmore, as a slice of territory was taken off when neighboring Roaring Brook Township was organized and then a small portion was annexed to the city of Scranton.

Until the 1880s, the area around Dunmore was still a largely wooded area. With the exception of a few streets around the Corners and the Bunker Hill neighborhood, most of the land comprising Dunmore was forested. The Hollywood section was covered in trees and underbrush, and chestnut trees abounded throughout the town. It was not until the development of the lands of the Pennsylvania Coal Company during that decade that Dunmore began to take shape. Dunmore's largest growth is credited to the Pennsylvania Coal Company, the Gravity Railroad, and the Erie Railroad.

In Thomas Murray's 1928 *History of Lackawanna County*, he claimed that one day Dunmore and the neighboring city of Scranton would be consolidated with Scranton swallowing up its suburb. As of 2012, this prophecy has not come true. Dunmore celebrated its centennial as a borough in 1962 and is poised to celebrate its 150th anniversary in 2012.

What was once a small wooded outpost has now come into its own as a town unique unto itself with its own history, culture, and traditions. This book aims not to be a complete history of the borough of Dunmore, as some images and details have, unfortunately, been lost due to the passage of time. Rather, this book aims to be a commemoration of Dunmore—remembering its past, embracing its present, and celebrating its future.

One

The Birth of a Borough

When Dunmore became a borough in 1862, it was largely thanks to the Pennsylvania Coal Company and its Gravity Railroad, which ran between Pittston and Hawley and passed through Dunmore. The first mayor, or burgess, was Calvin Spencer, and the first borough clerk was F.D. Brown. Edward Loughlin was named justice of the peace for Dunmore in 1865, and the first borough hall on Blakely Street was built in 1887.

While early Dunmore was much different than it is today, there were still many industries that helped it reach its borough status. For example, Stephen Tripp, for whom Tripp Street is named, built the first sawmill and gristmill in what was then known as Bucktown at what eventually became the No. 6 plane of the Pennsylvania Coal Company.

John B. Smith of the Pennsylvania Coal Company is largely credited with helping Dunmore receive its borough status, having served as the head of the company since its opening in 1845 until his death in 1895. Because of the Pennsylvania Coal Company, Dunmore needed a post office, which opened on December 17, 1849, with George Howell as postmaster.

During the 1880s, Dunmore also became home to the *Dunmore Pioneer*, which was its first newspaper and was launched by Frank P. Woodward. The newspaper's offices burned down on June 27, 1889, and Woodward did not rebuild. The *Dunmorean*, a weekly newspaper that still exists today, was opened in 1912 by the Barrett family.

Social life in Dunmore also grew rapidly after becoming a borough, with the borough's first uniformed baseball team, the Dunmore Greeleys, being formed in 1877 and Moosic Lake, once known as Cobb's Pond, being purchased by Timothy Burke, John M. Burke, and Frank Silliman Jr. in the early 1900s. At the time, the lake could be reached by a steam railroad that connected with the Scranton Railway Company's trolley road at its East Drinker Street terminal in Dunmore.

This chapter contains a sampling of the earliest images from Dunmore's past, focusing on the Pennsylvania Coal Company and the Gravity and Erie Railroads as well as showing the various settlers, industries, and businesses that helped shape Dunmore into what it is today.

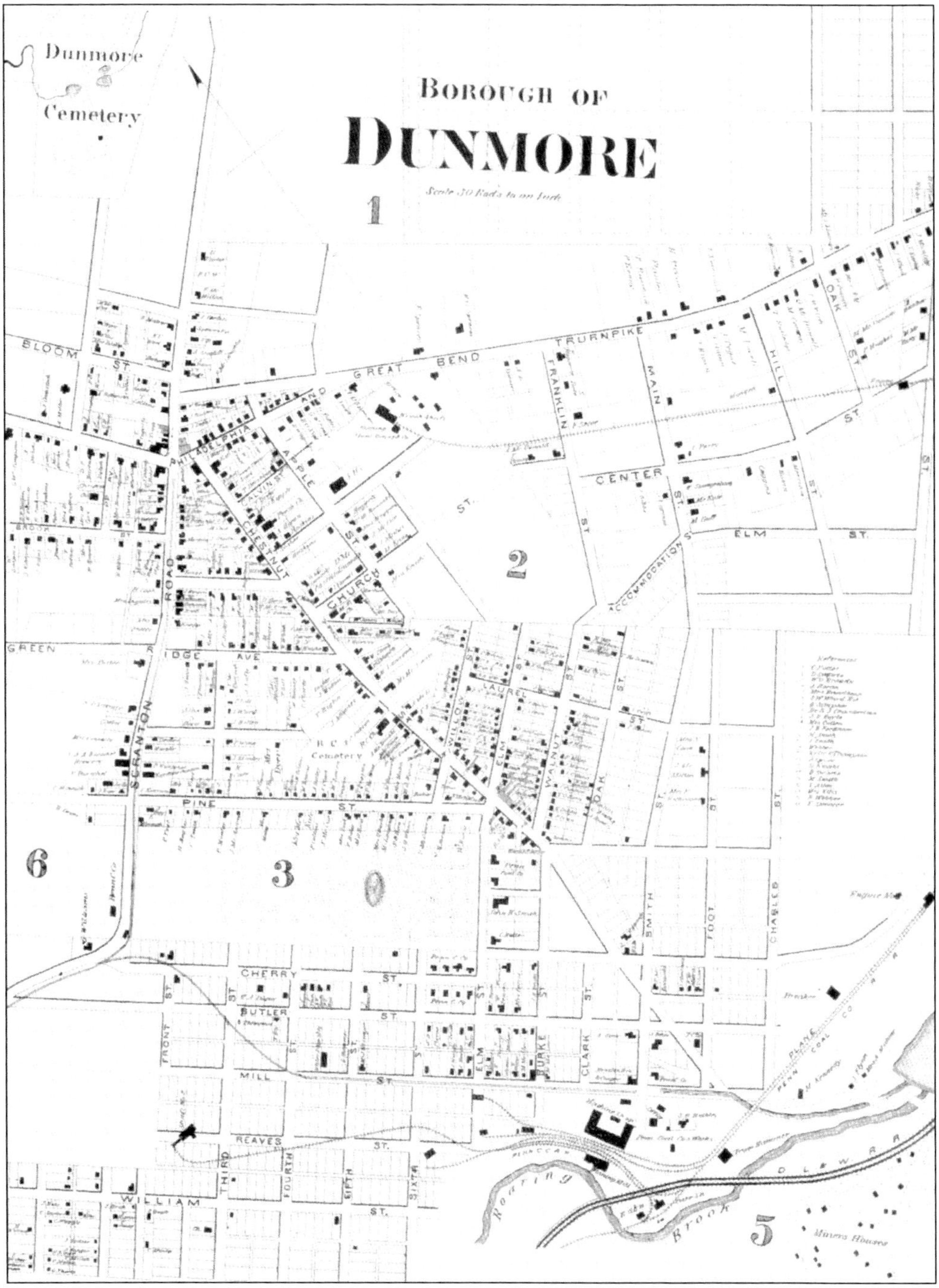

Printed before Blakely Street and Drinker Street received their names, this 1873 map of Dunmore shows the town 11 years after its incorporation as a borough. This map shows Blakely Street as Scranton Road. Drinker Street was the Philadelphia and Great Bend Turnpike at the time. Other notable street changes are Brook Street (present-day Delaware Street) and Bloom Street (present-day Electric Street). (Courtesy of Joe and Dolly Michalczyk.)

Dunmore boasts a large Irish population, so much so that the borough became the sister city of Dunmore, County Galway, Ireland. Many residents believe that the town received its name from its Irish counterpart, but it is generally agreed that Dunmore received its name from Charles Augustus Murray, Fifth Earl of Dunmore, Viscount Fincastle, and Baron of Blair, who, along with Henry Drinker (from whom Drinker Street received its name), was interested in developing land in Northeastern Pennsylvania in the late 1700s. (Courtesy of Dunmore Borough.)

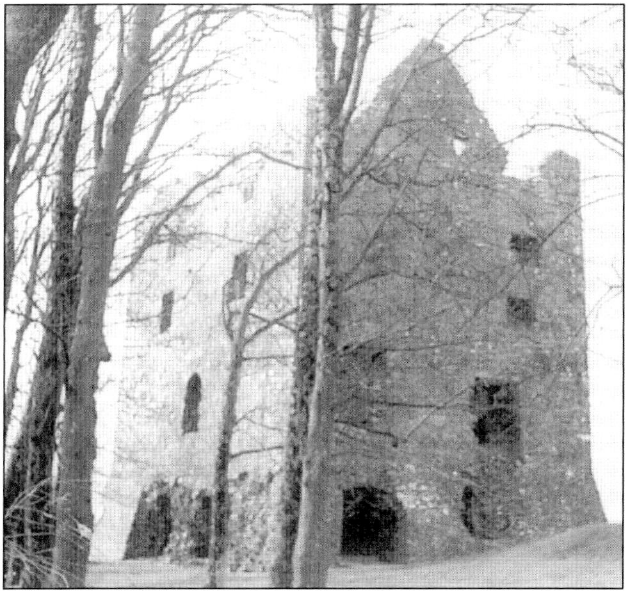

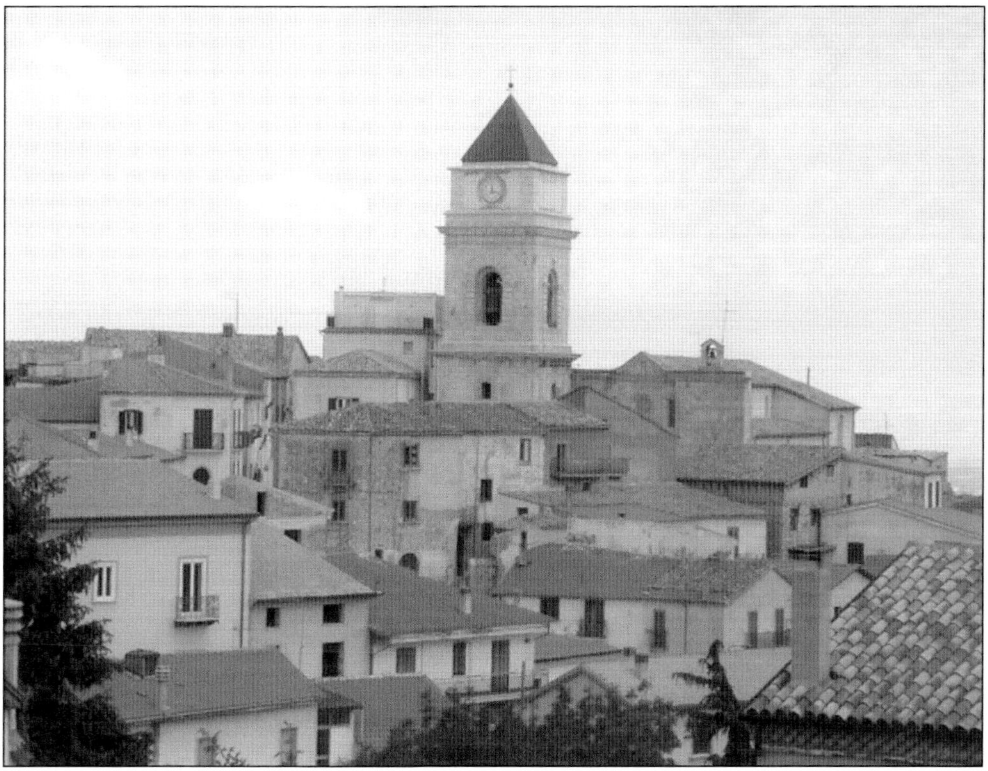

According to census records, Dunmore's predominant ethnicity is Italian. Pictured is the town of Guardia dei Lombardi, located in the province of Avellino in the Campania region of Italy, from where many residents of Dunmore's Bunker Hill neighborhood claim their ancestry. Other notable Italian towns represented by the population of Dunmore include Calitri, also located in the province of Avellino in the Campania region of Italy; San Cataldo, located in the province of Caltanissetta in Sicily; and various towns in the regions of Calabria and Abruzzo. (Author.)

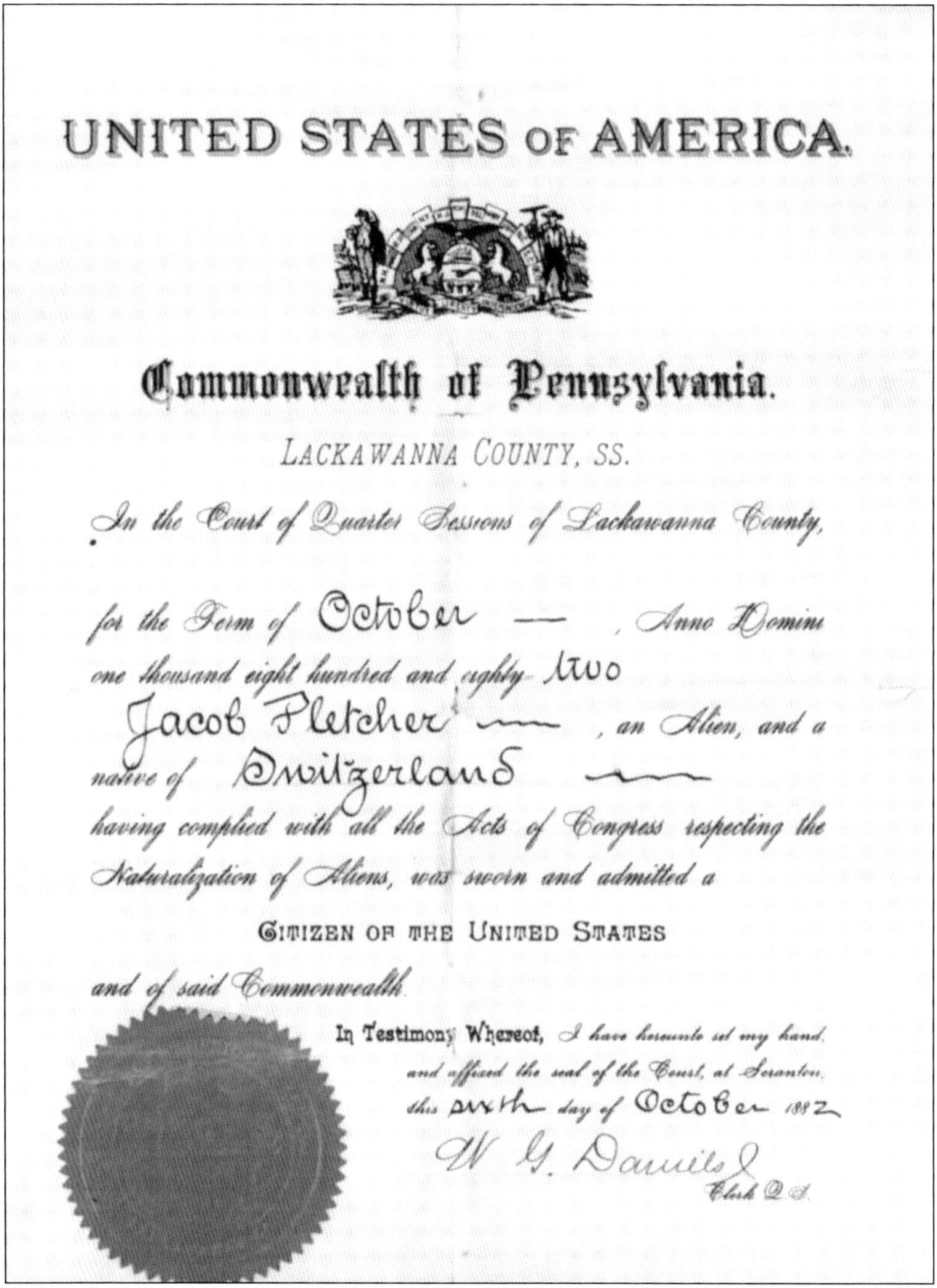

UNITED STATES OF AMERICA.

Commonwealth of Pennsylvania.

LACKAWANNA COUNTY, SS.

In the Court of Quarter Sessions of Lackawanna County,

for the Term of October —, Anno Domini one thousand eight hundred and eighty-two Jacob Pletcher —, an Alien, and a native of Switzerland — having complied with all the Acts of Congress respecting the Naturalization of Aliens, was sworn and admitted a

CITIZEN OF THE UNITED STATES

and of said Commonwealth.

In Testimony Whereof, I have hereunto set my hand, and affixed the seal of the Court, at Scranton, this sixth day of October 1882

W. G. Daniels

Clerk Q. S.

Despite its large Italian and Irish populations, residents of Dunmore can claim ancestry from many countries. This is the 1882 declaration of citizenship for Jacob Pletcher, who settled in Dunmore after arriving from Switzerland. Pletcher was a fireman at the stationary engine on the No. 11 plane of the Pennsylvania Gravity Railroad in Dunmore and served as a patrolman on the Dunmore police force during the 1890s. (Courtesy of the Dunmore Historical Society.)

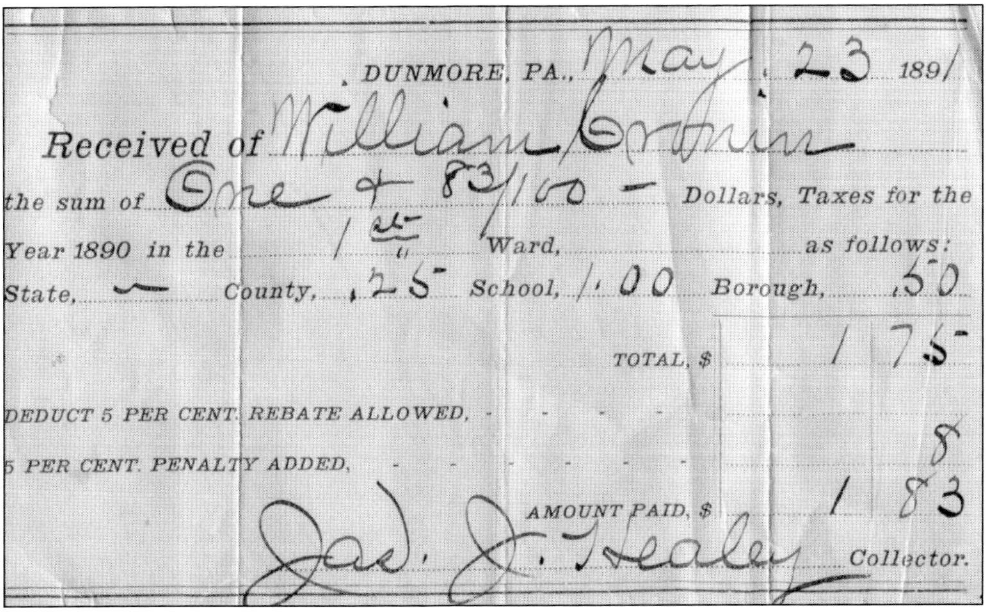
DUNMORE, PA., May 23 1891

Received of William Cronin

the sum of One + 83/100 — Dollars, Taxes for the

Year 1890 in the 1st Ward, as follows:

State, — County, .25 School, 1.00 Borough, .50

TOTAL, $ 1 75

DEDUCT 5 PER CENT. REBATE ALLOWED,

5 PER CENT. PENALTY ADDED, 8

AMOUNT PAID, $ 1 83

Jas. J. Healey Collector.

This tax receipt, dated May 23, 1891, shows that William Cronin, a resident of Dunmore's First Ward, paid $1.83 in taxes to the borough for 1890. At the time, the First Ward of Dunmore was mainly located in the area of Dunmore Cemetery. (Courtesy of Sam Valenza.)

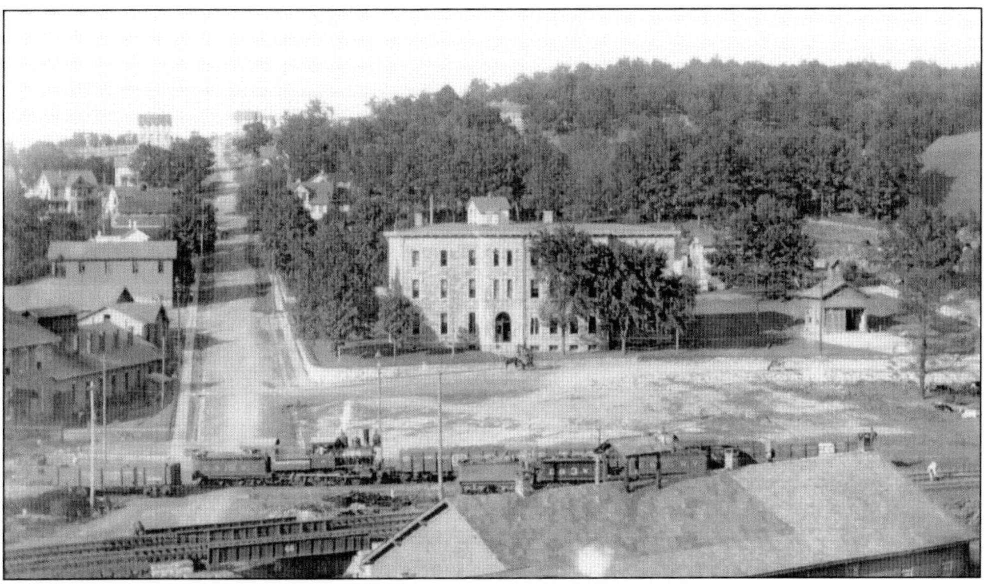

The Pennsylvania Coal Company was partly responsible for Dunmore's growth from a small outpost en route to Philadelphia and New York. This photograph of the Pennsylvania Coal Company offices was taken in the early 1900s and shows its expansion around the area of Smith and Mill Streets as more and more coal began to be mined in Dunmore. (Courtesy of the Dunmore Historical Society.)

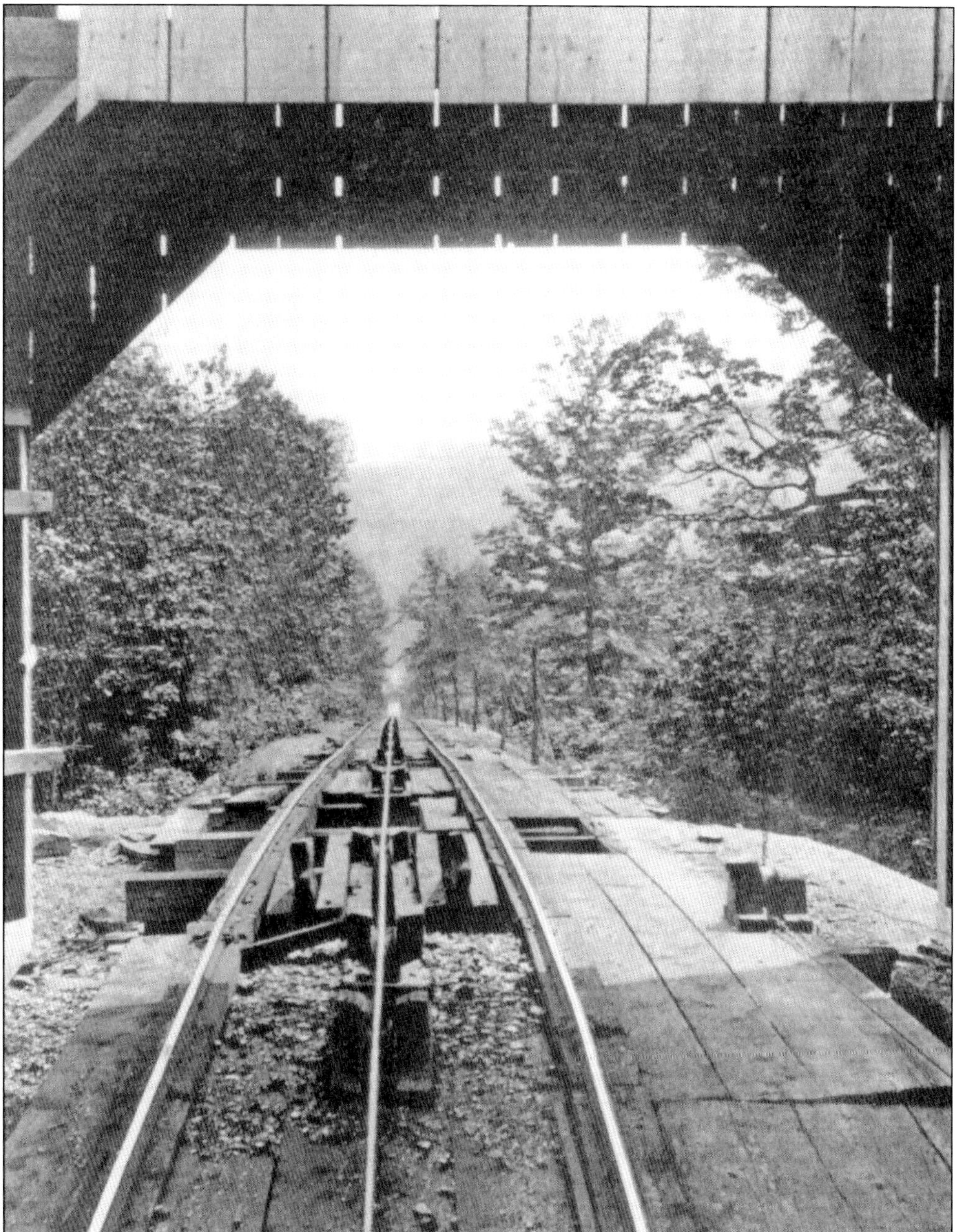

This is a view down the No. 10 plane of the Pennsylvania Coal Company's Gravity Railroad, which ran along the Moosic Mountains in the vicinity of the present-day Best Western Scranton East Hotel and Convention Center (formerly the Holiday Inn of Dunmore). The Pennsylvania Coal Company opened the Gravity Railroad between Pittston and Hawley, entering Dunmore at the No. 6 plane, in 1849 with the first train being run on June 10, 1850. (Courtesy of the Dunmore Historical Society.)

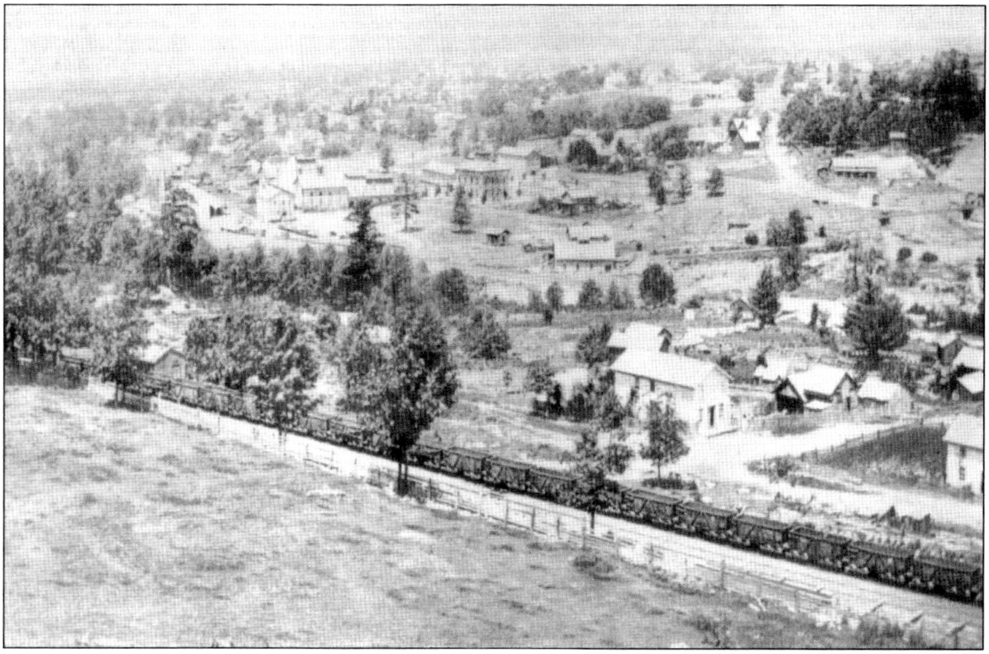

Seen here is a panoramic view of the No. 6 plane of the Pennsylvania Coal Company. The No. 6 plane was partially located in the Bunker Hill neighborhood of Dunmore. The first coal mined in Dunmore was from the drifts at the outcrop of the three Dunmore veins on the hill east of the former Pennsylvania Coal Company offices in 1850 and was loaded on Gravity railroad cars from a trestle about 300 feet from the foot of the No. 6 plane. (Courtesy of the Dunmore Historical Society.)

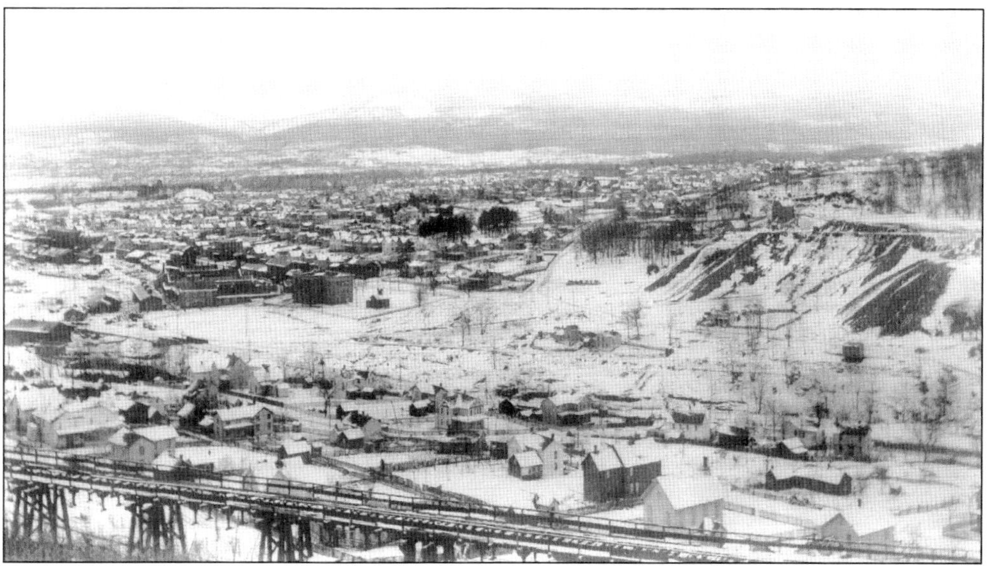

This is a view of the Pennsylvania Coal Company's mines from Dunmore's Elmhurst Boulevard. The Spencer Shaft, sunk in 1855, was the oldest of the Pennsylvania Coal Company mines. Other notable mines were the Gypsy Grove Shaft, which was sunk in 1857; the No. 5 shaft, which was sunk in 1882; and the No. 1 shaft, which was sunk in 1885. The breaker at the mines was completed in 1888. (Courtesy of Karl Wegforth.)

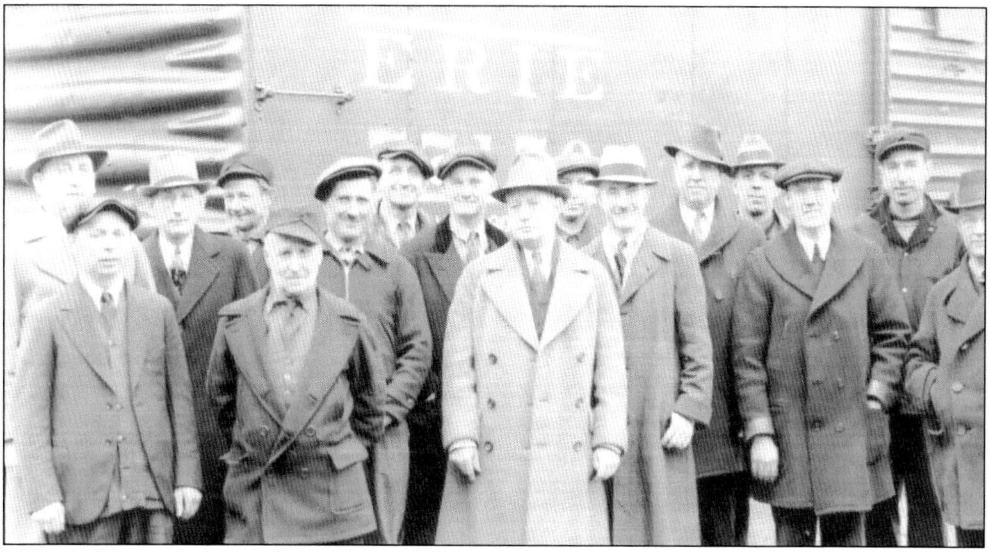

The Gravity Railroad was absorbed by the Erie & Wyoming Valley Railroad Company in 1884, which was the same year that the Erie Shops were built along Mill Street. Besides transporting large quantities of coal, the Erie ran several passenger trains daily, reaching Wilkes-Barre, Scranton, Pittston, Hawley, and Honesdale. It also made connections for New York and Philadelphia with other railroads and helped to develop Lake Ariel in Wayne County as a popular summer recreation spot in Northeastern Pennsylvania. (Courtesy of Karl Wegforth.)

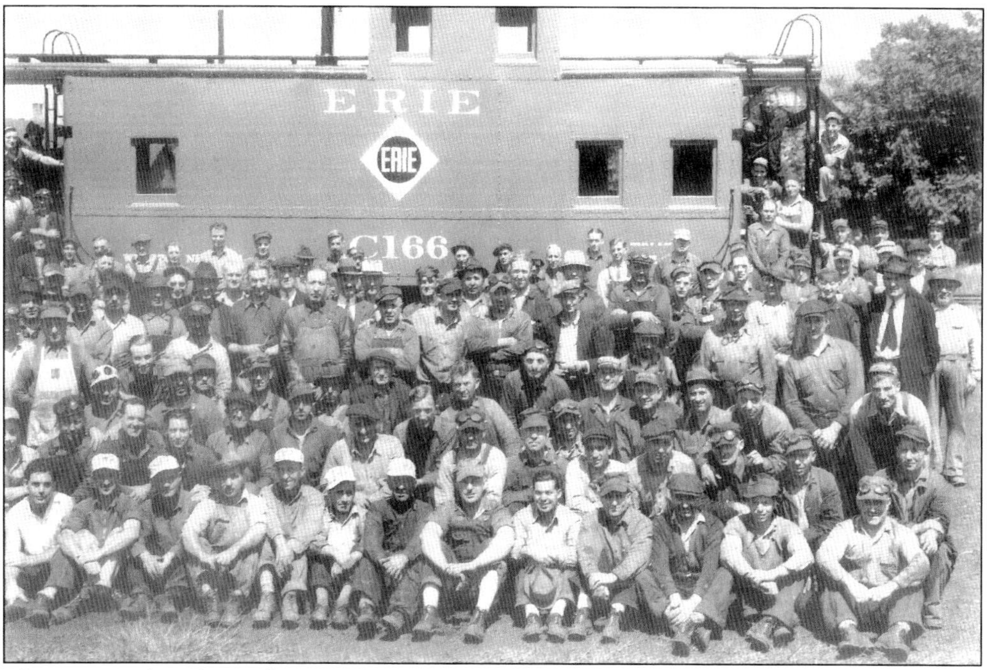

The main yards and roundhouses of the Erie & Wyoming Valley Railroad Company were located in Dunmore. The company was a threat to the dominance of larger anthracite carrying roads until it was acquired by the Erie Company in 1901, which was the same year that the Erie Shops, seen here, were opened in Dunmore. Most cars for the Erie Company were built at the Erie Shops in Dunmore. (Courtesy of Karl Wegforth.)

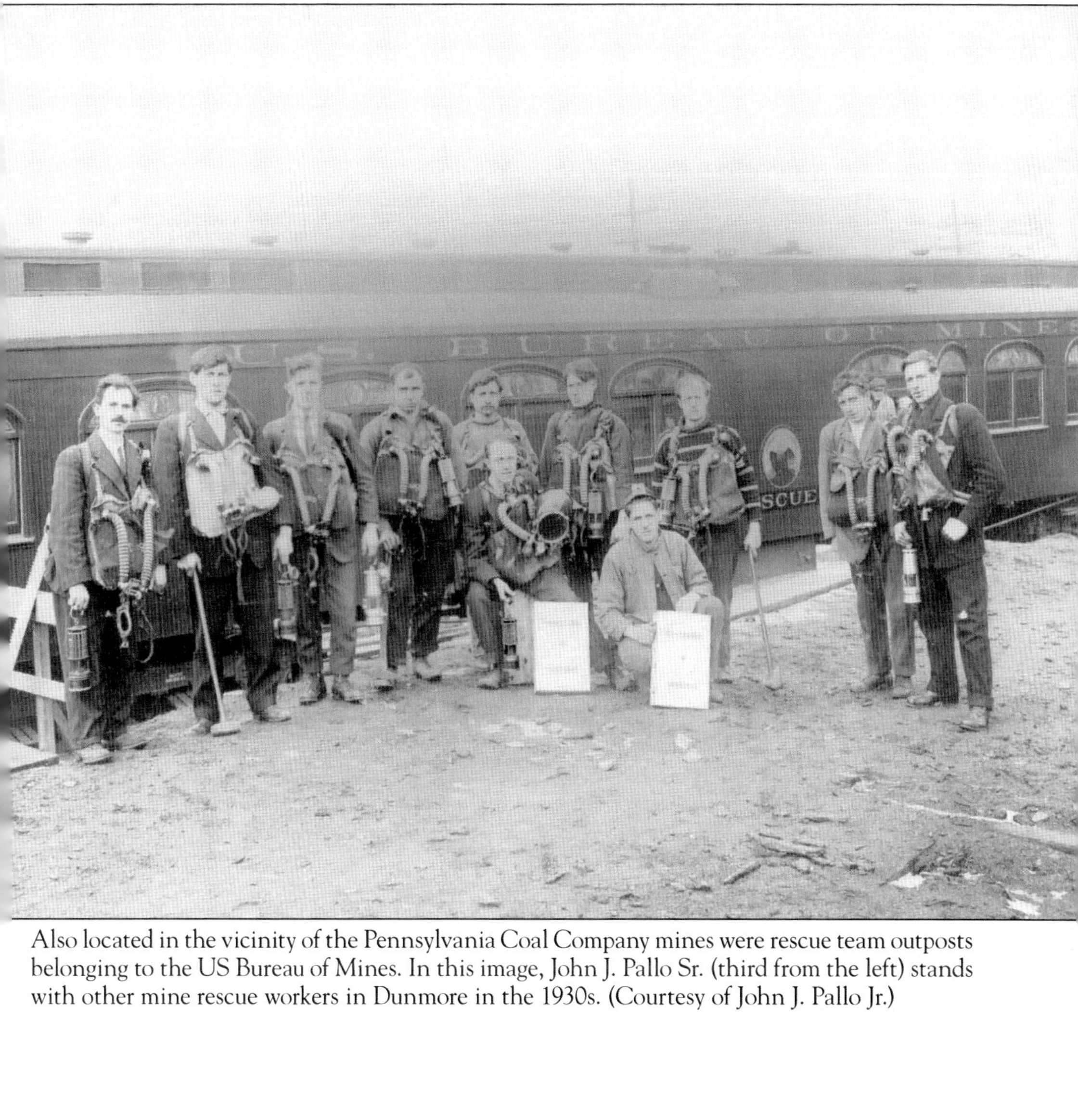

Also located in the vicinity of the Pennsylvania Coal Company mines were rescue team outposts belonging to the US Bureau of Mines. In this image, John J. Pallo Sr. (third from the left) stands with other mine rescue workers in Dunmore in the 1930s. (Courtesy of John J. Pallo Jr.)

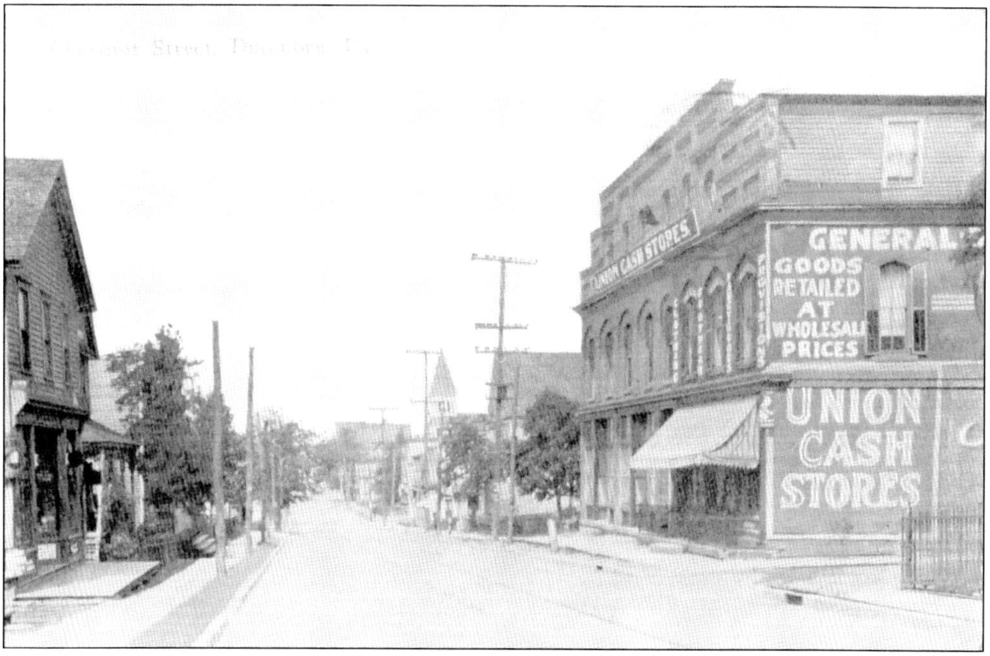

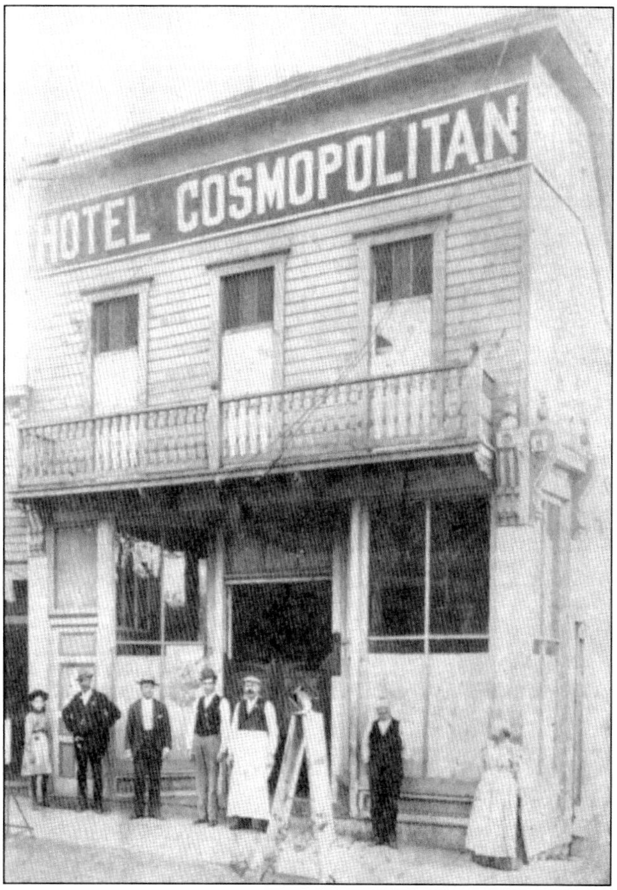

At the turn of the century, Chestnut Street was already one of Dunmore's main streets. In this photograph, old trolley tracks can be seen on the street and St. Mary of Mount Carmel Church is visible in the distance. (Courtesy of Dunmore Borough.)

The Hotel Cosmopolitan was owned by Paddy Ragan, one of Dunmore's best-known hotel keepers in the early 1900s, and was located at Dunmore Corners at the intersection of Drinker and Blakely Streets. Dunmore Corners was where the town's original hotels were located, including Allsworth's Inn, which, in the late 1700s and early 1800s, was where many travelers passing through Dunmore stayed the night. At that time, Dunmore was known as "Bucktown" because of the many deer that were seen in the area. (Courtesy of the Dunmore Historical Society.)

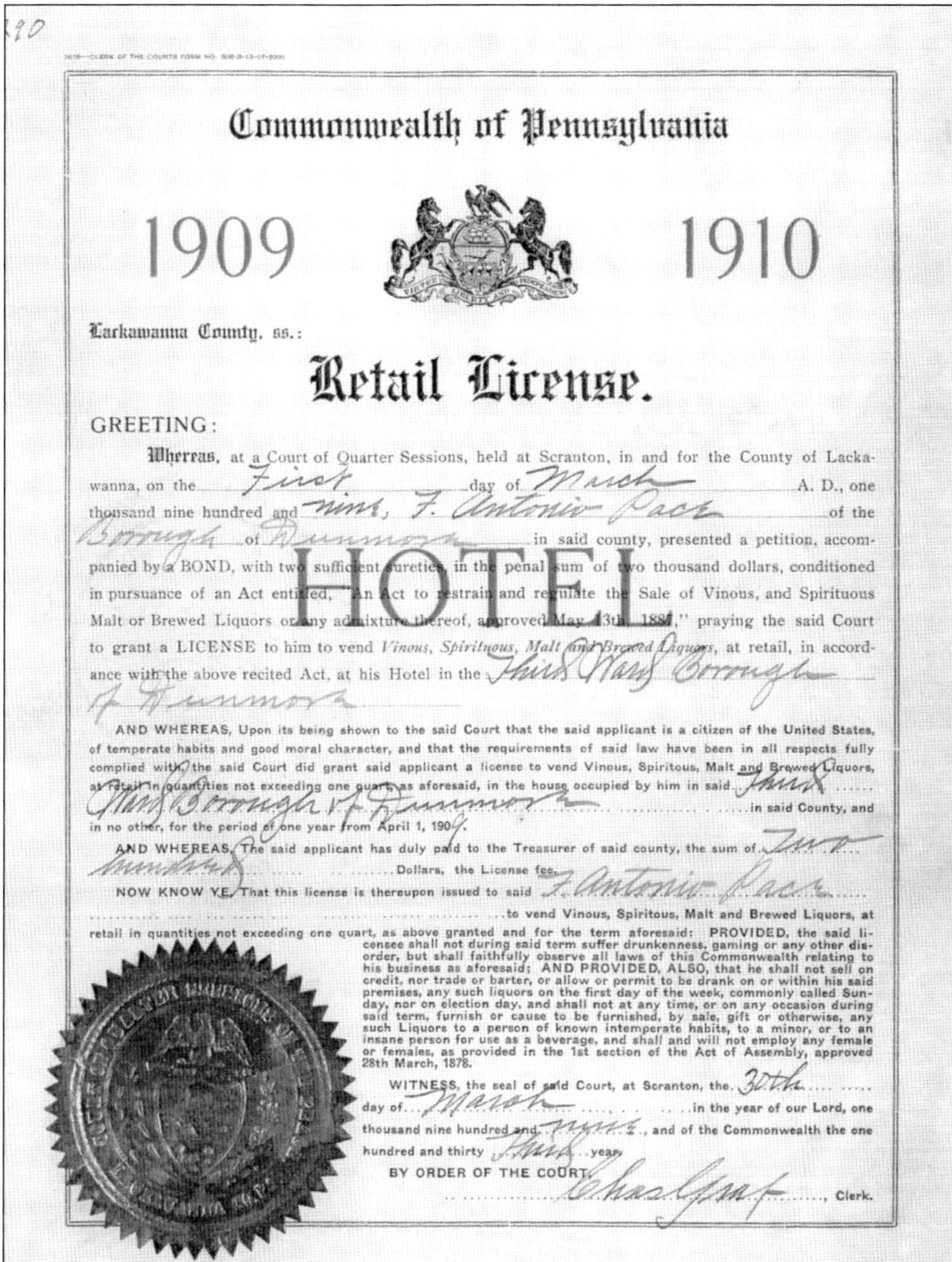

Commonwealth of Pennsylvania

1909 1910

Lackawanna County, ss.:

Retail License.

GREETING:

Whereas, at a Court of Quarter Sessions, held at Scranton, in and for the County of Lackawanna, on the First day of March A. D., one thousand nine hundred and nine, F. Antonio Pace of the Borough of Dunmore in said county, presented a petition, accompanied by a BOND, with two sufficient sureties, in the penal sum of two thousand dollars, conditioned in pursuance of an Act entitled, "An Act to restrain and regulate the Sale of Vinous, and Spirituous Malt or Brewed Liquors or any admixture thereof, approved May 13th, 1887," praying the said Court to grant a LICENSE to him to vend *Vinous, Spirituous, Malt and Brewed Liquors*, at retail, in accordance with the above recited Act, at his Hotel in the Third Ward Borough of Dunmore

HOTEL

AND WHEREAS, Upon its being shown to the said Court that the said applicant is a citizen of the United States, of temperate habits and good moral character, and that the requirements of said law have been in all respects fully complied with, the said Court did grant said applicant a license to vend Vinous, Spiritous, Malt and Brewed Liquors, at retail in quantities not exceeding one quart, as aforesaid, in the house occupied by him in said Third Ward Borough of Dunmore in said County, and in no other, for the period of one year from April 1, 1909.

AND WHEREAS, The said applicant has duly paid to the Treasurer of said county, the sum of Two hundred Dollars, the License fee.

NOW KNOW YE, That this license is thereupon issued to said F. Antonio Pace to vend Vinous, Spiritous, Malt and Brewed Liquors, at retail in quantities not exceeding one quart, as above granted and for the term aforesaid: PROVIDED, the said licensee shall not during said term suffer drunkenness, gaming or any other disorder, but shall faithfully observe all laws of this Commonwealth relating to his business as aforesaid; AND PROVIDED, ALSO, that he shall not sell on credit, nor trade or barter, or allow or permit to be drank on or within his said premises, any such liquors on the first day of the week, commonly called Sunday, nor on election day, and shall not at any time, or on any occasion during said term, furnish or cause to be furnished, by sale, gift or otherwise, any such Liquors to a person of known intemperate habits, to a minor, or to an insane person for use as a beverage, and shall and will not employ any female or females, as provided in the 1st section of the Act of Assembly, approved 28th March, 1878.

WITNESS, the seal of said Court, at Scranton, the 30th day of March in the year of our Lord, one thousand nine hundred and nine, and of the Commonwealth the one hundred and thirty third year.

BY ORDER OF THE COURT,

Chas Graf, Clerk.

Another popular Dunmore hotel during the early 1900s was owned by Antonio Pace. Seen here is his 1909–1910 retail license, which allowed him to serve alcohol in the bar that was located on the ground floor of the hotel. (Courtesy of the Dunmore Historical Society.)

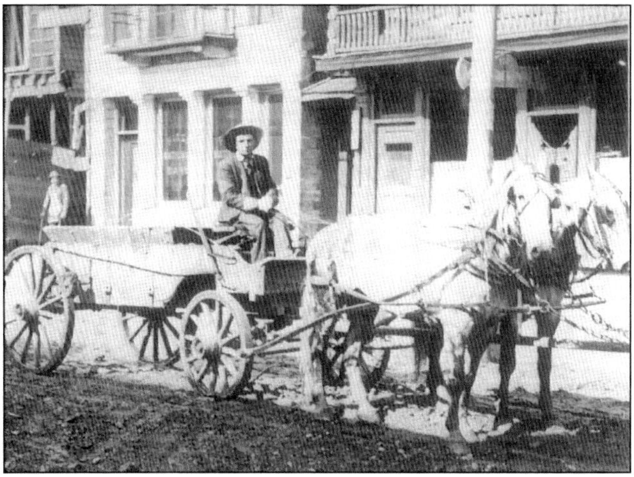

The Dunmore Corners business district was bustling even in the early 1900s, as seen in this photograph from 1908 where a resident posed on Drinker Street outside the Metropole Hotel. Present-day Bone Court can be seen in the background. (Courtesy of Dunmore Borough.)

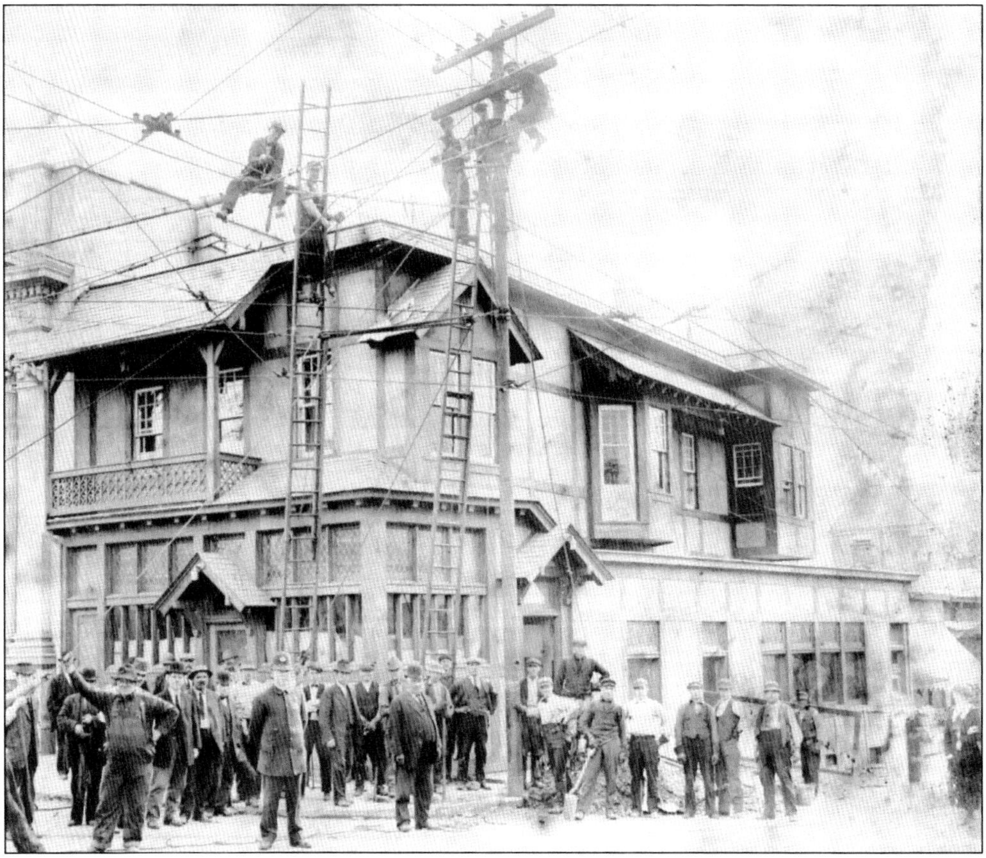

Michael J. Mangan, seen in the upper left-hand corner of this photograph sitting on top of the wires, was a linesman for the American Bell Telephone Company, later American Telephone and Telegraph (AT&T). In this 1913 photograph, the Hotel Gortellita can be seen in the background with Bell workers standing outside of it. By 1913, Paddy Ragan had remodeled the Hotel Cosmopolitan and renamed it the Hotel Gortellita. The First National Community Bank of Dunmore now occupies the site of the hotel; the building was destroyed when the bank expanded. (Courtesy of Catherine G. Quinnan.)

Members of the First Christian Church of Dunmore pose on the steps of their original church in this c. 1910 photograph. The First Christian Church of Dunmore was built in 1858 and eventually became known as the Tripp Avenue Christian Church until it was decommissioned in 2008. (Courtesy of the Dunmore Historical Society.)

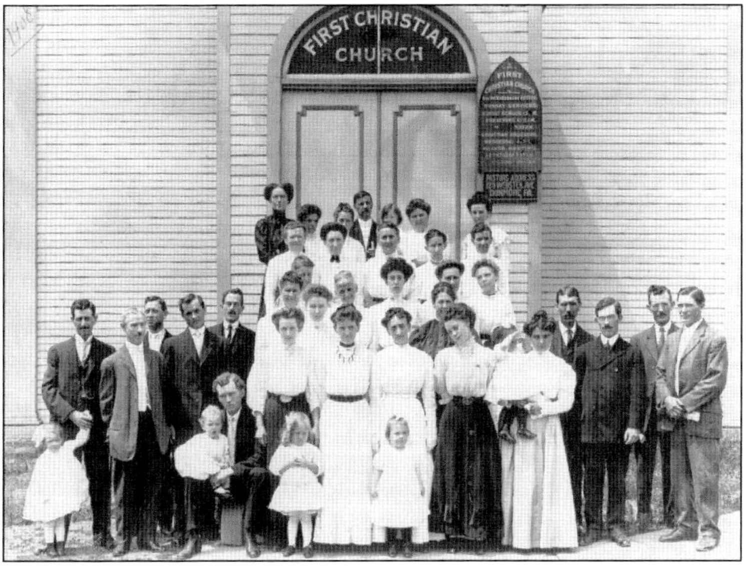

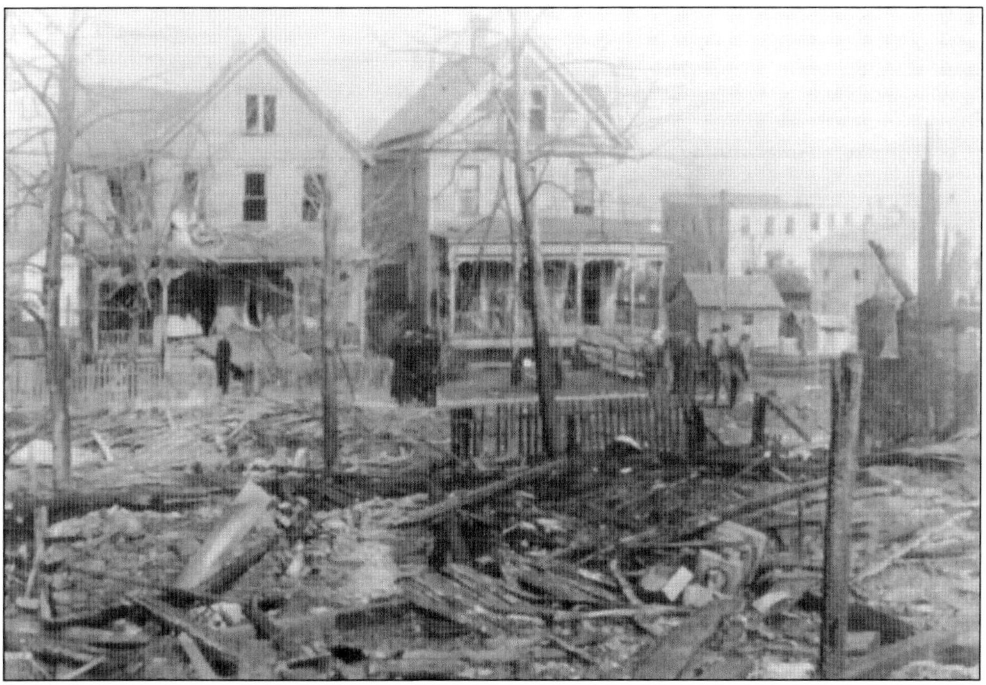

In what was called "Dunmore's Worst Tragedy," an explosion destroyed a home at 242 Elm Street on the morning of March 12, 1912. The rubble from the explosion can be seen in this photograph. The blast shattered many windows in the area and caused the three-story home to burn to the ground. Nine people were killed. The explosion was attributed to a gas leak with the gas following a water pipe into the home. (Author.)

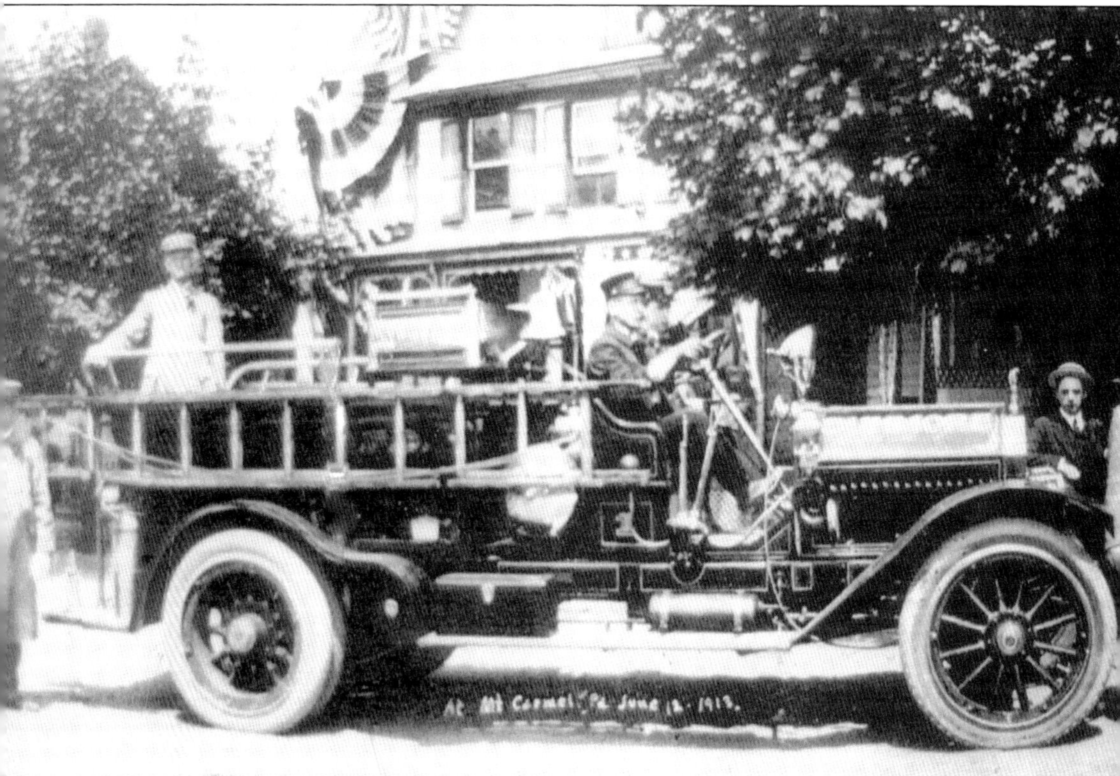

In this June 12, 1913, photograph, the Neptune Fire Company, which was located on Blakely Street, traveled to Mount Carmel, Pennsylvania, to participate in a parade. The Neptune Chemical Company was organized on October 1, 1887, and changed its name to the Neptune Fire Company in the early 1890s. The Neptune Fire Company was the first fire department to be recognized by Dunmore Borough. (Courtesy of Dunmore Borough.)

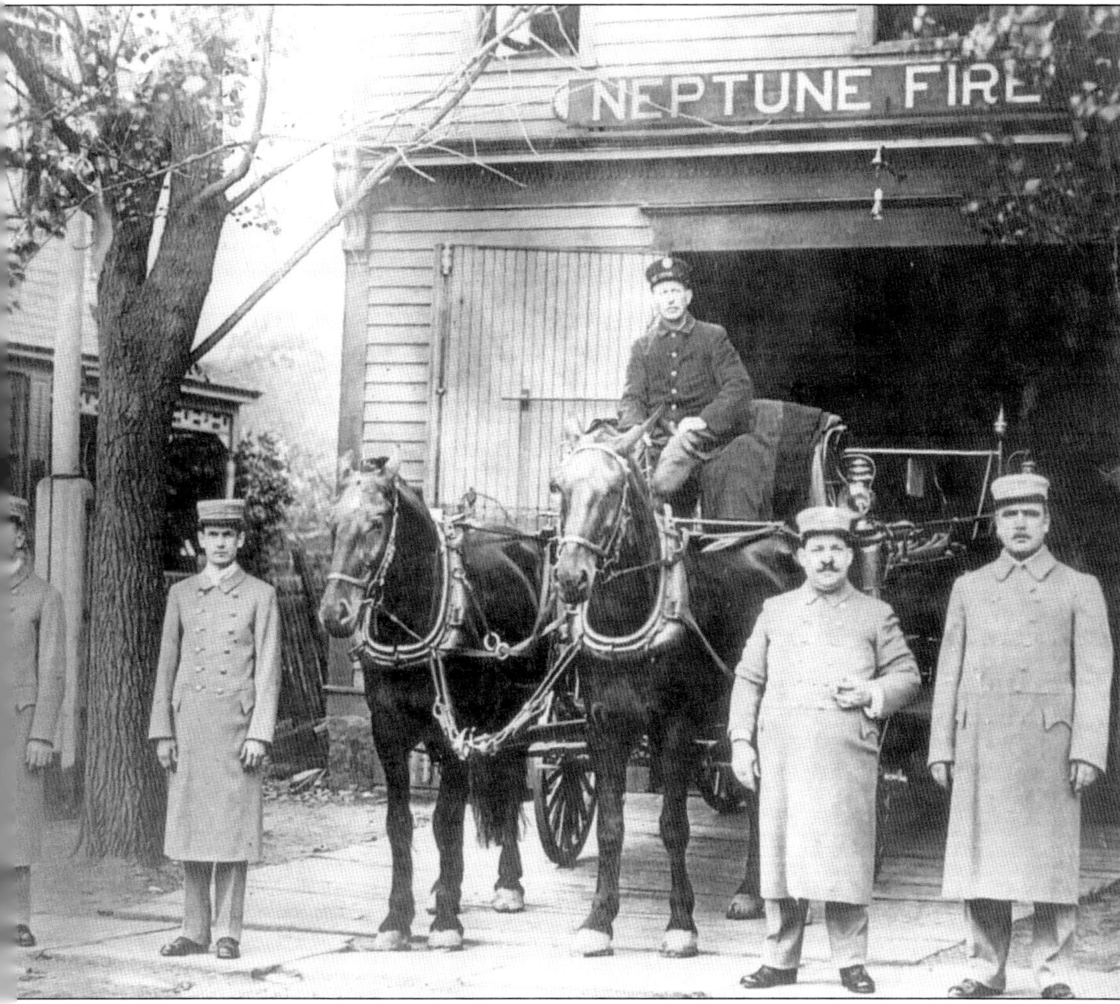

This image shows members of the Neptune Fire Company outside of their headquarters on Blakely Street at the turn of the century. Other fire departments that were located in Dunmore include the Columbia Hose Company, which was Dunmore's first fire department after relying solely on bucket brigades; the Electric Engine Company No. 4; the John B. Smith Hose Company' the O.S. Johnson Hose Company; and the Eclipse Hose Company. (Courtesy of the Dunmore Historical Society.)

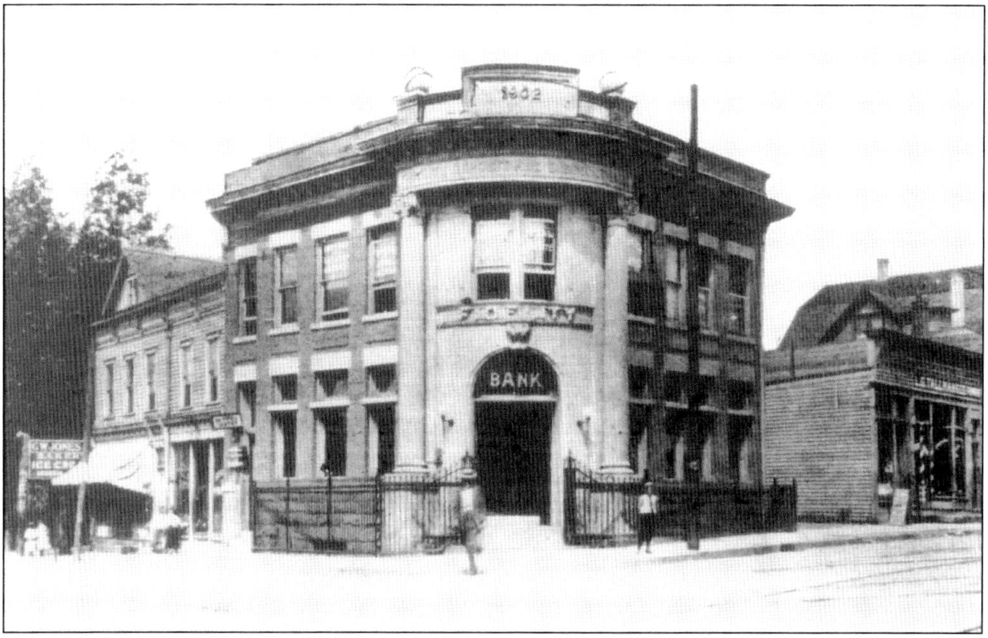

The Fidelity Deposit and Discount Bank has been located at Dunmore Corners at Drinker and Blakely Streets since 1903. Before its opening on May 11, 1903, Dunmore residents used the banks in the nearby city of Scranton for their banking needs. The first president of Fidelity Deposit and Discount Bank was Patrick J. Horan. (Courtesy of Fidelity Deposit and Discount Bank.)

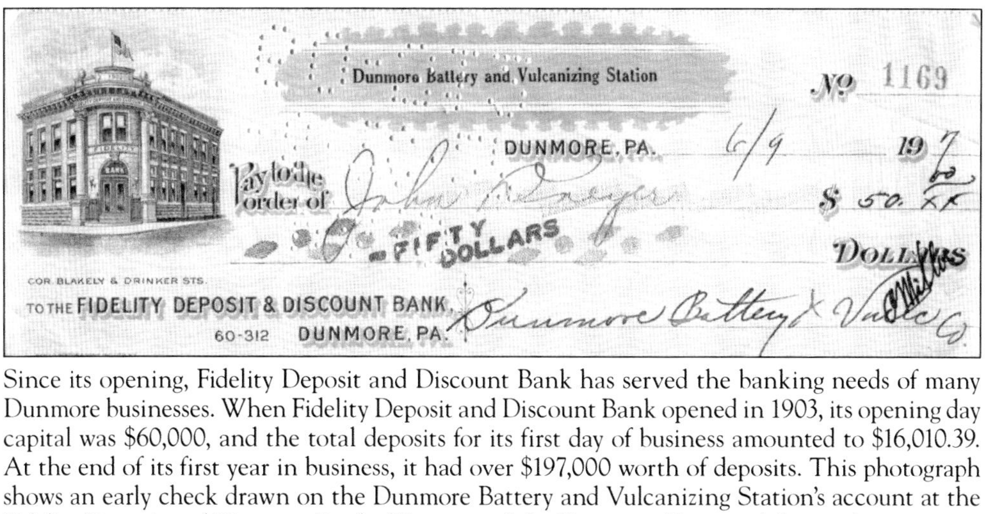

Since its opening, Fidelity Deposit and Discount Bank has served the banking needs of many Dunmore businesses. When Fidelity Deposit and Discount Bank opened in 1903, its opening day capital was $60,000, and the total deposits for its first day of business amounted to $16,010.39. At the end of its first year in business, it had over $197,000 worth of deposits. This photograph shows an early check drawn on the Dunmore Battery and Vulcanizing Station's account at the Fidelity Deposit and Discount Bank. (Courtesy of the Dunmore Historical Society.)

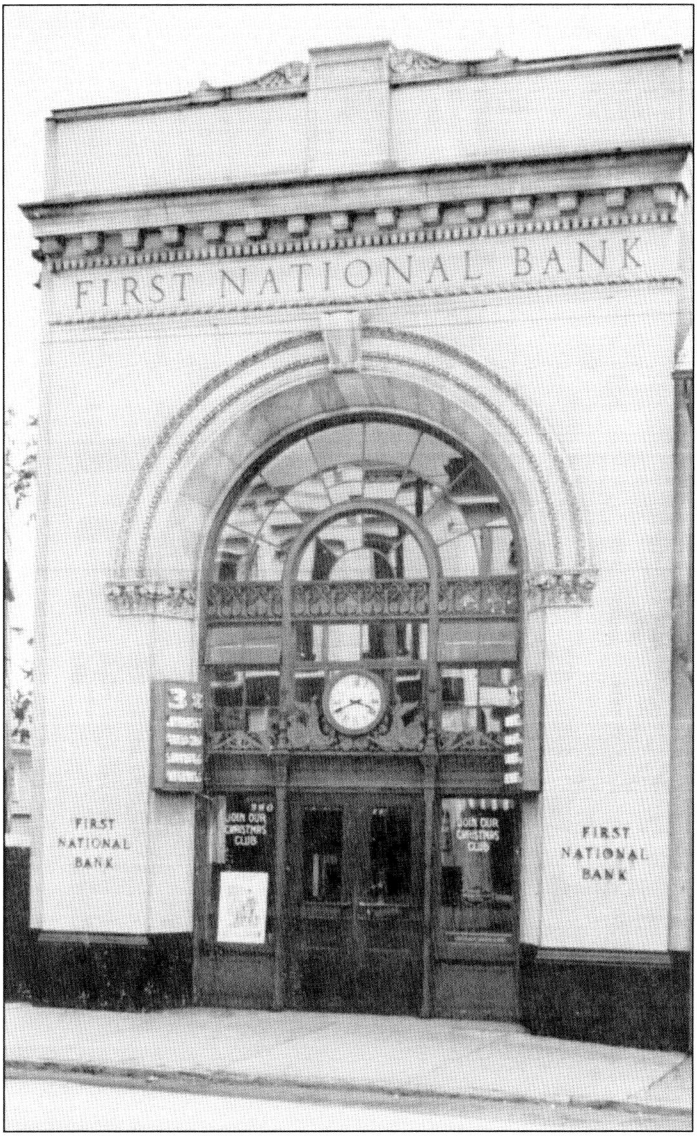

The First National Bank of Dunmore (today known as First National Community Bank or FNCB) was opened across the street from the Fidelity Deposit and Discount Bank at Dunmore Corners on November 1, 1910. The first president of the First National Bank was M.J. Murray. (Courtesy of the First National Community Bank, Dunmore.)

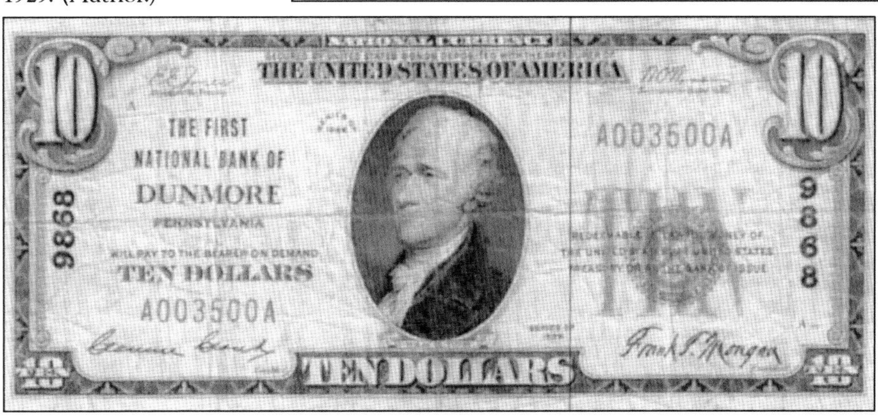

Between 1863 and 1929, the US government allowed banks to issue their own currency, called National Bank Notes. The National Bank Notes looked exactly like traditional American currency, except they were printed by smaller banks and circulated at the same time as Federal Reserve Bank Notes, which is the currency still in use today. Pictured is a National Bank Note from the First National Bank of Dunmore, printed in 1929. (Author.)

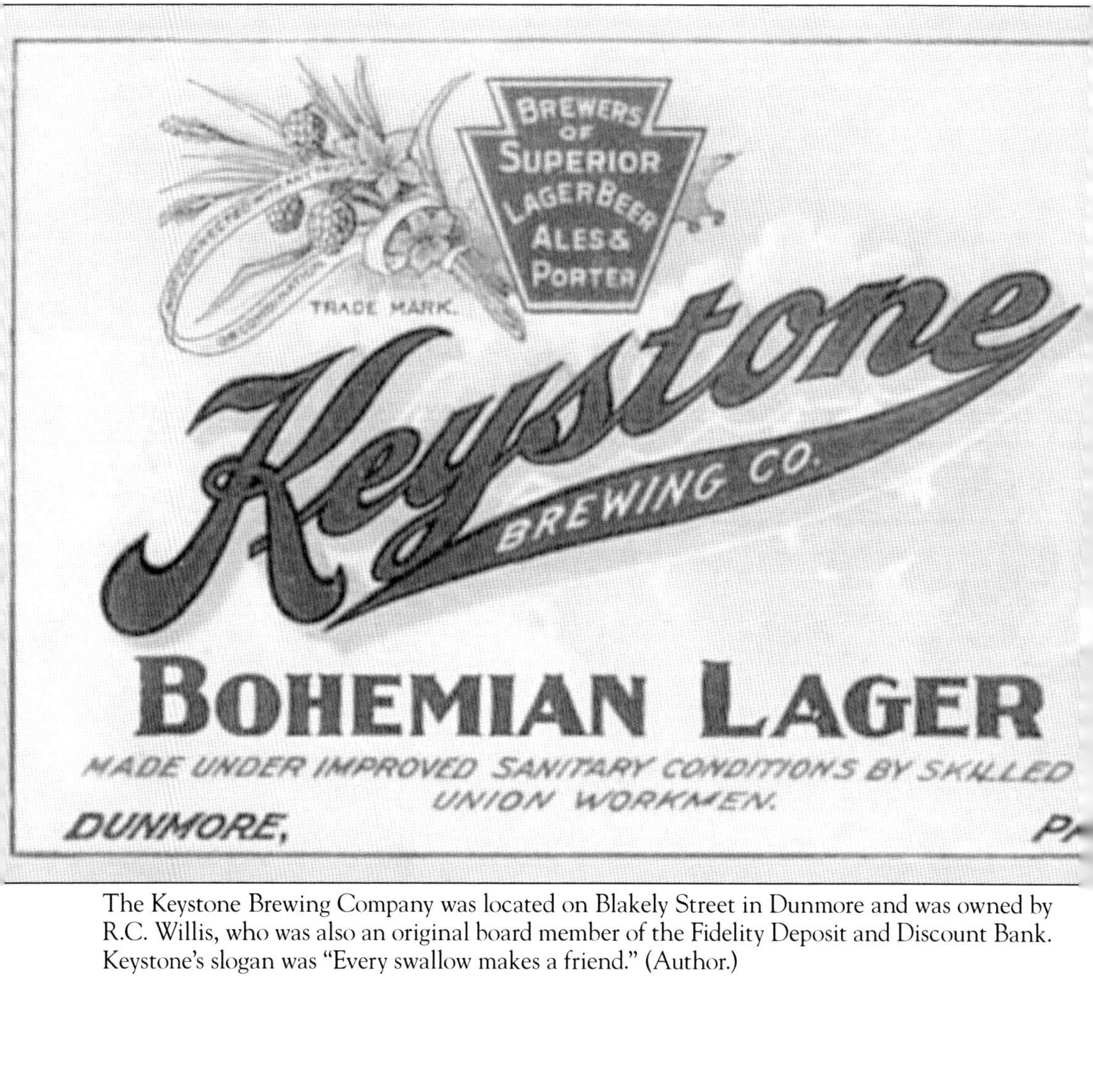

The Keystone Brewing Company was located on Blakely Street in Dunmore and was owned by R.C. Willis, who was also an original board member of the Fidelity Deposit and Discount Bank. Keystone's slogan was "Every swallow makes a friend." (Author.)

Two

BUCKTOWN

Although "Bucktown" was the original name for Dunmore, it still remains a popular nickname for the borough to this day and can be said to symbolize the life and culture of the town itself.

By the 1930s, Dunmore had grown so much in size that it was considered the most populous of the Scranton suburbs. Many churches and businesses had come to call Dunmore home, including those seen in this chapter. Other notable churches include the Dunmore Presbyterian Church on Chestnut Street, Temple Israel on Drinker Street, and St. Michael's Byzantine Catholic Church on Drinker Street.

Another prominent feature of Dunmore was St. Joseph's Children and Maternity Hospital, now known as St. Joseph's Center. Located on Adams Avenue, the property was sold to the hospital for $1 by the Pennsylvania Coal Company in the 1890s with the stipulation that it would revert back to the coal company if it was not used for charitable purposes.

Dunmore also boasts a large number of civic and fraternal organizations, including the Dunmore Lions Club, which was founded on May 22, 1952, and the Dunmore Rotary, which was founded in October 1937. Dunmore also once had a chapter of UNICO National, the largest Italian American service organization in the United States. Dunmore's chapter was formed in 1957 but has since been absorbed by the Scranton Chapter, which is the largest chapter of UNICO National with over 400 members.

The Keystone Industrial Park, which opened in Dunmore in the 1960s, is also credited with expanding the industrial makeup of the borough.

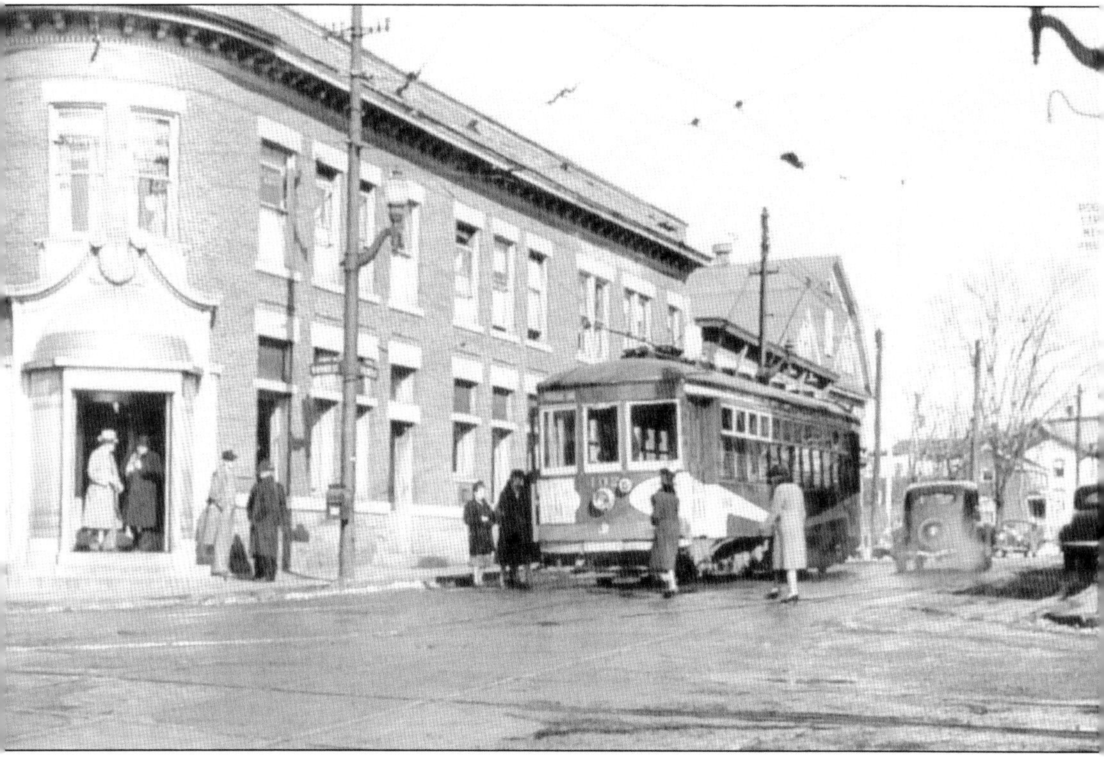

Scranton Transit Company Car No. 402 stops to pick up and discharge passengers in front of Fidelity Deposit and Discount Bank at the corner of North Blakely Street and Drinker Street in February 1939. The car operated on the Dunmore Suburban Line and traveled only a few blocks from the end of the line at Warren Street. It would then turn right on Drinker Street and go toward Electric Street before turning south on Adams Avenue. It would eventually share trackage with the Green Ridge Suburban line to go into downtown Scranton. Service on the Dunmore Suburban Line ended on October 7, 1950, and service on Scranton's final electric rail line, the Green Ridge Suburban, ended on December 18, 1954. (Courtesy of Fidelity Deposit and Discount Bank.)

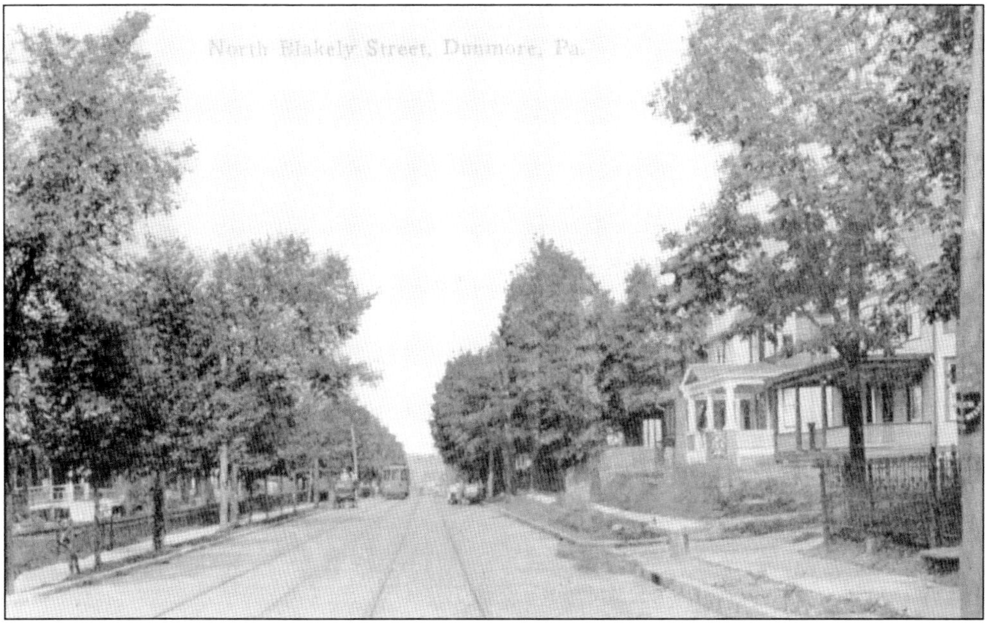

One of the many trolleys that served Dunmore can be seen in the distance in this undated photograph of North Blakely Street. (Courtesy of Karl Wegforth.)

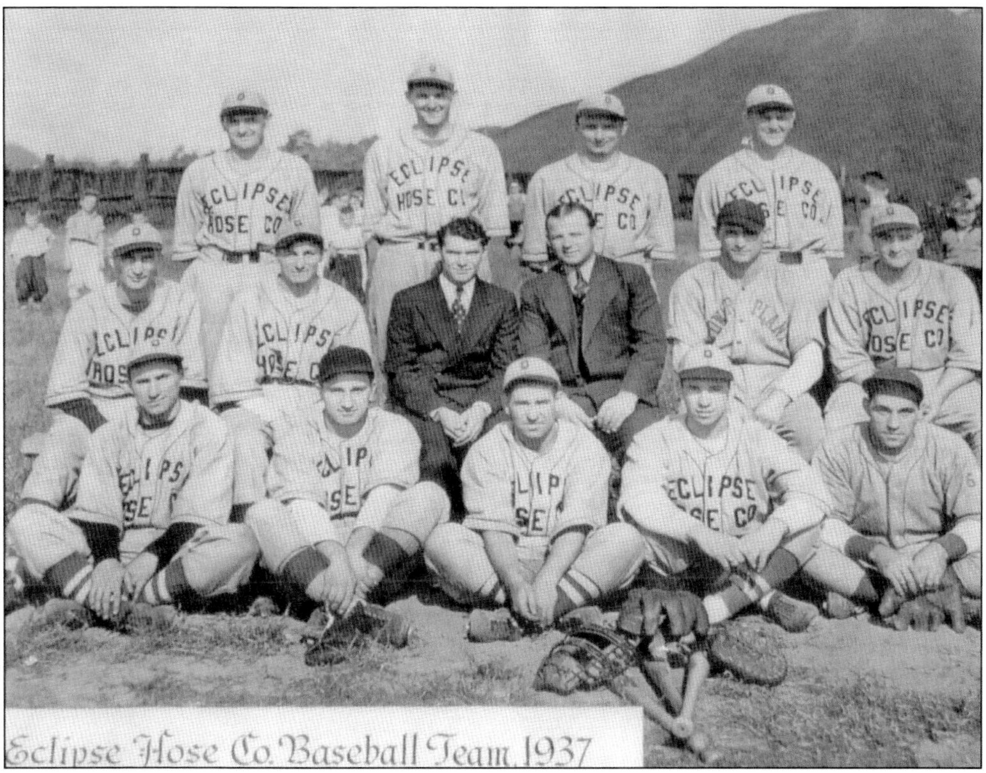

Players and managers of the Eclipse Hose Company baseball team can be seen in this 1937 photograph. The Eclipse Hose Company was organized in 1911. (Courtesy of the Dunmore Historical Society.)

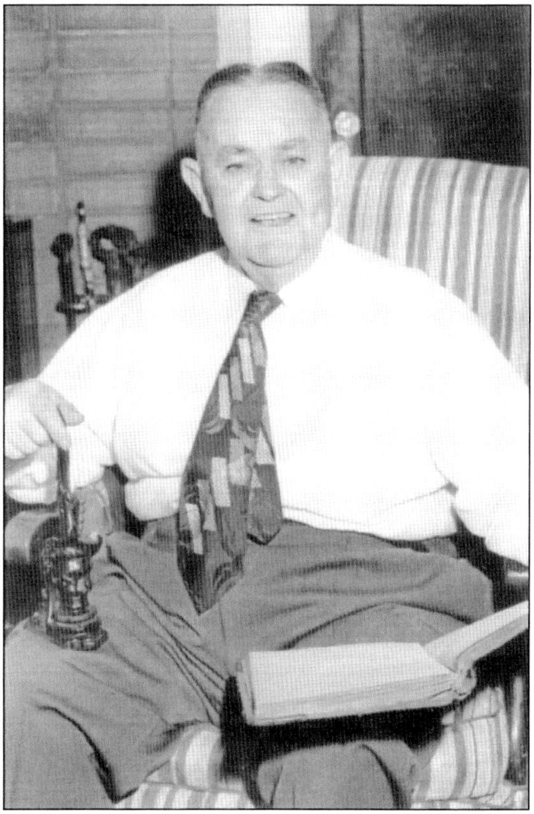

P.C. Mellody lived in the Johnson's Patch neighborhood of Dunmore and was the secretary of the O.S. Johnson Hose Company. Mellody came to the United States from Ireland and was known throughout Dunmore as being a gifted and humorous storyteller. (Courtesy of Geralyn Swinick.)

P.C. Mellody can be seen at the far left in this photograph of the O.S. Johnson Hose Company's reunion dinner on May 29, 1961, at the former Billy's Restaurant in Dunmore. The O.S. Johnson Hose Company was located on West Grove Street in Dunmore's Johnson's Patch neighborhood and changed its name around 1920 to the Thomas F. Quinn Hose Company. The O.S. Johnson Hose Company was founded in 1901. (Courtesy of Geralyn Swinick.)

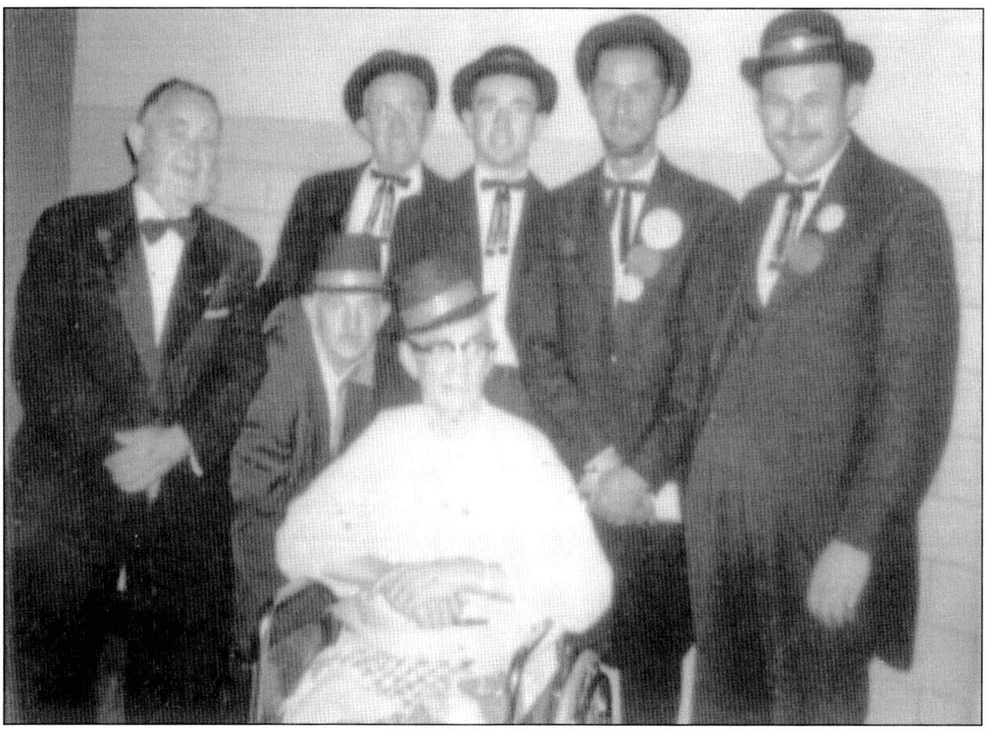

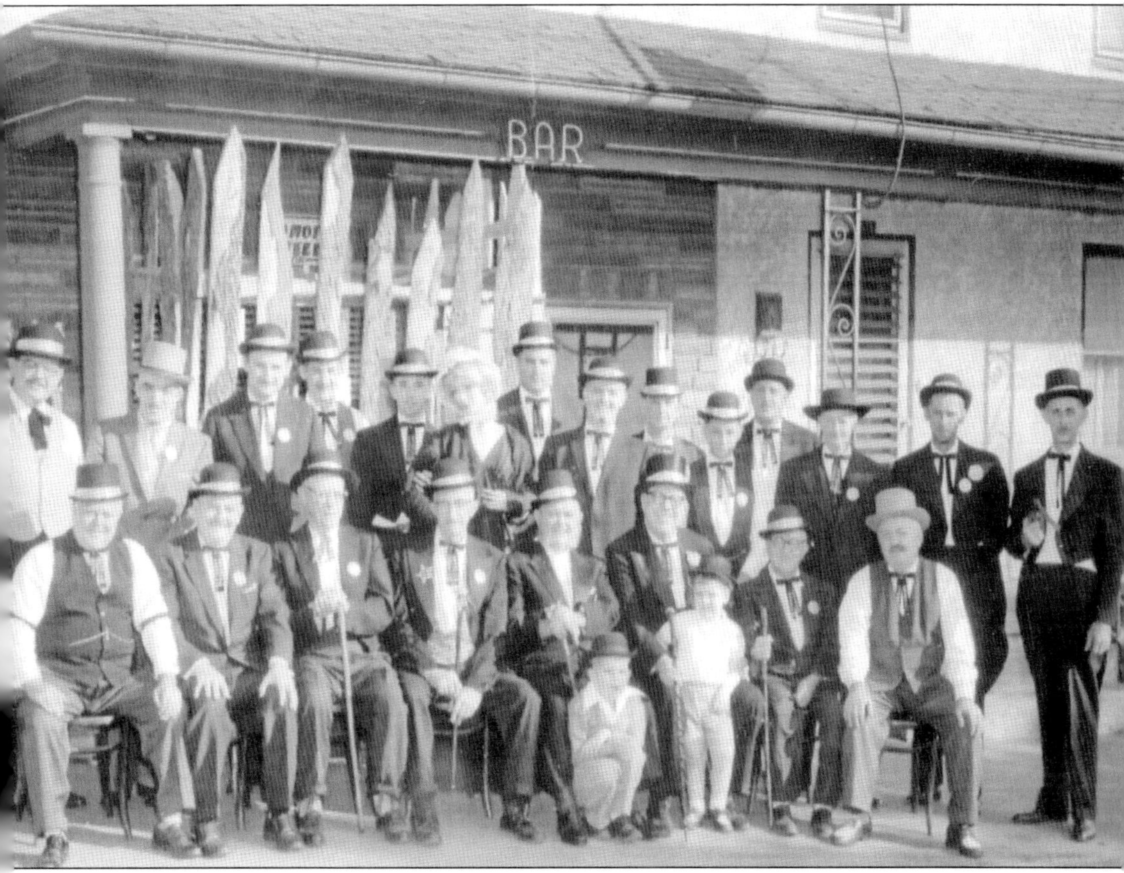

Retired members of the O.S. Johnson Hose Company gather outside of Casey's Bar on Blakely Street in 1962. (Courtesy of Geralyn Swinick.)

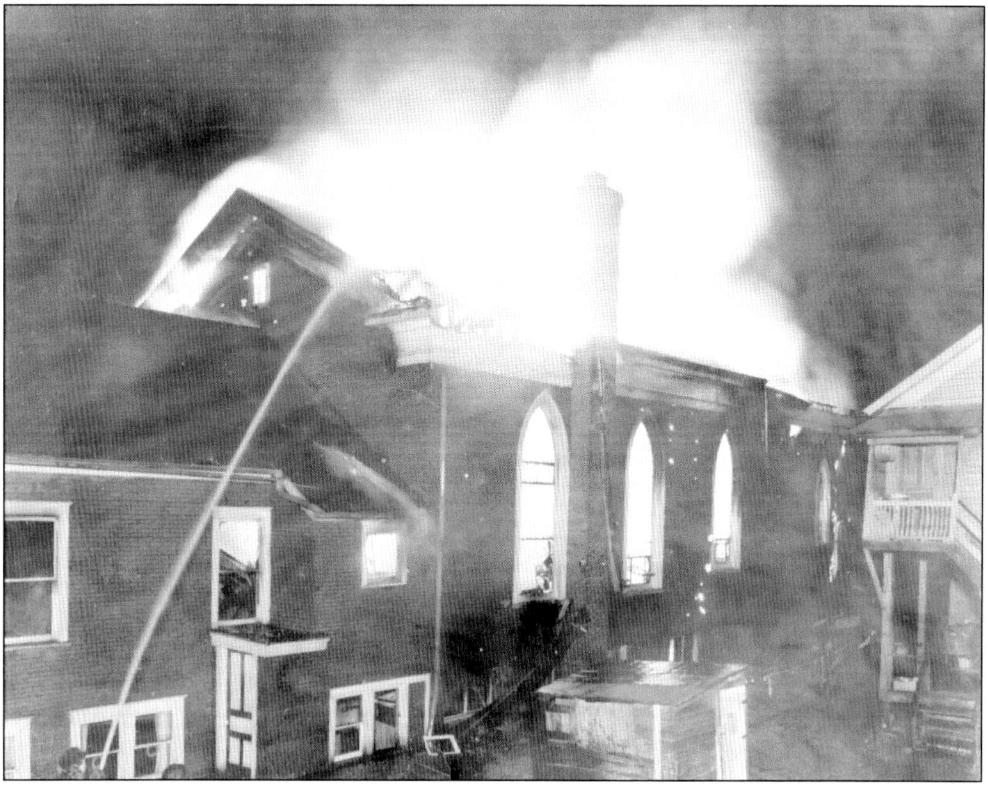

The Tripp Avenue Christian Church was organized in 1856 as the First Christian Church of Dunmore. Tragically, the church's original building caught fire on December 20, 1936, and was destroyed. (Courtesy of the Dunmore Historical Society.)

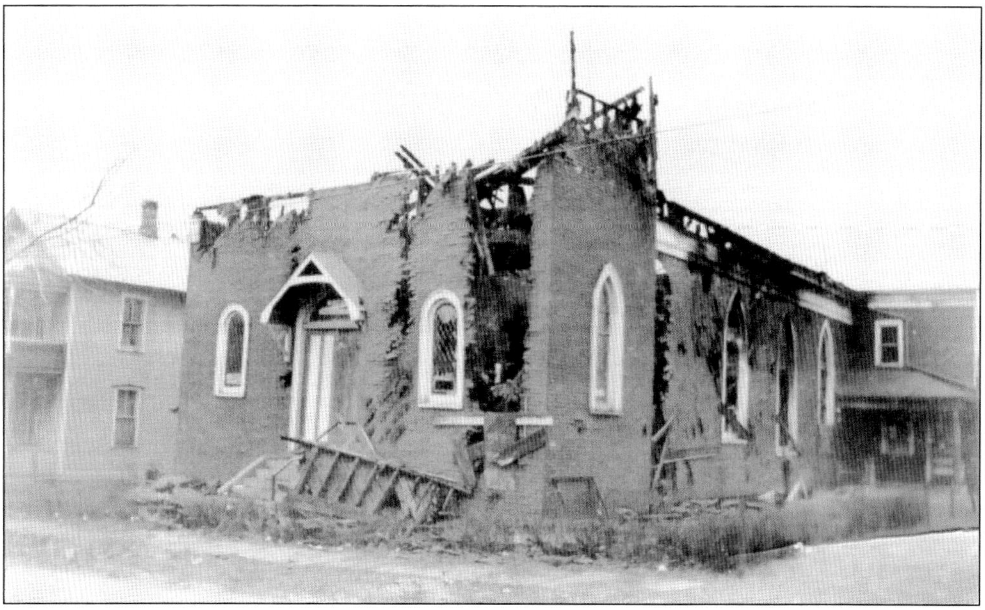

The Tripp Avenue Christian Church was rebuilt in 1937 and dedicated on January 9, 1938. The cause of the 1936 fire was never determined. (Courtesy of the Dunmore Historical Society.)

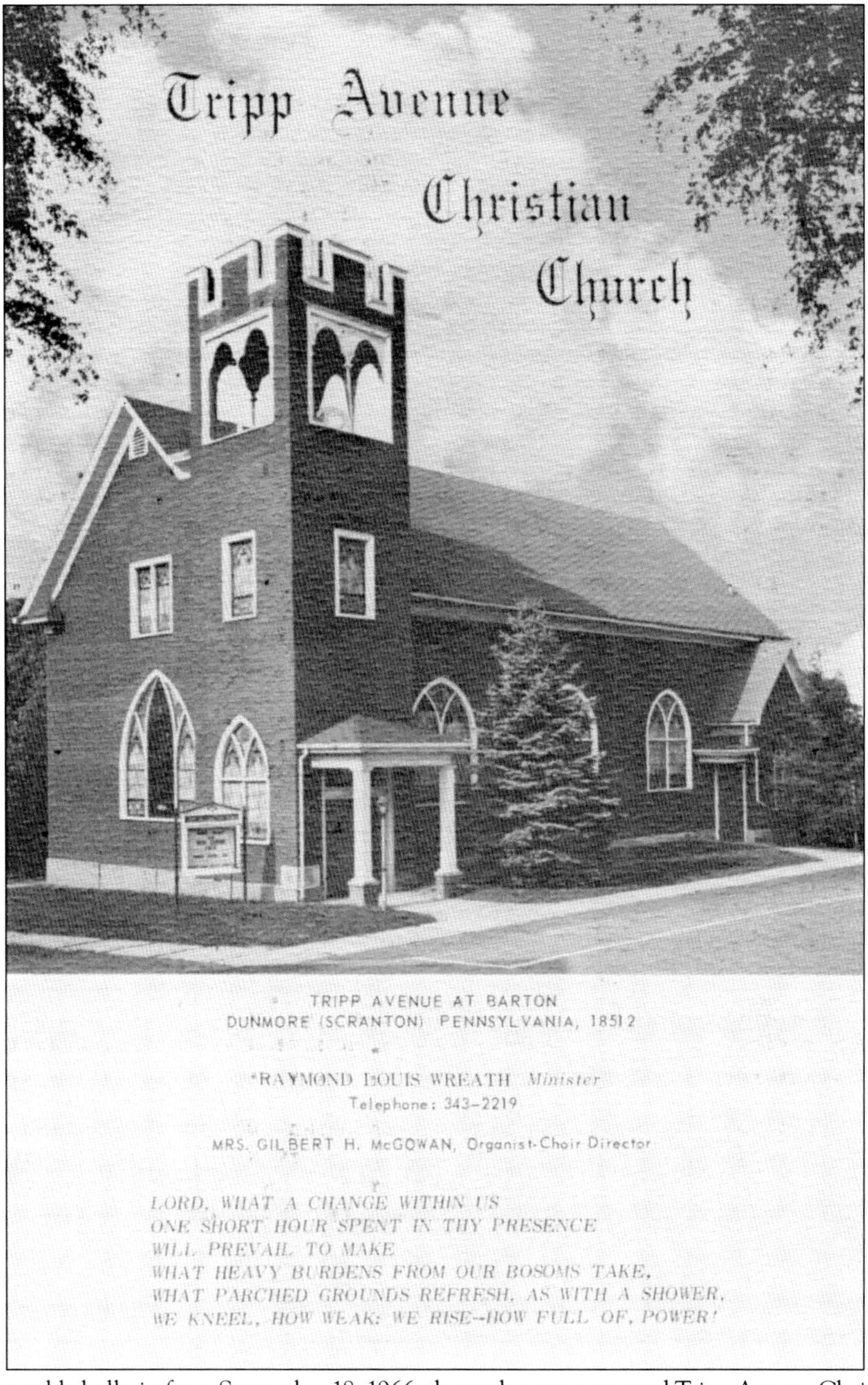

Tripp Avenue Christian Church

TRIPP AVENUE AT BARTON
DUNMORE (SCRANTON) PENNSYLVANIA, 18512

*RAYMOND LOUIS WREATH *Minister*
Telephone: 343-2219

MRS. GILBERT H. McGOWAN, Organist-Choir Director

*LORD, WHAT A CHANGE WITHIN US
ONE SHORT HOUR SPENT IN THY PRESENCE
WILL PREVAIL TO MAKE
WHAT HEAVY BURDENS FROM OUR BOSOMS TAKE,
WHAT PARCHED GROUNDS REFRESH, AS WITH A SHOWER,
WE KNEEL, HOW WEAK; WE RISE--HOW FULL OF, POWER!*

This weekly bulletin from September 18, 1966, shows the reconstructed Tripp Avenue Christian Church. Services were held in this building until September 28, 2008, when the church was deconsecrated and the congregation disbanded. Incidentally, September 28, 2008, was also the church's 150th anniversary. The Tripp Avenue Christian Church building is now the home of the Dunmore Historical Society. (Courtesy of the Dunmore Historical Society.)

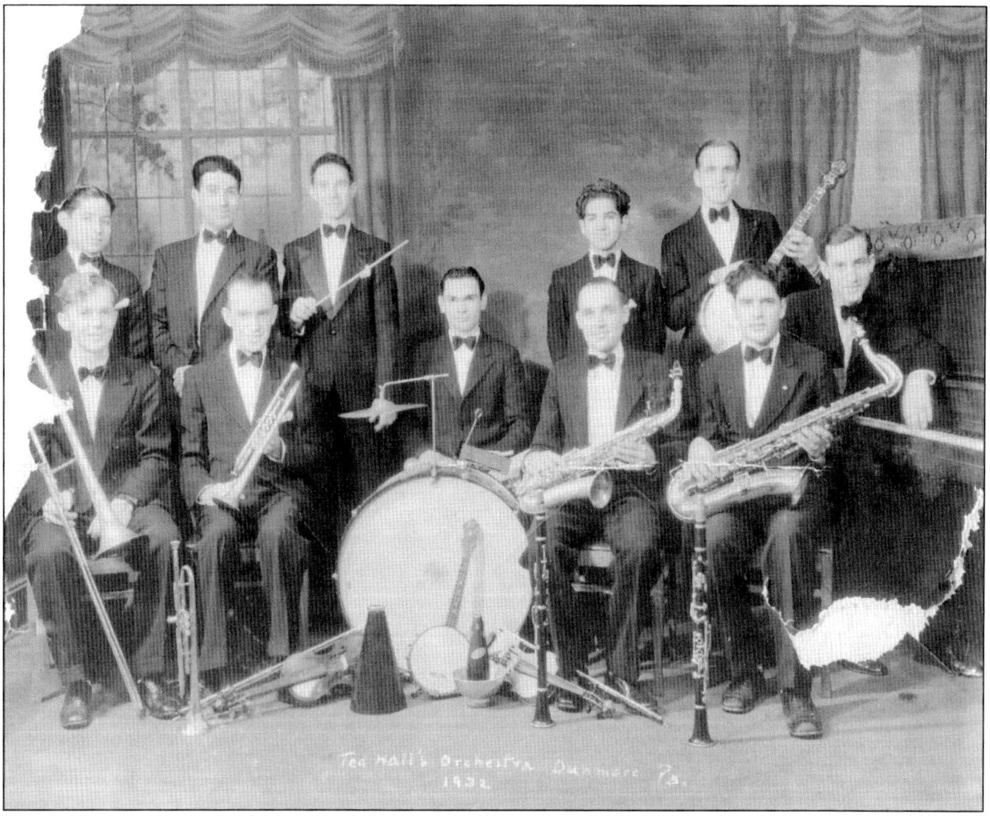

The Ted Hall Orchestra of Dunmore poses for this 1932 photograph. The Ted Hall Orchestra was one of the many Dunmore-based bands that were popular locally throughout the 1930s and 1940s. (Courtesy of the Dunmore Historical Society.)

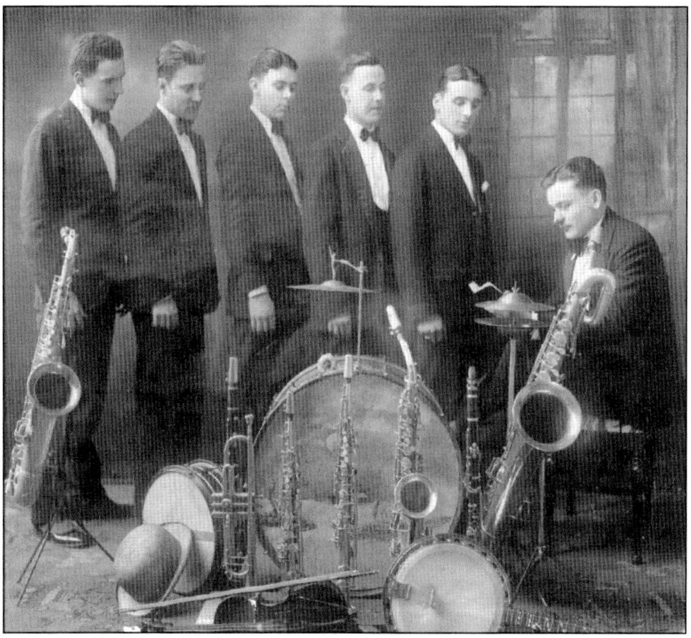

Eddie Getz and His Blue Jackets was another Dunmore-based band from the 1930s. In this photograph, Donato DelRosario of Dunmore is second from the right. (Courtesy of Rosemary Summa.)

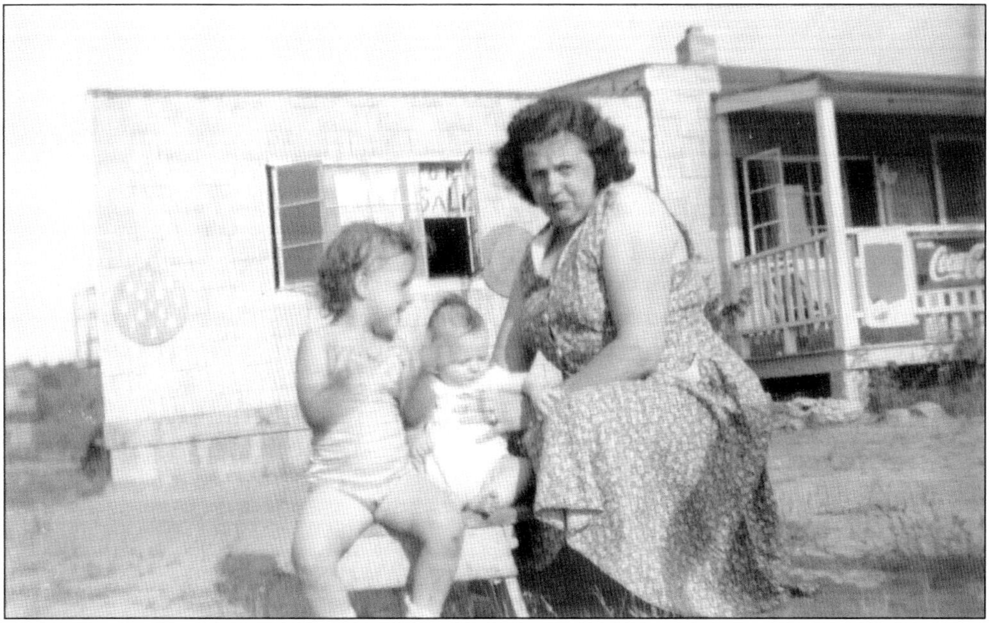

One popular spot in Dunmore during the 1940s and 1950s was Mullen's Field. Pictured from left to right are Anne Helene and Joann Santarsiero with their mother, Ann Tur Santarsiero. (Courtesy of Joseph Santarsiero.)

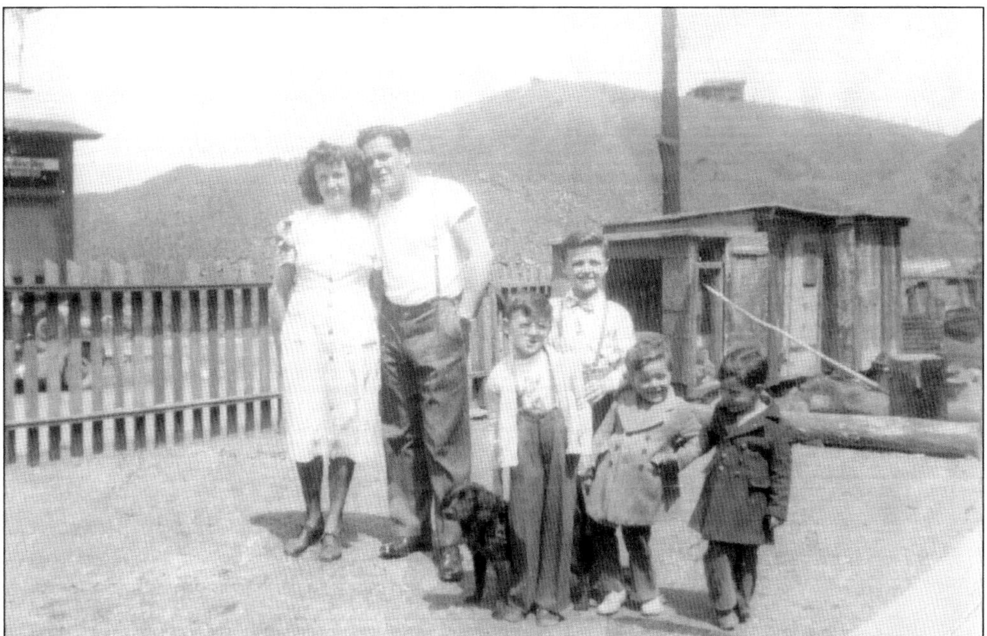

During the 1940s, there was a culm dump in the rear of Allen Street near the vicinity of the Meadowside Coal Breaker that was a popular hangout. Pictured from left to right, Ann Tur Santarsiero, Frank F. Santarsiero, Robert Santarsiero, William Santarsiero, Joseph Santarsiero, and Jack Tur stand in front of the culm dump. (Courtesy of Joseph Santarsiero.)

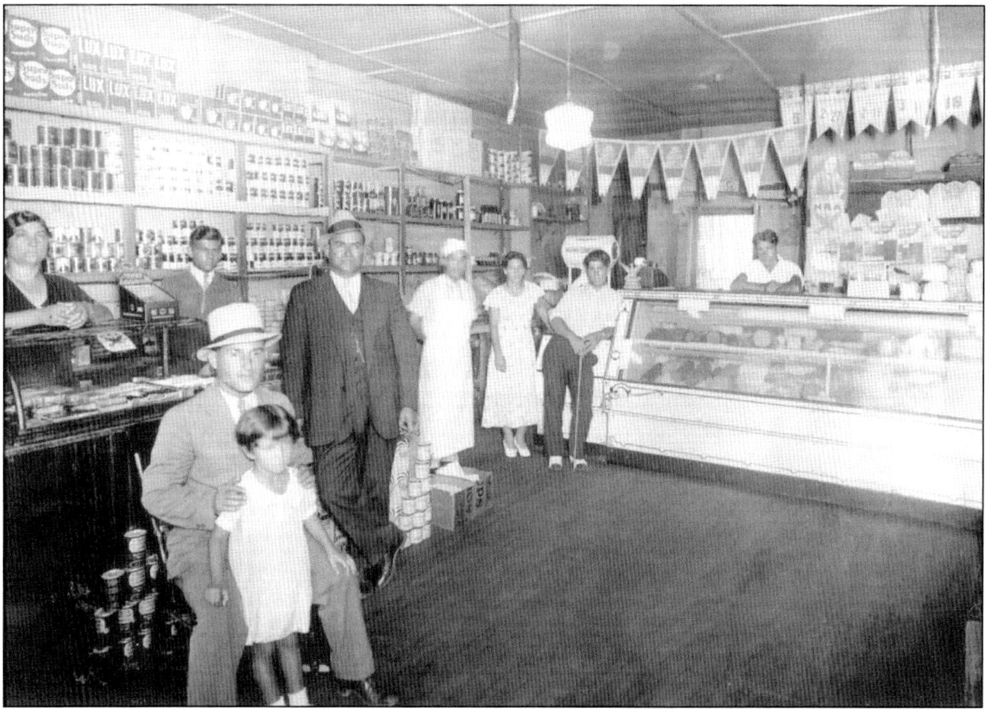

John Fortuna's grocery store was located on the corner of Burke and Butler Streets in Dunmore. Seated are Anthony D'Arienzo and Frances D'Arienzo Tomko. Standing from left to right are Erasmo "Raymond" D'Arienzo, John Fortuna, Bernetta Angerson D'Arienzo, and Phil "Casey" D'Arienzo. Behind the counters are, from left to right, Louise Fortuna, Nick Franco, and Anthony Calabro. (Courtesy of Philip D'Arienzo and Joe and Frances Tomko.)

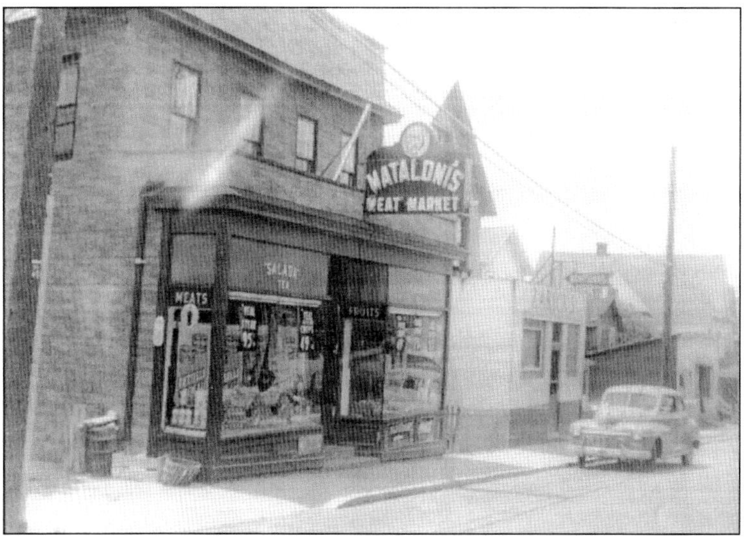

Mataloni's Meat Market was located on Drinker Street in Dunmore during the 1950s and 1960s. (Courtesy of the Mataloni family.)

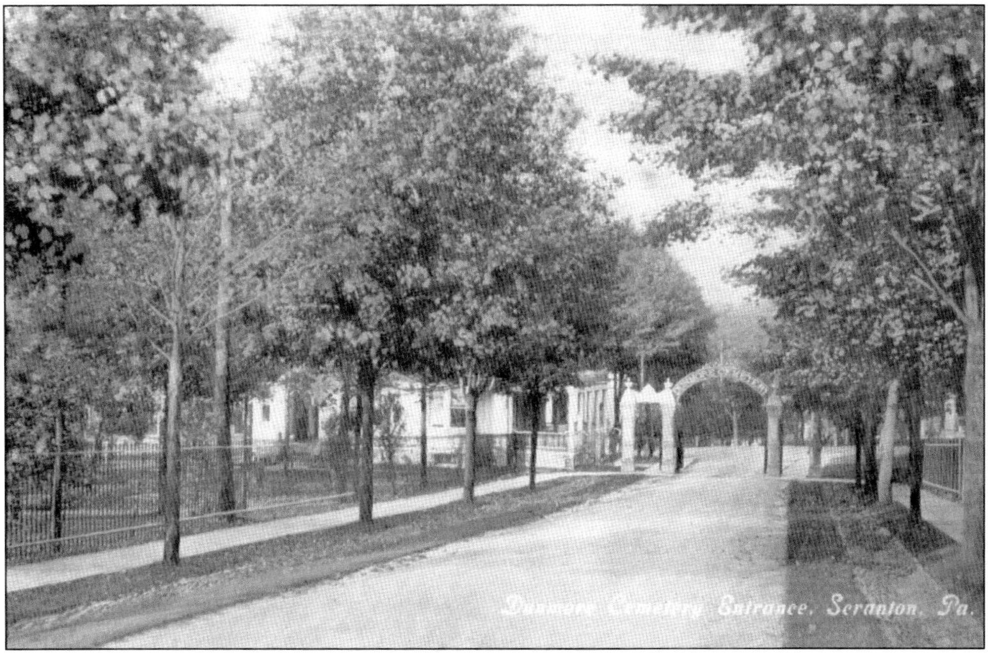

The Dunmore Cemetery is the oldest and largest cemetery in Dunmore. It was begun in 1828 on land that was donated by Levi Depuy. The first person to be buried at Dunmore Cemetery is believed to be Gabriel Dunning. George Whitfield Scranton, for whom the city of Scranton is named, is also interred in Dunmore Cemetery. (Courtesy of the Dunmore Historical Society.)

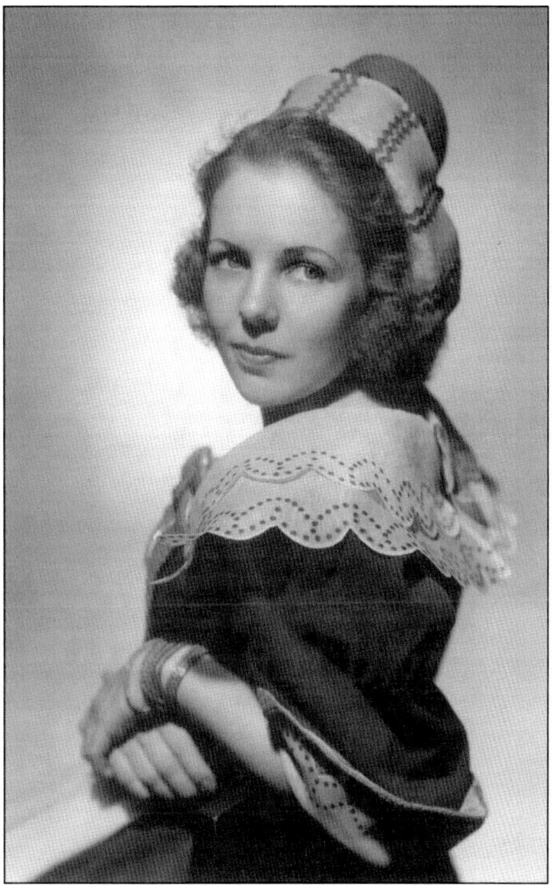

Jeanne Madden poses in costume as Tina Tienhoven from *Knickerbocker Holiday*, a musical by Kurt Weill and Maxwell Anderson, in this 1938 photograph by Ben Pinchot. Madden was originally from Scranton and became a famous Hollywood actress in the 1930s and 1940s. Madden died on January 15, 1989, and is buried in Dunmore's Forest Hill Cemetery. Forest Hill Cemetery is also the final resting place of many Civil War veterans and of Daniel Protheroe, one of Wales's most famous composers and conductors. (Courtesy of the Weill-Lenya Research Center, Kurt Weill Foundation for Music, New York.)

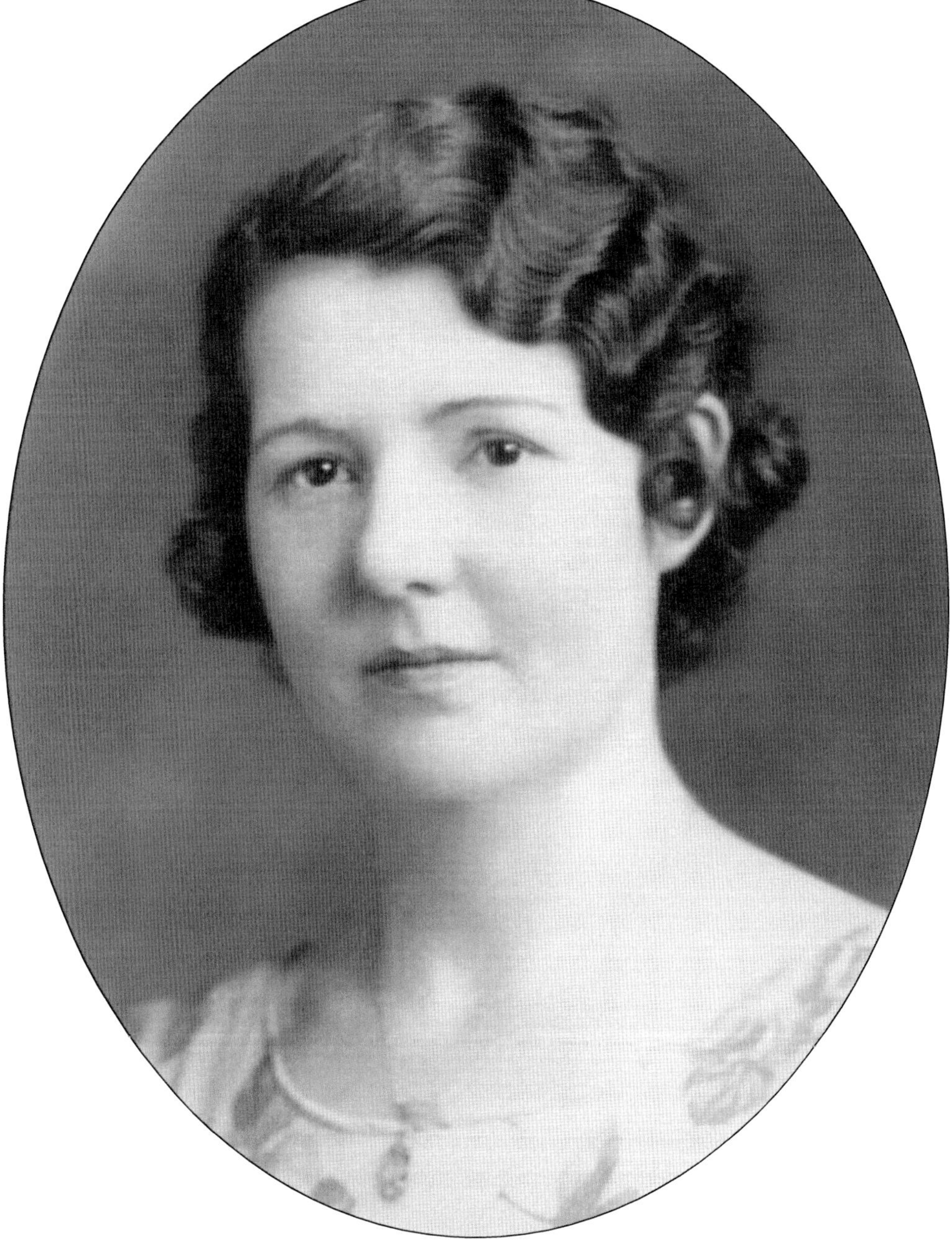

Gertrude Jones Hawk of Dunmore was born in 1903. Her father died while she was still a child, and her mother suffered from a severe heart ailment. To help her family, young Gertrude went to work at a local candy store at the age of 12. She married Elmer Hawk in 1922. At the height of the Great Depression in 1936, Gertrude felt that she should try to help her family by earning money on the side. Gertrude Hawk Chocolates is now an award-winning company with stores throughout Pennsylvania, New York, and New Jersey. (Courtesy of Gertrude Hawk Chocolates.)

This photograph shows the original candy kitchen of Gertrude Hawk Chocolates, located on Mark Avenue in Dunmore's Bunker Hill section. When Gertrude and Elmer Hawk's son Elmer Hawk Jr. returned home from World War II after having been a German prisoner of war for over a year and a half, he decided to go into business with his parents and used the money he received for serving in the US military to purchase equipment to expand the small business. (Courtesy of Gertrude Hawk Chocolates.)

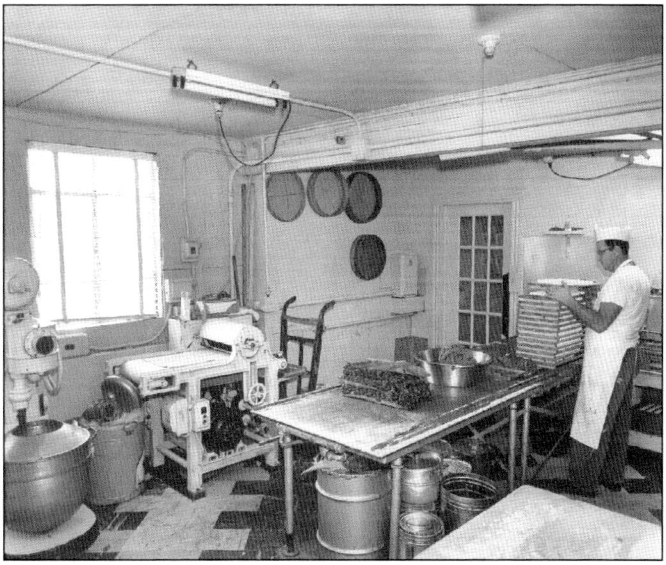

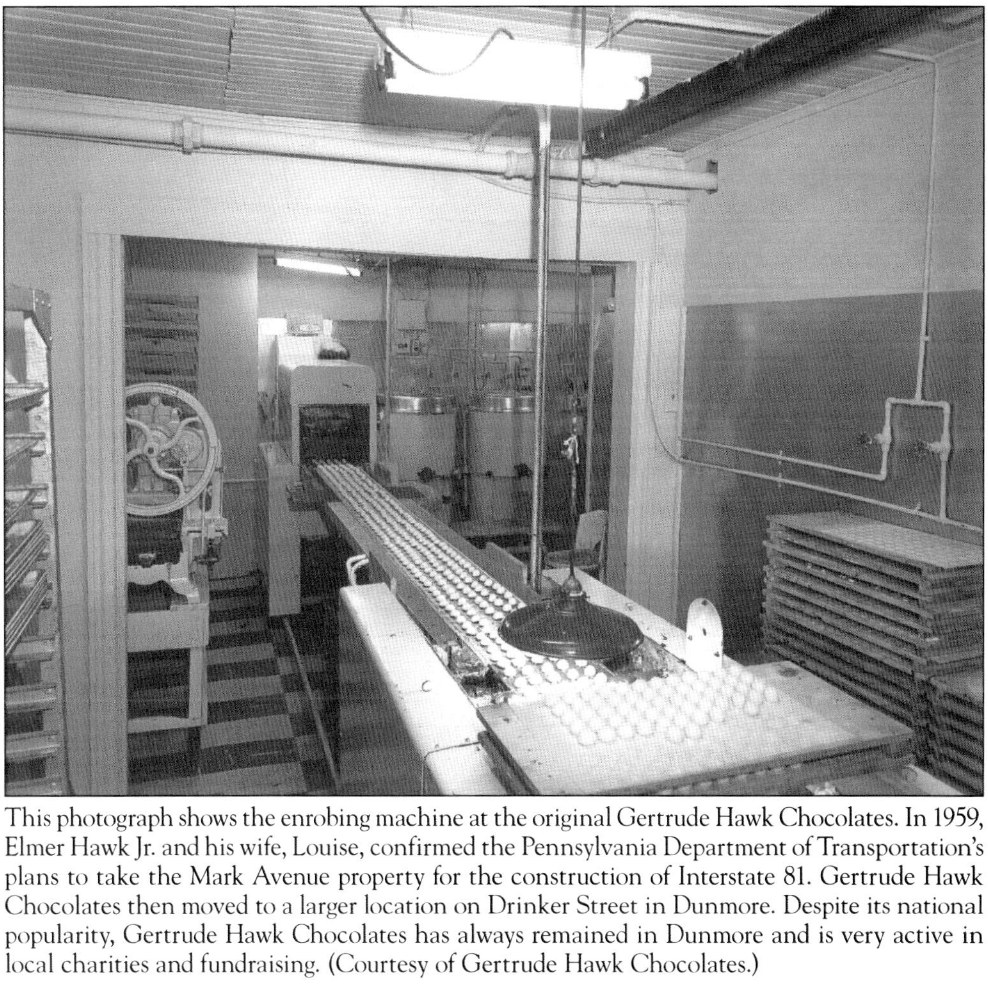

This photograph shows the enrobing machine at the original Gertrude Hawk Chocolates. In 1959, Elmer Hawk Jr. and his wife, Louise, confirmed the Pennsylvania Department of Transportation's plans to take the Mark Avenue property for the construction of Interstate 81. Gertrude Hawk Chocolates then moved to a larger location on Drinker Street in Dunmore. Despite its national popularity, Gertrude Hawk Chocolates has always remained in Dunmore and is very active in local charities and fundraising. (Courtesy of Gertrude Hawk Chocolates.)

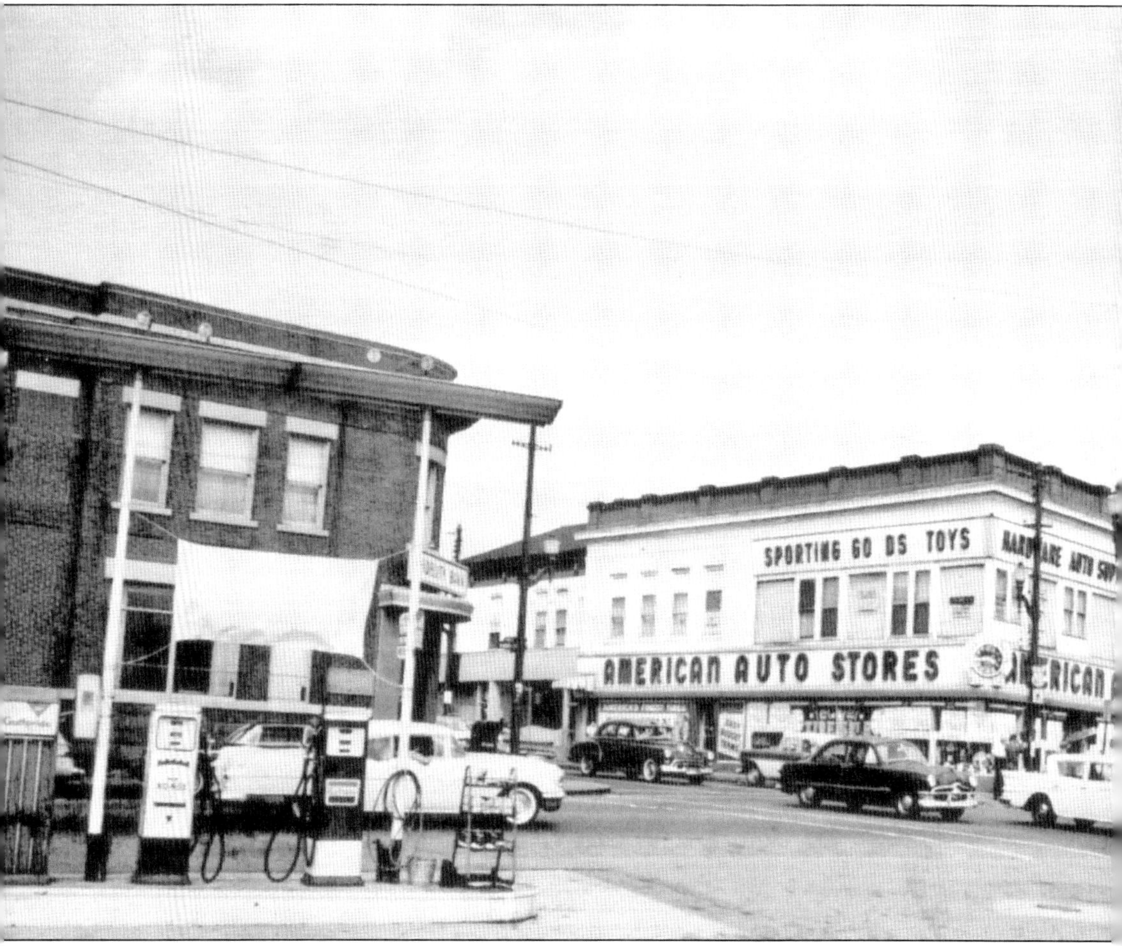

Dunmore Corners is pictured in 1959. (Courtesy of Dunmore Borough.)

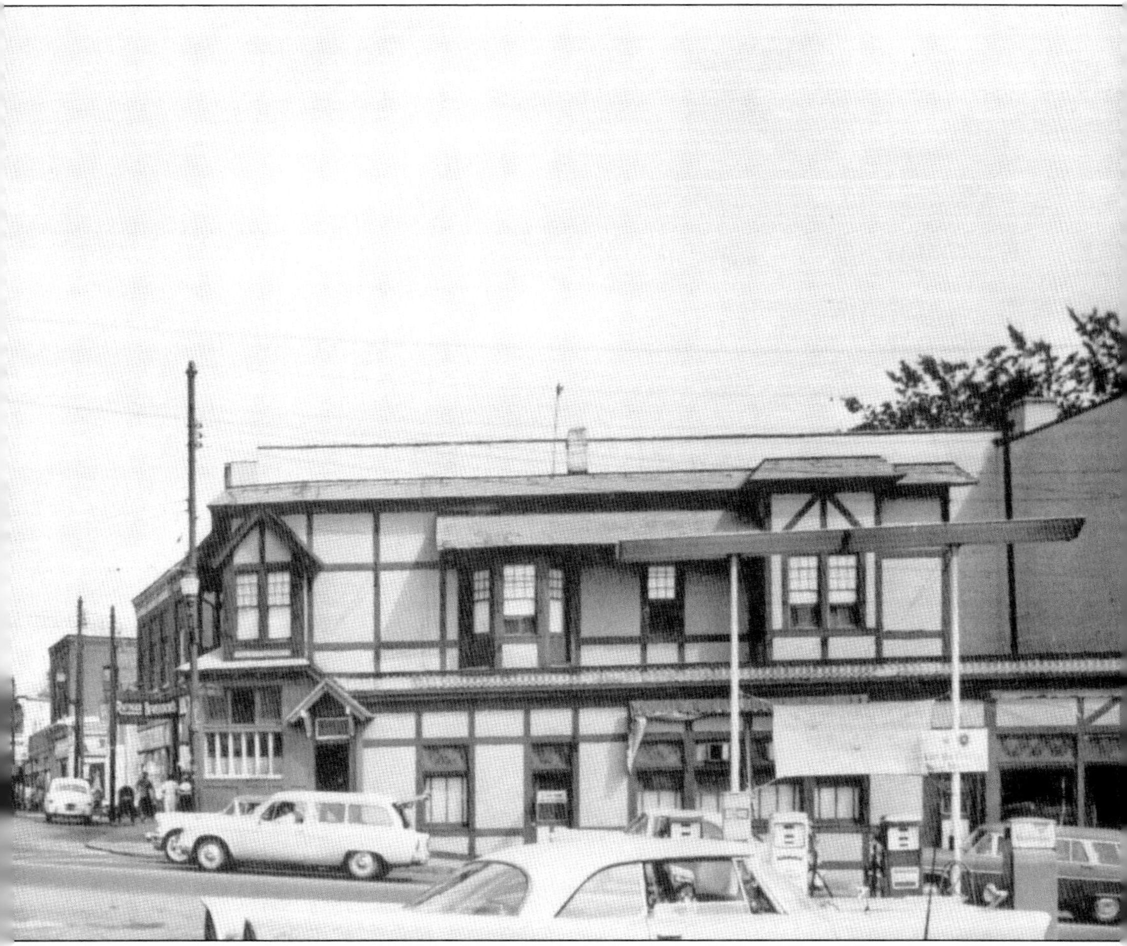

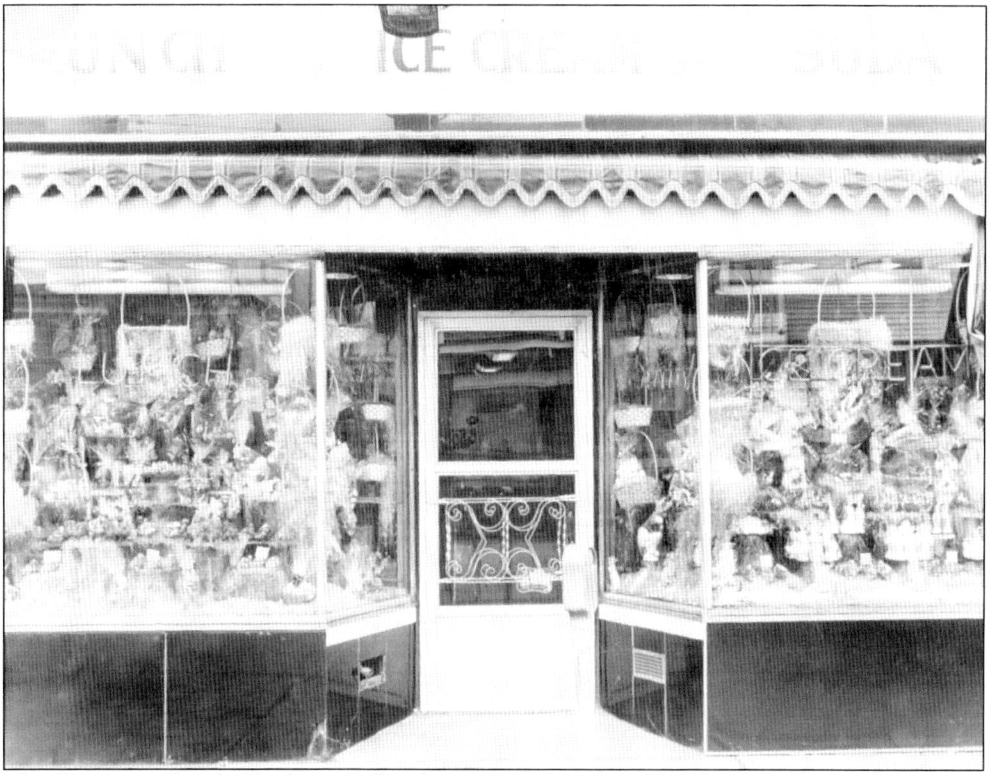

The Dunmore Candy Kitchen on Drinker Street was owned by the Perrella family since its opening in 1904 until the 2000s. The exterior of the shop has remained largely unchanged since the 1960s. (Courtesy of the Dunmore Historical Society.)

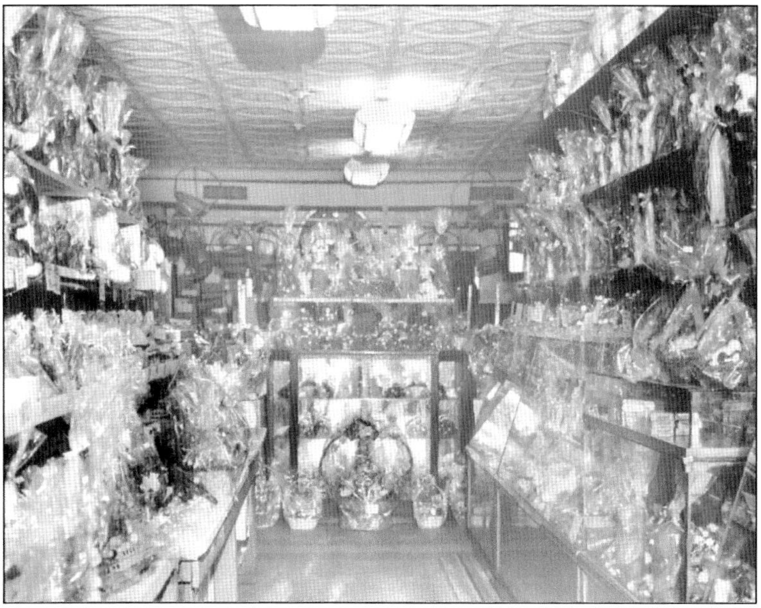

Owner Lou Perrella was known for his array of Easter baskets in the entryway of the Dunmore Candy Kitchen. In this 1960s photograph, Easter baskets go up to the ceiling in preparation for one of the largest chocolate holidays of the year. (Courtesy of the Dunmore Historical Society.)

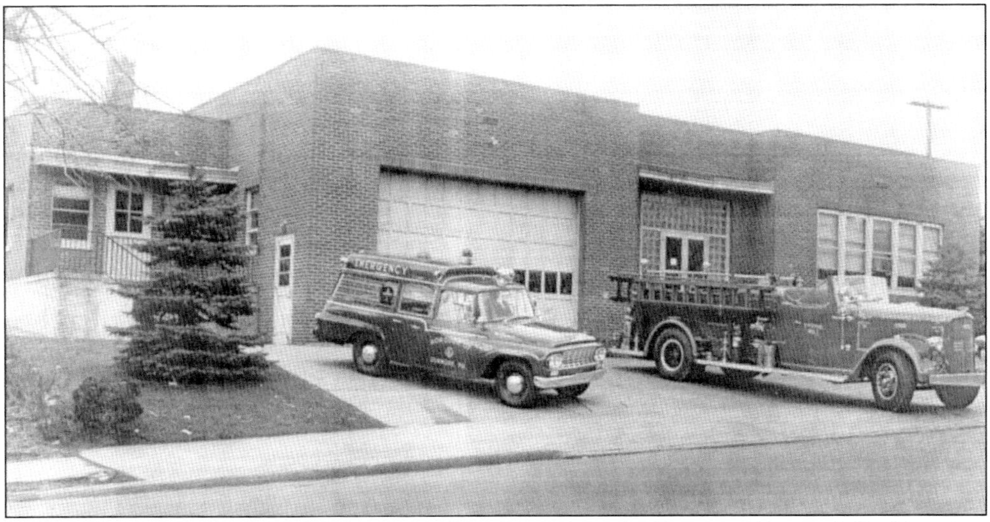

The Dunmore Borough Building is pictured in the 1950s. The Dunmore Borough Building has always occupied the same spot on Blakely Street since the borough's incorporation in 1862. (Courtesy of the Dunmore Historical Society.)

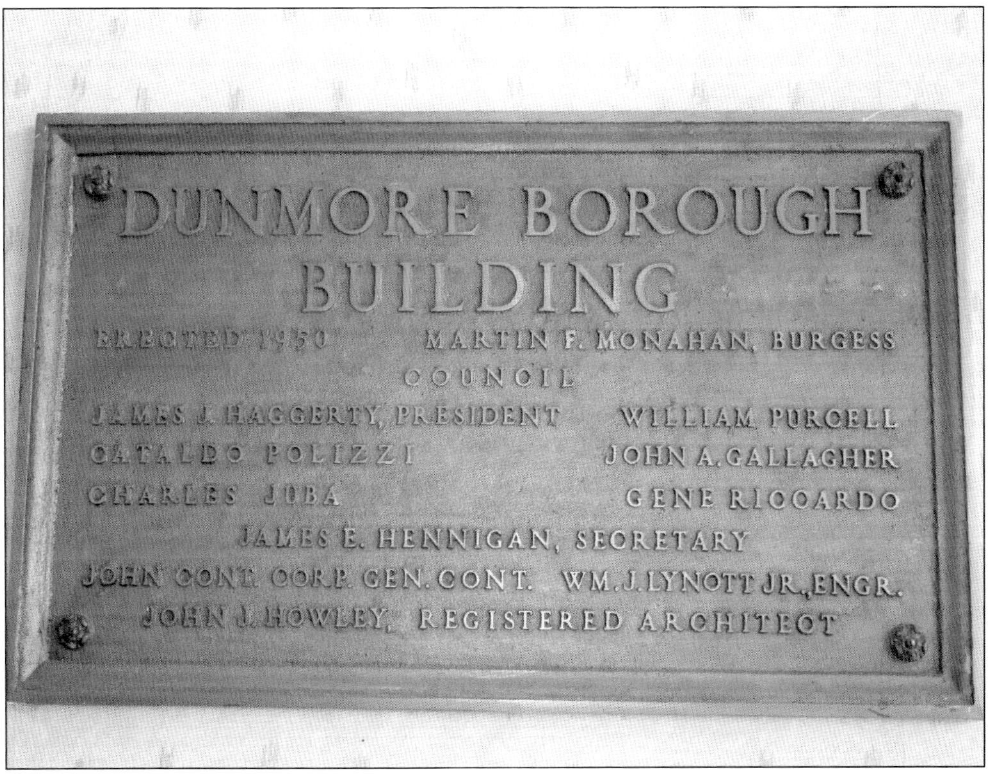

This photograph shows the new cornerstone that was installed in the Dunmore Borough Building in 1950 following its reconstruction and remodeling. (Courtesy of Dunmore Borough.)

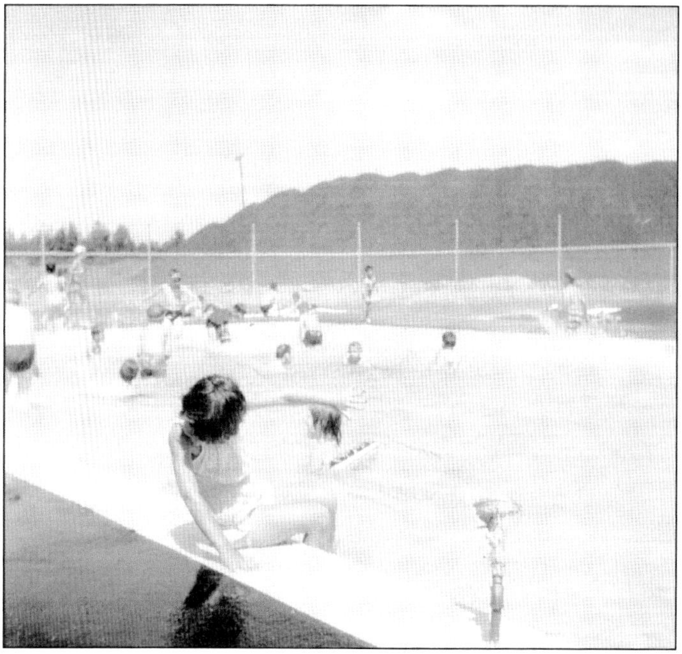

The Sherwood Youth Association, a private, nonprofit organization, was formed in 1958 by a group of neighbors who wanted to transform an old culm dump, located on the corner of Sherwood Avenue and Barnard Streets in Dunmore, into a park for the community. The land was purchased from the Mid Valley Coal Company, and the association ran various fundraisers to pay the mortgage. Children are pictured here playing at the park's pool in 1961. (Courtesy of the Sherwood Youth Association.)

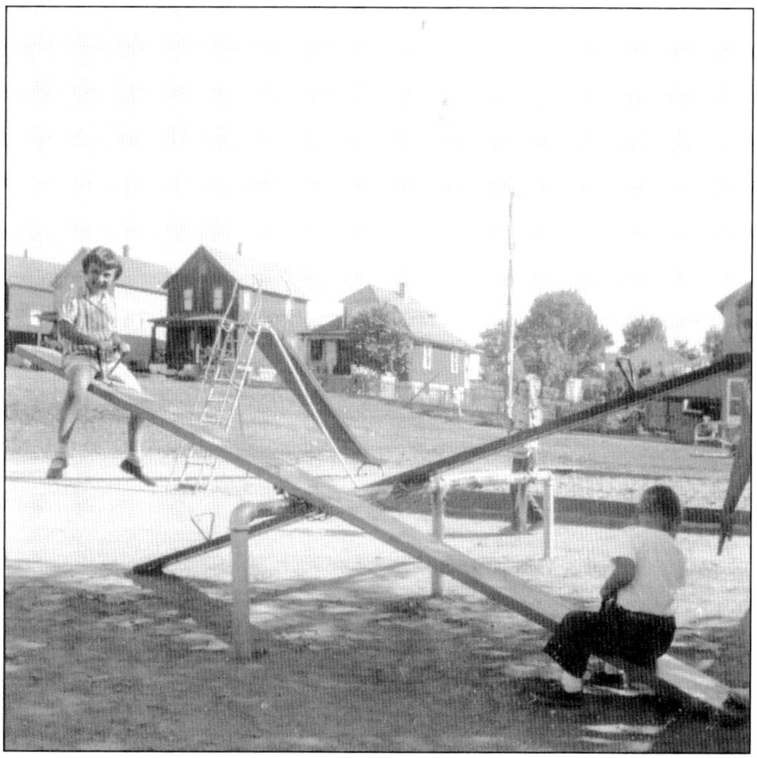

Although Sherwood Park began as a rather small enterprise, through the efforts of the Sherwood Youth Association it eventually grew to include a playground, basketball courts, softball, baseball, and soccer fields, and a pavilion for picnics. (Courtesy of the Sherwood Youth Association.)

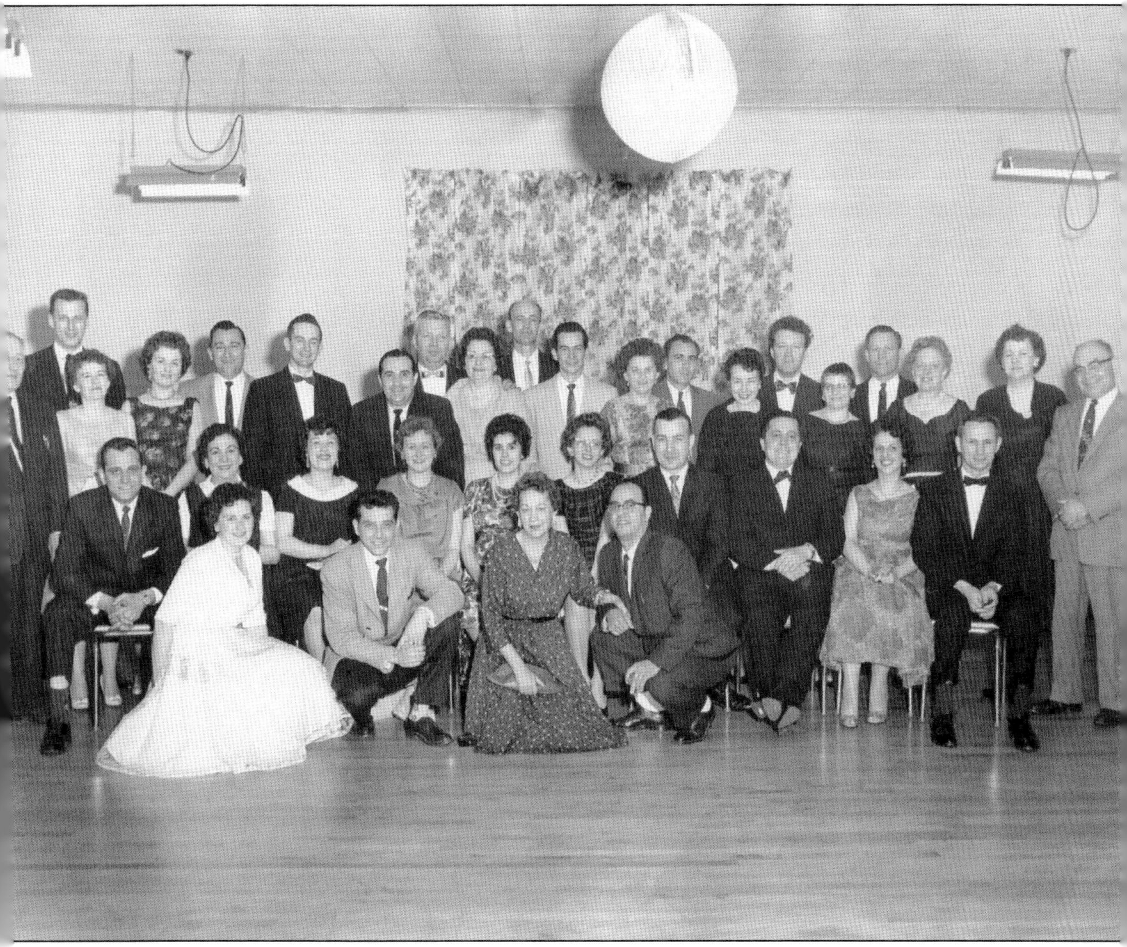

Officers and auxiliary officers of the Sherwood Youth Association gather for a party in 1961. The charter members of the Sherwood Youth Association were Joseph Dunda, George Kofel, Anthony Michalek, Vincent Metallo, Andrew Hudak, Patrick DeMarco, Edward Kraycer, Leonard DeMarco, Leonard Melia, Eustachio Arduino, Daniel Sacco, Michael Martarano, and Matthew Sienkiewich. (Courtesy of the Sherwood Youth Association.)

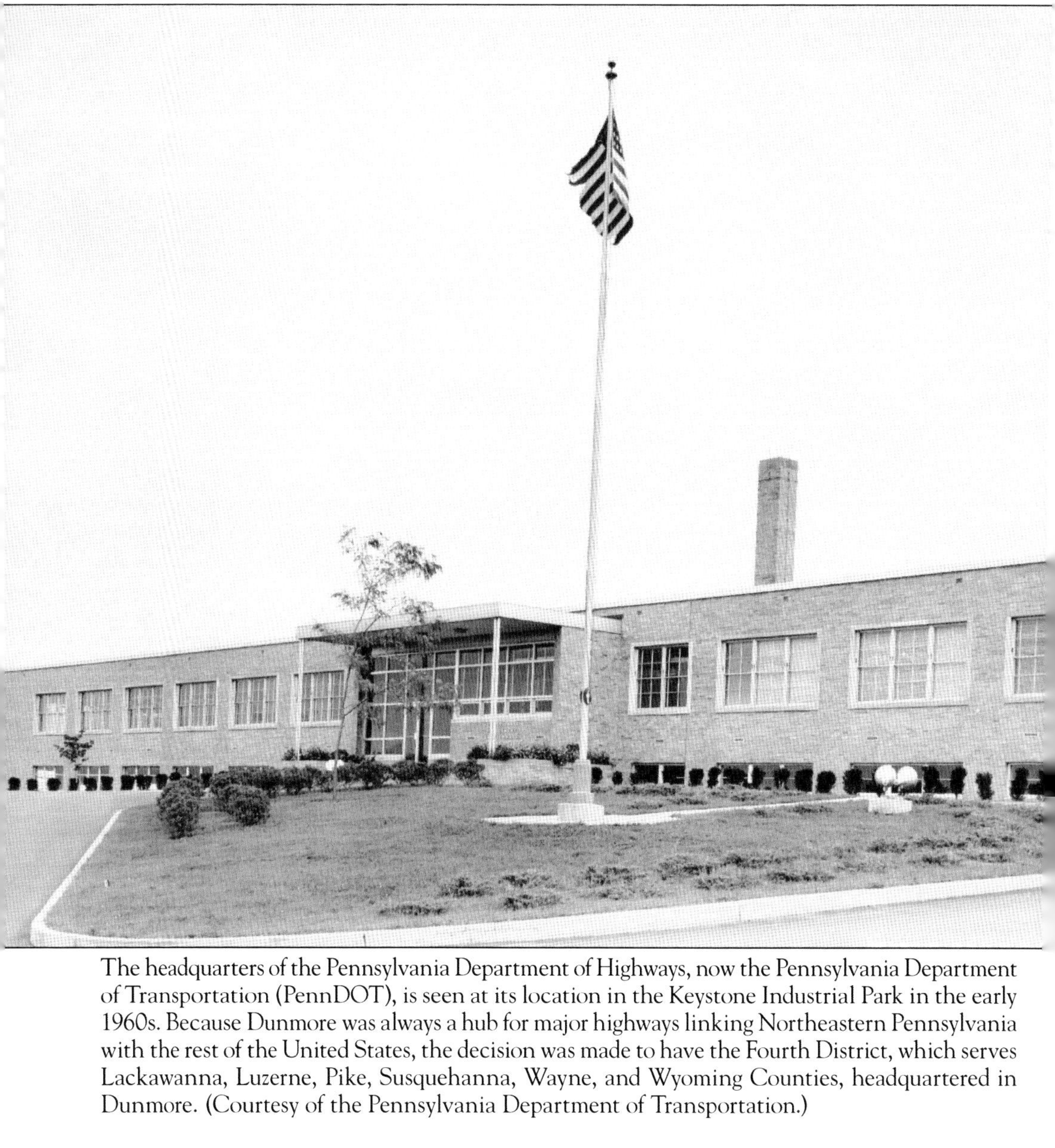

The headquarters of the Pennsylvania Department of Highways, now the Pennsylvania Department of Transportation (PennDOT), is seen at its location in the Keystone Industrial Park in the early 1960s. Because Dunmore was always a hub for major highways linking Northeastern Pennsylvania with the rest of the United States, the decision was made to have the Fourth District, which serves Lackawanna, Luzerne, Pike, Susquehanna, Wayne, and Wyoming Counties, headquartered in Dunmore. (Courtesy of the Pennsylvania Department of Transportation.)

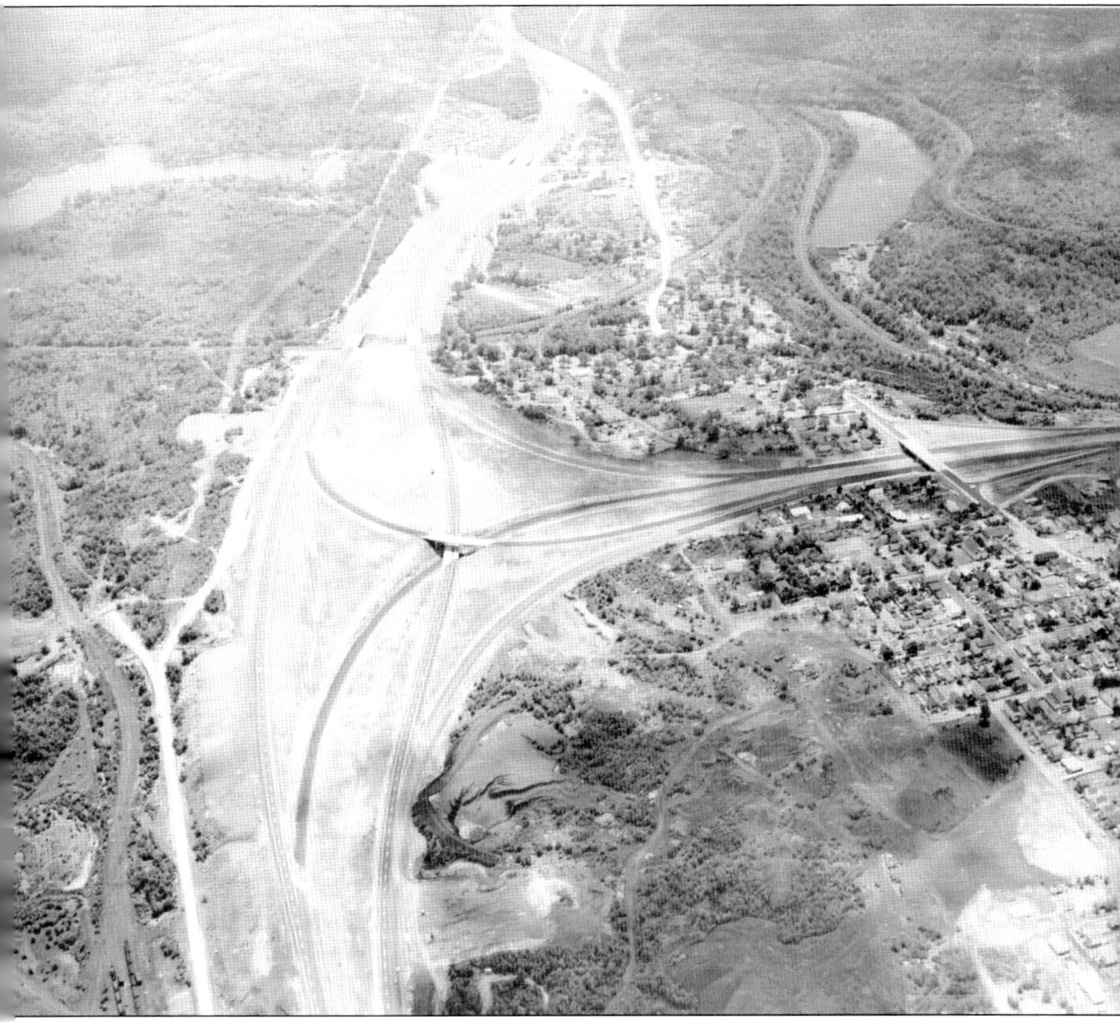

For residents of Northeastern Pennsylvania, Interstate 81 is one of the major highways of the region. At Dunmore, Interstate 81 intersects with Interstates 84 and 380. Construction on the "Cumberland Valley Freeway-Anthracite Expressway-Penn Can Highway" link between Hagerstown, Maryland, and Binghamton, New York, began in Pennsylvania in 1958 and took over 17 years to complete, eventually bearing the name "Interstate 81." Shown following its construction in the 1960s is the current exit 187 at Dunmore with Interstate 81 running from the bottom to the right. (Courtesy of the Pennsylvania Department of Transportation.)

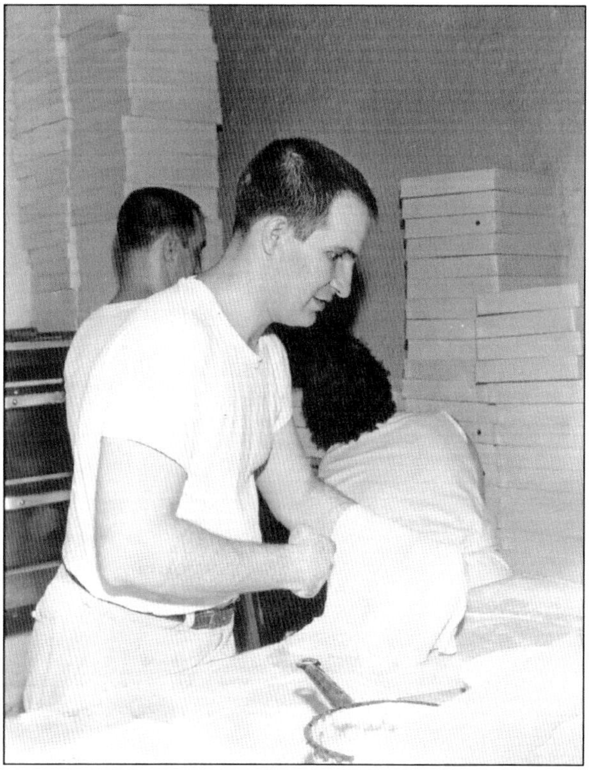

Salvatore J. Nardozzi Sr. opened Nardozzi's Pizza on Dunmore's Blakely Street in 1959. A popular hangout for Dunmore High School students before and after home games, Nardozzi's Pizza is best known for its authentic hearth-baked Neapolitan-style pizza. (Courtesy of Salvatore J. Nardozzi Jr.)

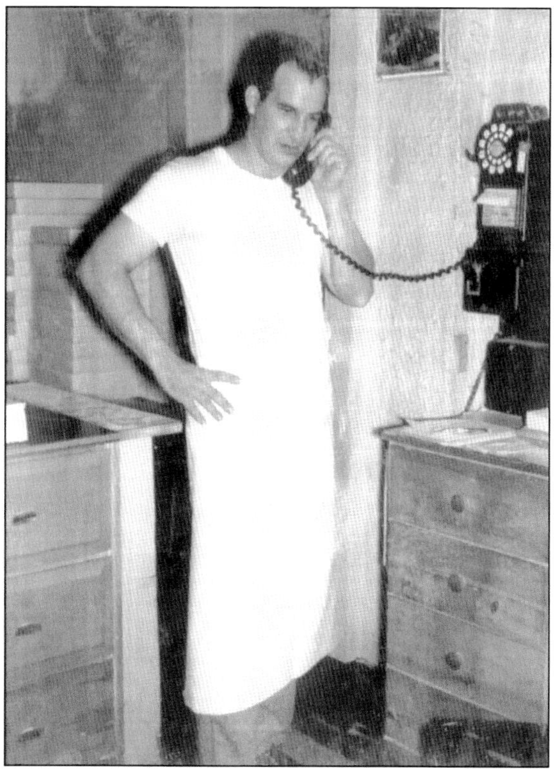

Although Salvatore J. Nardozzi Sr. passed away in 2005, his son Salvatore J. Nardozzi Jr. still makes pizza in the pizzeria's original location with his father's original recipe. Salvatore J. Nardozzi Sr. is pictured taking phone orders during the 1960s. (Courtesy of Salvatore J. Narzozzi Jr.)

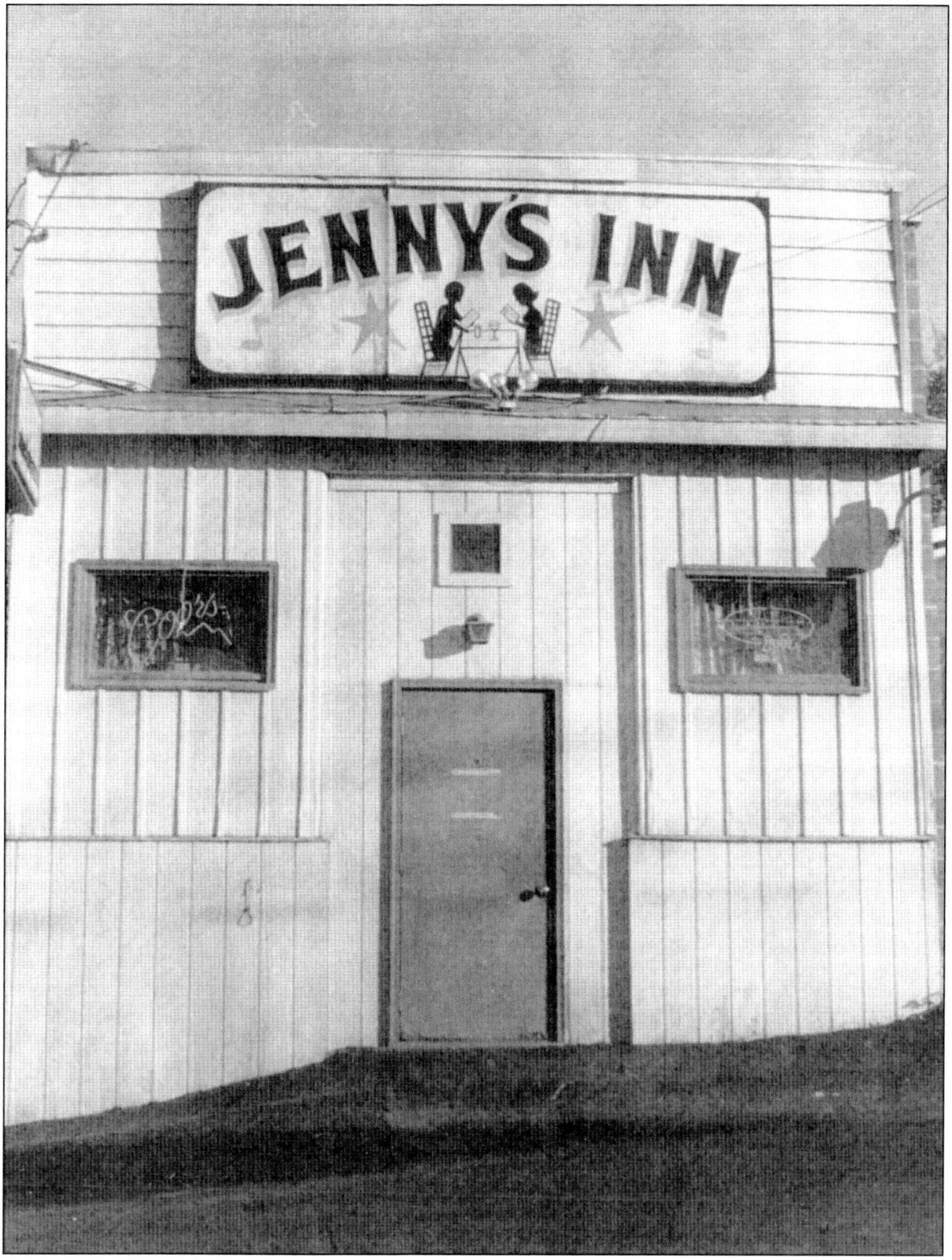

Jenny's Inn, located in the Bunker Hill section of Dunmore, was a popular restaurant for many years until its closing in the 2000s. Owned by Peter Castellano with his sister Mary Castellano Coviello as cook, the restaurant featured homemade pastas and sauces, with Mary giving guests free *pizza fritta* at the end of their meals. The building was torn down in early 2011. (Courtesy of Karl Wegforth.)

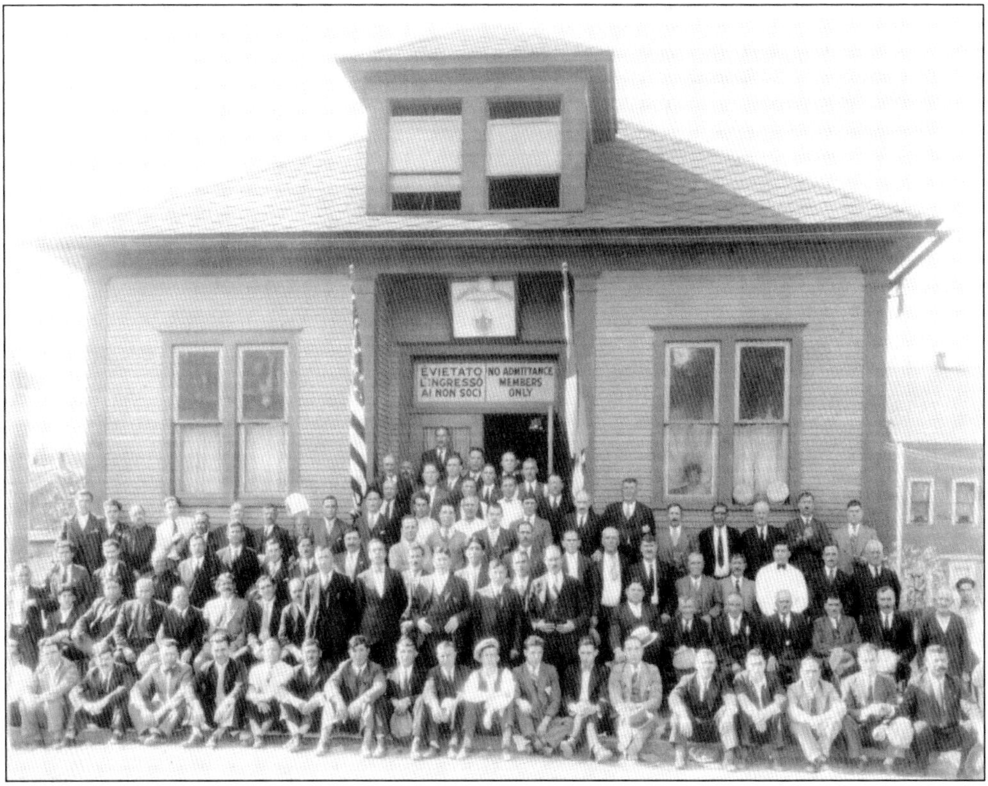

A large number of the Italian population of Dunmore can trace its roots to San Cataldo, Sicily. In 1904, a group of men from San Cataldo organized the "Società San Cataldese Cooperativa di Mutuo Soccorso" as a way to promote good will, civic betterment, and beneficial purposes to its members in case of sickness, accident, or death from the funds they collected among members. The Commonwealth of Pennsylvania formally recognized the San Cataldo Club as a club on May 15, 1906. In this photograph, members stand outside the San Cataldo Clubhouse on Elizabeth Street in Dunmore in 1929. (Courtesy of Santo "Sandy" Cancelleri.)

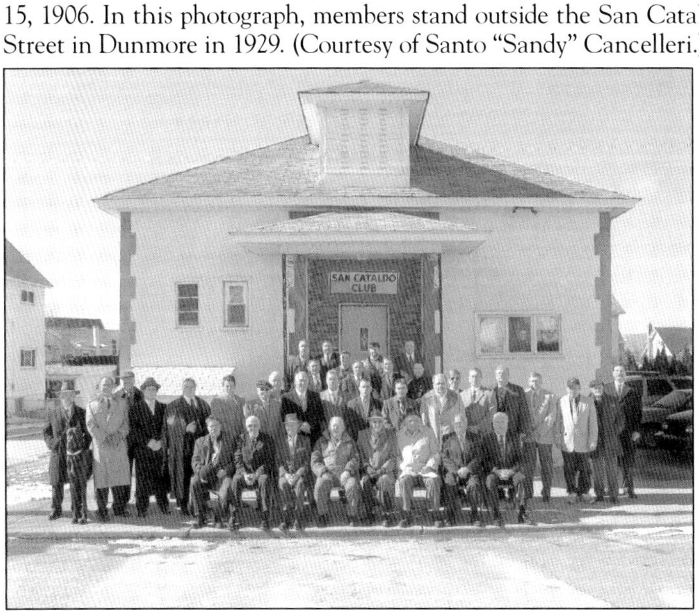

Descendants of the original members of the San Cataldo Club as well as current club members stand outside the San Cataldo Clubhouse on Elizabeth Street in Dunmore in 2006 in celebration of the club's centennial. (Courtesy of Santo "Sandy" Cancelleri.)

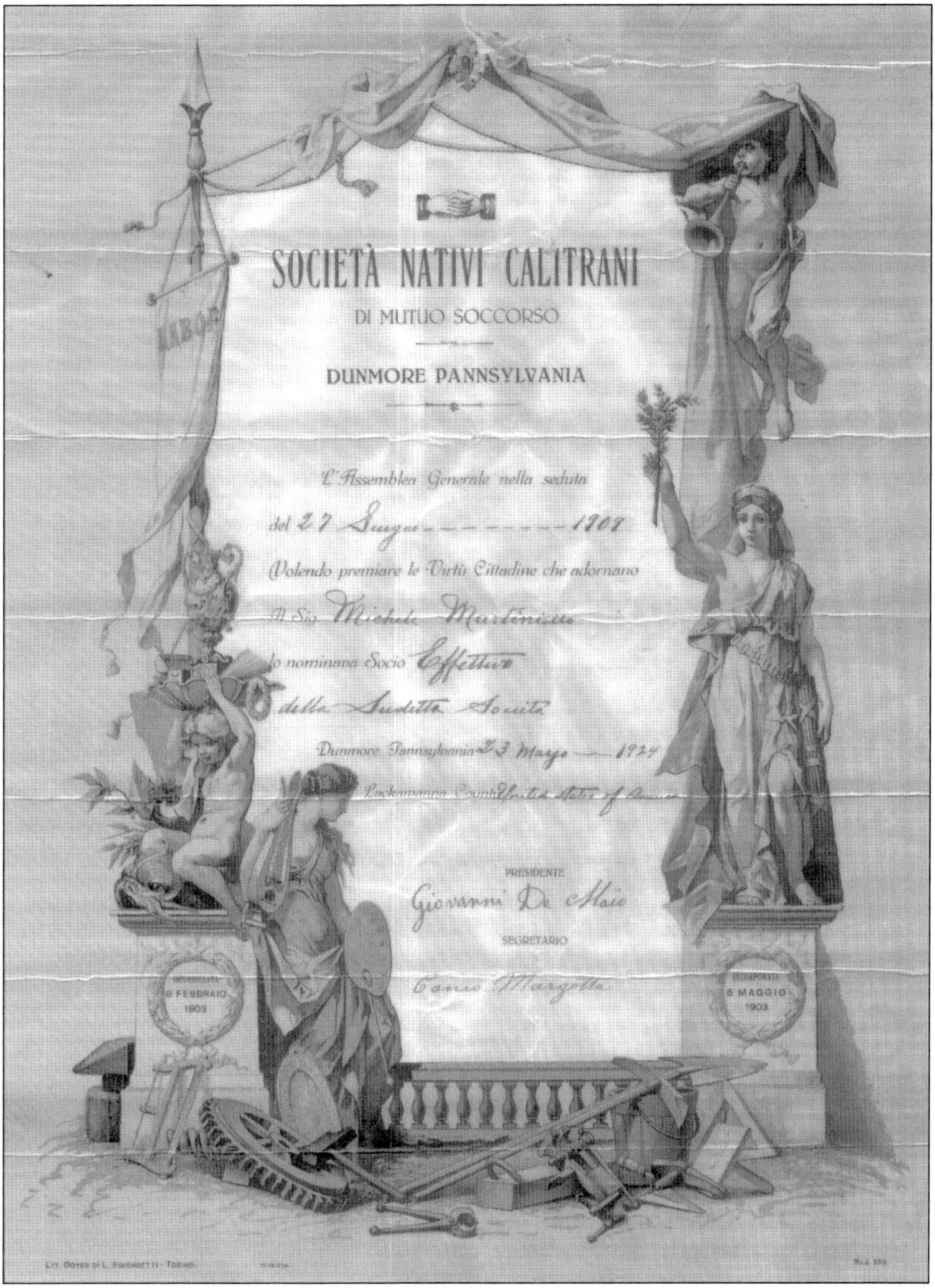

Another mutual aid society among Dunmore's Italian population was the "Società Nativi Calitrani di Mutuo Soccorso," which was incorporated in Dunmore on May 6, 1903. This document is the membership approval for Michele Martiniello, dated May 23, 1924. (Courtesy of the Dunmore Historical Society.)

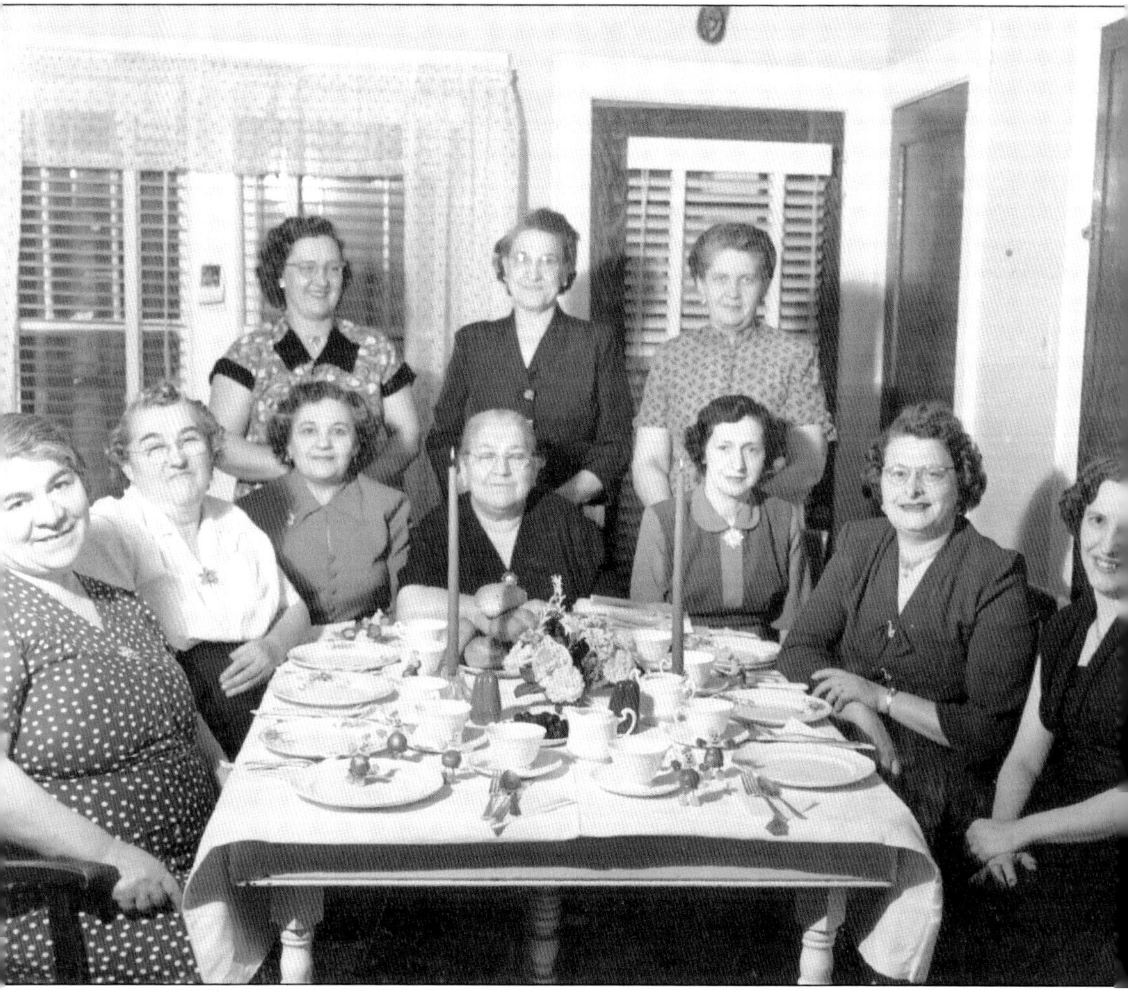

A group of members of the women's auxiliary of the Calitrani Club meet in the 1940s. Pictured from left to right are (first row) Concetta Sabata, Julia Russomano, Antoinette Margotta, Rosa Nicolais Rose Cianci DelRosario, Anna Cianci, and Katy Cianci; (second row) Margaret Simsick, Antoinette Vitaletti, and Norma Green. The club met once a month in members' homes. (Courtesy of Rosemary Summa.)

Francis Xavier Kranick, MD, practiced family medicine at 526 East Drinker Street from 1955 until his death in 1988. Kranick was a 1943 graduate of Dunmore High School and served in the US Army during World War II. He received his medical degree from the University of Pennsylvania in 1953 and served with the US Air Force for two years, discharged with the rank of captain. In 1971, he joined with four other physicians to form Professional Medical Associates in Scranton. He also served as the director of the emergency care unit at the former Mercy Hospital, Scranton, from 1976 to 1980, resuming work there in January 1988, just before his death. (Courtesy of Ellen Coyle.)

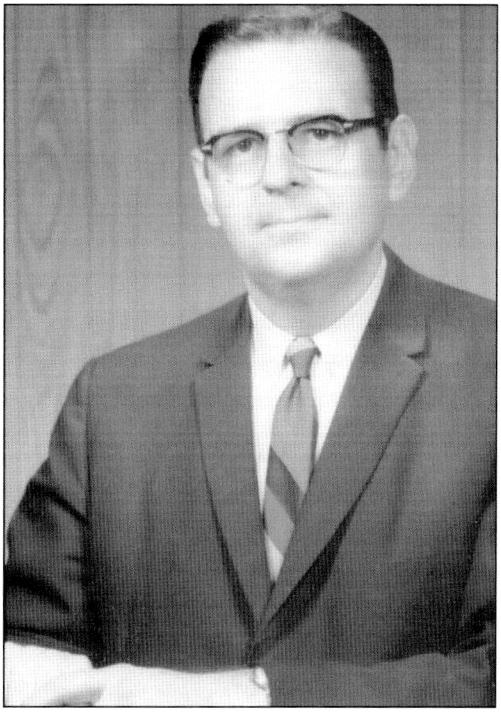

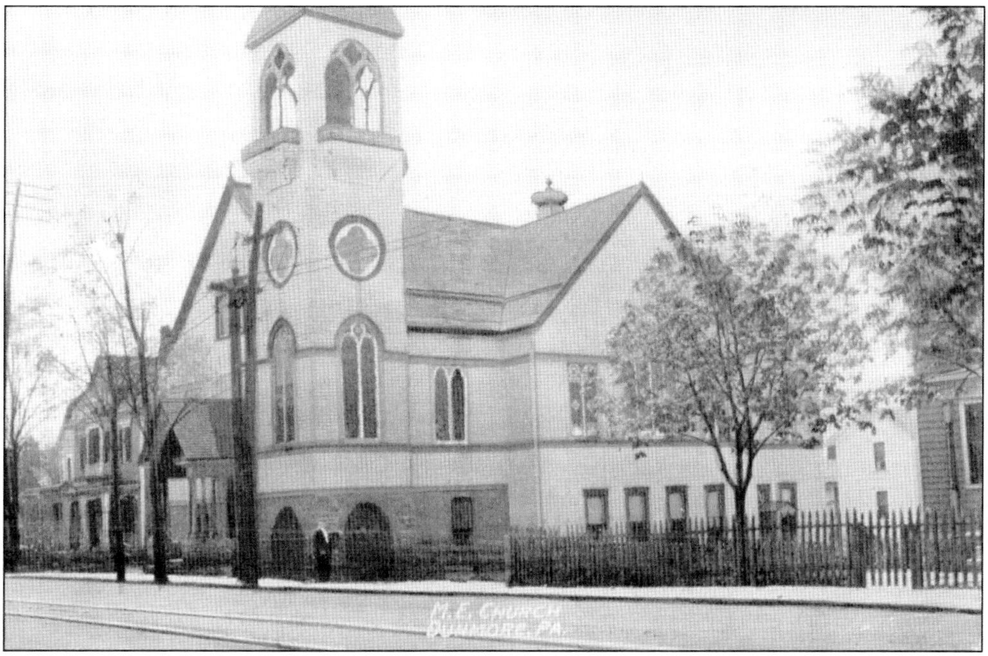

The Dunmore Methodist Church began as a mission in 1851 on North Blakely Street. In 1854, Edward Spencer donated a lot on Chestnut Street, where the Dunmore Presbyterian Church now stands, on the condition that the pews were free. In 1859, the first Dunmore Methodist Church was built at that location. In 1888, the church's current property at the corner of South Blakely and Rigg Streets was purchased, and the present church was built that year. (Courtesy of the Dunmore Historical Society.)

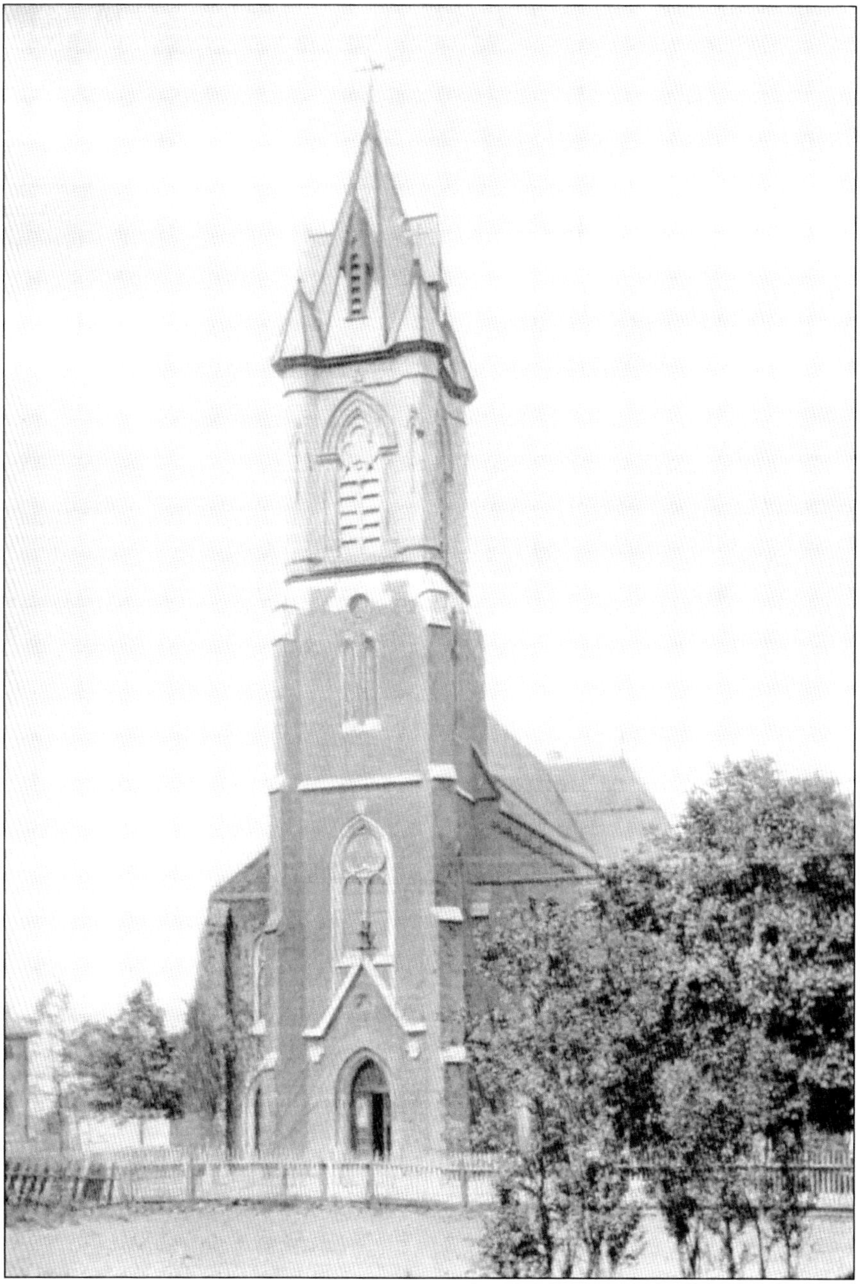

Roman Catholicism grew in Dunmore thanks to the creation of the Gravity Railroad and the opening of the mines. The first Catholics to settle in Dunmore originally hailed from Carbondale and used to go to Scranton to attend services. In 1855, the land for what is now known as Our Lady of Mount Carmel Parish was purchased from Charles Potter. The first church built on that parcel of land was named St. Simon the Apostle. Bishop John N. Neumann, who was eventually canonized a saint in the Catholic Church, personally came to dedicate the original St. Simon's Church on July 26, 1857. This photograph shows the new St. Mary of Mount Carmel Church, which is located on the site of the original St. Simon the Apostle Church, during the early 1900s. (Courtesy of Sam Valenza.)

This photograph shows the original interior of St. Mary of Mount Carmel Church. Out of all of the Catholic churches in Dunmore, St. Mary of Mount Carmel is the oldest. The name of the church was changed from St. Simon the Apostle to St. Mary of Mount Carmel in 1874 in commemoration of the 150th anniversary of the adoption of the Feast of Our Lady of Mount Carmel in the Catholic Church. (Courtesy of Sam Valenza.)

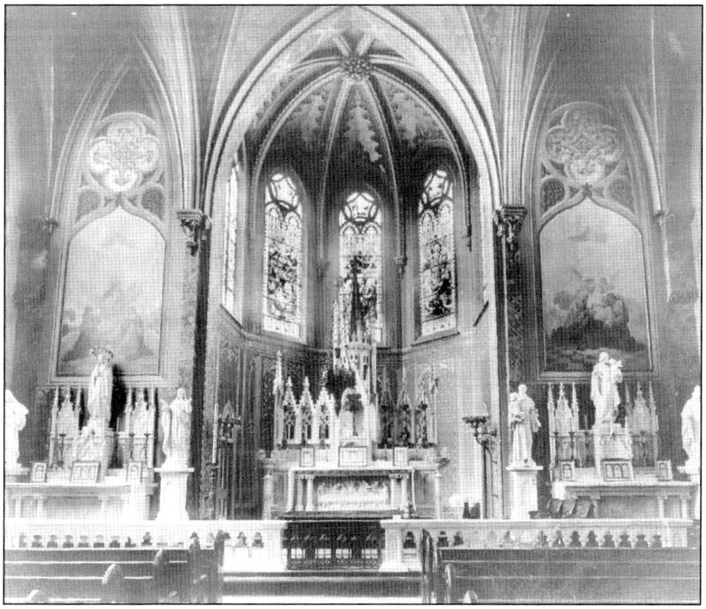

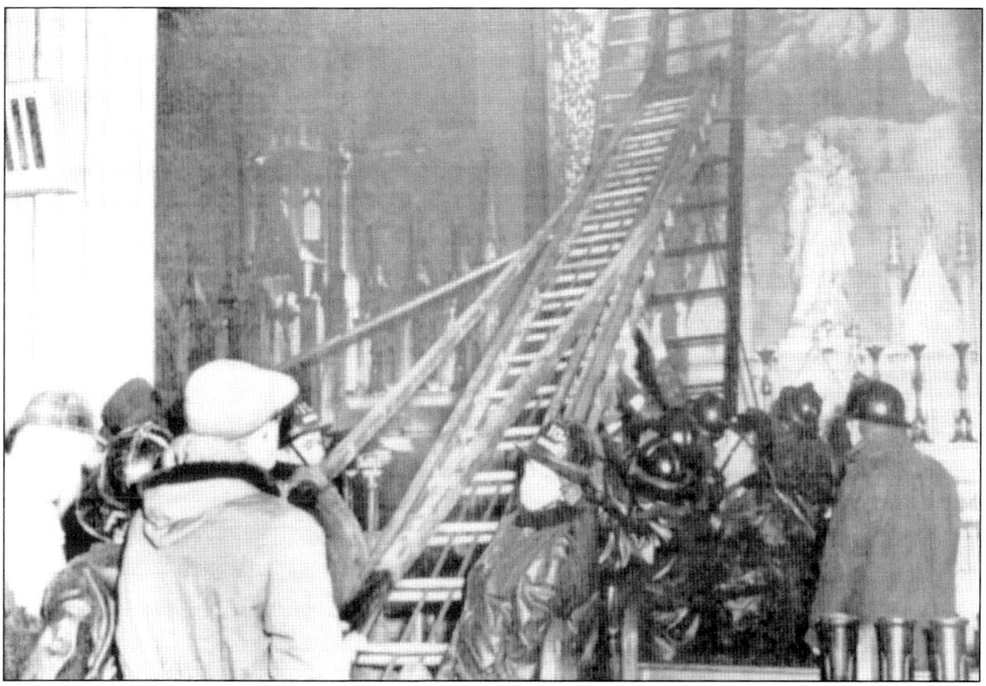

On February 21, 1959, a fire broke out in St. Mary of Mount Carmel Church after a short circuit in electrical wiring triggered the ringing of the church bell. The altar area of the church, as seen in the previous photograph, was completely destroyed and the estimated damage totaled well over $100,000. (Courtesy of Joe and Dolly Michalczyk.)

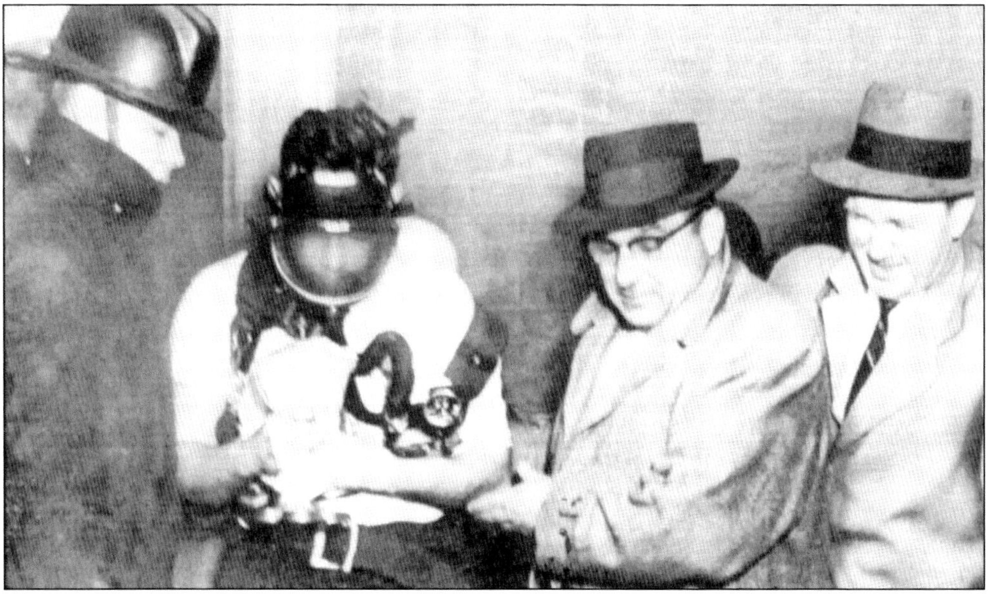

On the night of the fire at St. Mary of Mount Carmel Church, then-assistant pastor Fr. William Ward, age 27 at the time, entered the burning church in an attempt to save the Blessed Sacrament as well as other valuable items from the church. Having received an oxygen mask from a fireman, Father Ward succeeded in rescuing the Blessed Sacrament, relying on the sense of touch to get out of the burning church. Parishioner William Lavin, at Father Ward's right, assisted him when he got outside. (Courtesy of Joe and Dolly Michalczyk.)

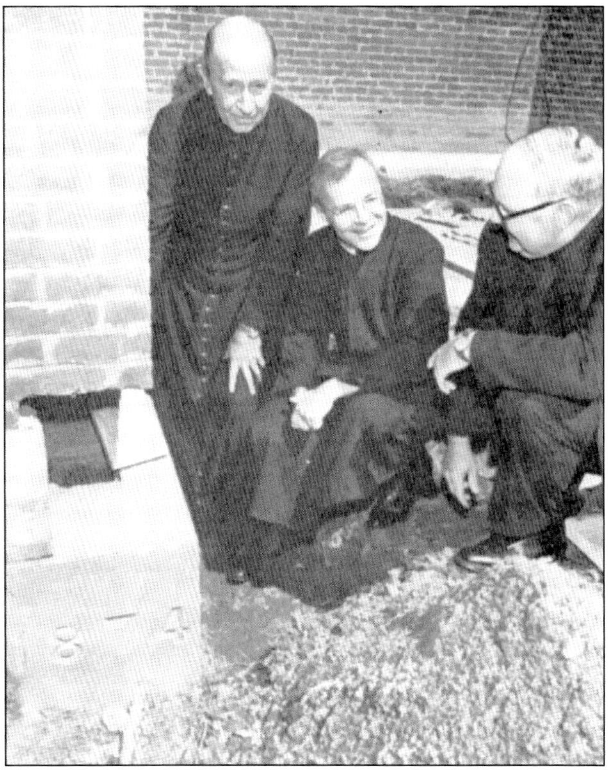

In preparation for St. Mary of Mount Carmel's centennial in 1974, then-assistant pastor Fr. Paul Flynn noticed this cornerstone after it had been exposed while new sidewalks around the church were being installed. The cornerstone, which reads "B.V.M. de Mont. Carmelo—1874," confirms the year that the church's name was changed from St. Simon the Apostle to St. Mary of Mount Carmel. The cornerstone had become hidden when the ground around St. Mary of Mount Carmel Church was leveled to make way for trolley tracks during the early 1900s. From left to right are Msgr. Charles Heid, then-pastor of St. Mary of Mount Carmel Church; assistant pastor Fr. Paul Flynn; and assistant pastor Fr. John Lipinski. (Courtesy of Sam Valenza and Joe and Dolly Michalczyk.)

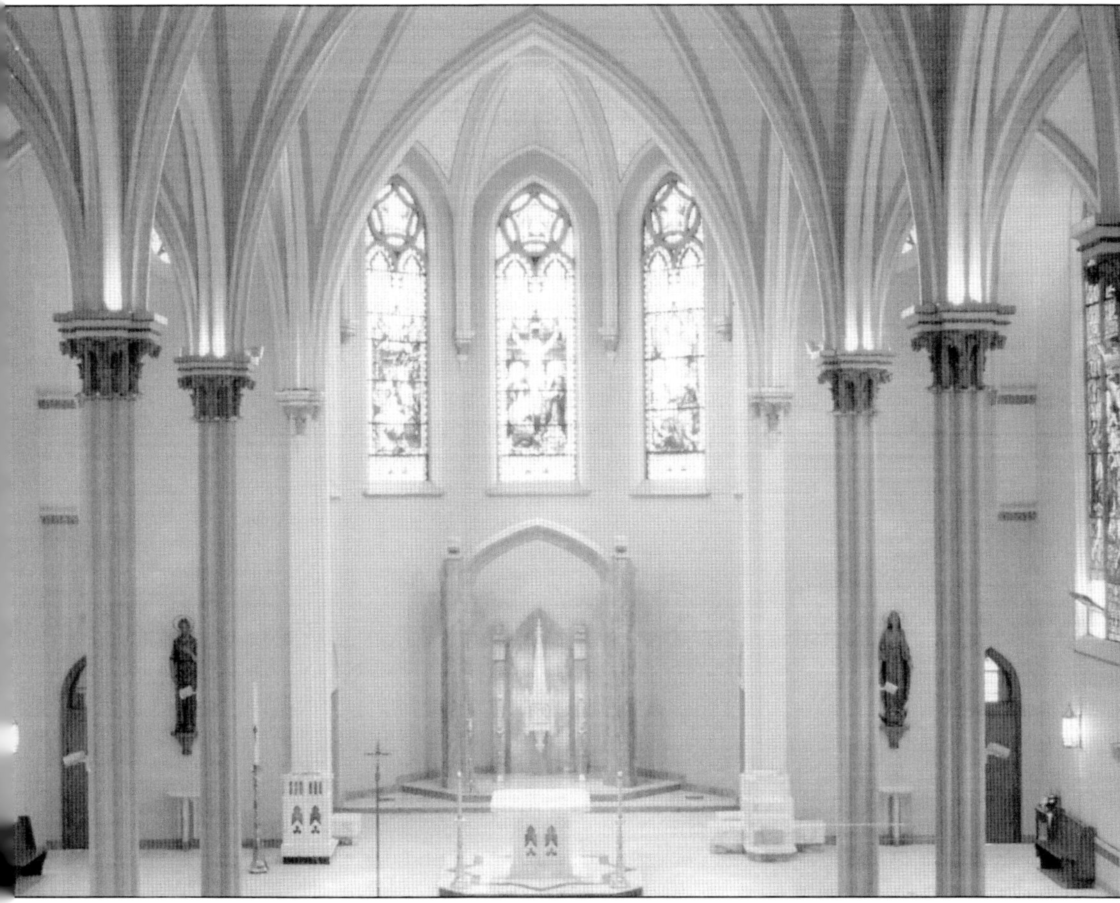

Here is the interior of St. Mary of Mount Carmel Church following extensive renovations after the 1959 fire and in preparation for both the 1974 centennial and the 125th anniversary of the church's construction in 1999. (Courtesy of Sam Valenza.)

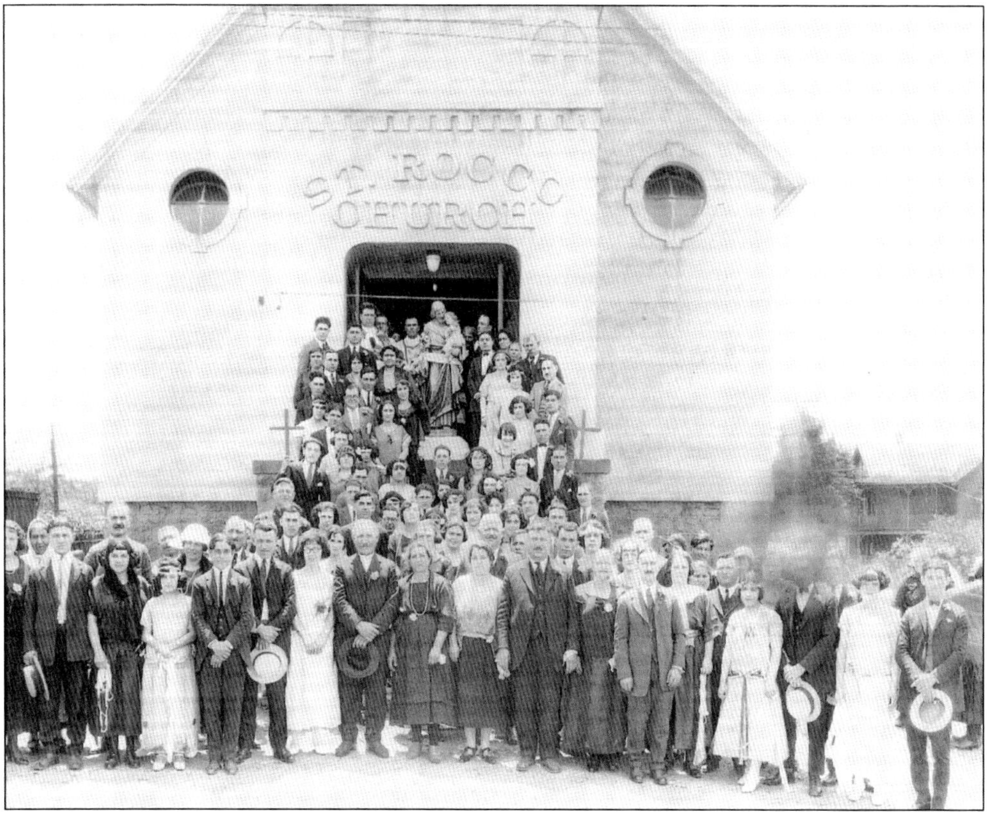

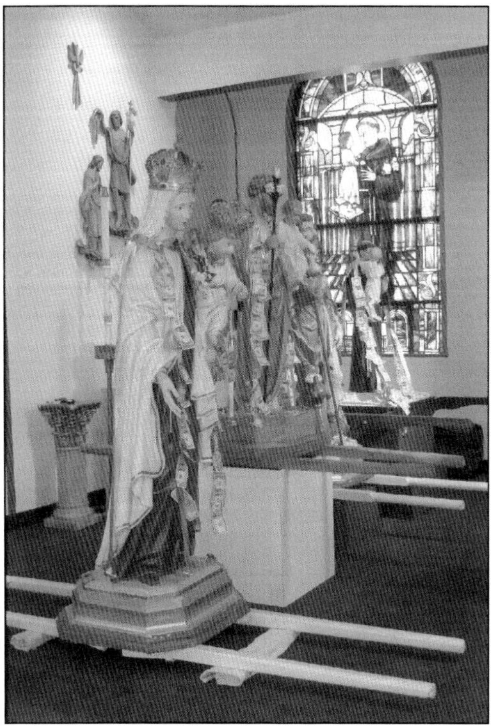

Newly arrived immigrants from Guardia dei Lombardi, Italy, stand in front of St. Rocco's Church in Dunmore's Bunker Hill neighborhood following the annual procession to St. Rocco, which takes place every August in both Dunmore and Guardia dei Lombardi. (Courtesy of Carlo Pisa.)

The statues of the Blessed Virgin Mary, St. Joseph, St. Rocco, and St. Anthony are seen on the altar at St. Rocco's Church in Dunmore's Bunker Hill following the annual procession to St. Rocco in 2008. The procession to St. Rocco has taken place every year at St. Rocco's Church since 1922. The statue of St. Anthony was added to the procession in 2008 to mark the parish's linkage with St. Anthony of Padua Parish in Dunmore. In 2010, St. Anthony of Padua Parish and St. Rocco's Parish united as one parish under the name of SS. Anthony and Rocco Parish with the procession continuing to take place every August. (Author.)

Here is the interior of St. Rocco's Church in the 1950s. St. Rocco's Parish was organized in 1904 by a group of young Italian men who immigrated to Dunmore's Bunker Hill from Guardia dei Lombardi, Italy, under the name "the Society of the Congregation of St. Rocco's Church." St. Rocco is the patron saint of Guardia dei Lombardi because, according to legend, he saved the town from a violent plague in 1656 that killed 1,110 of its 1,475 residents. (Courtesy of Carlo Pisa.)

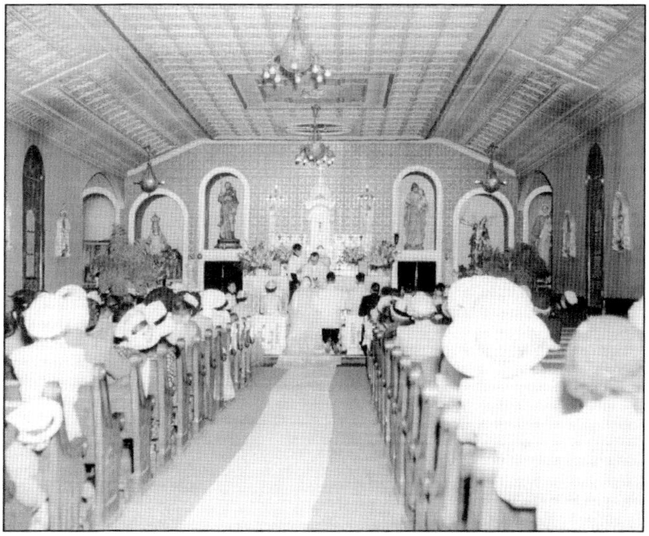

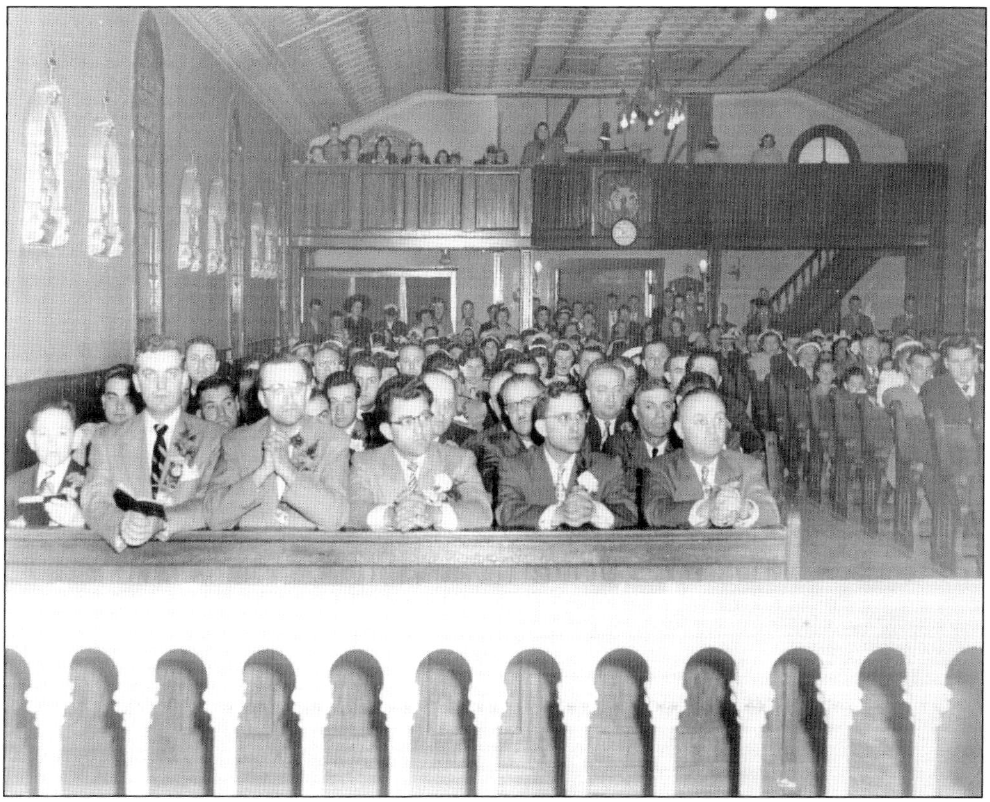

This is the rear of St. Rocco's Church as it appeared in the 1950s. The original choir loft no longer exists. The building itself was purchased in 1905 from the Dunmore Presbyterian Church, and extensive renovations were made under the first pastorate of Fr. Anthony Tombasco, who was pastor of St. Rocco's from 1967 until 1977 and again from 1984 until 2006. Extensive renovations also continued under the pastorate of Fr. Joseph Cipriano, who was pastor of St. Rocco's from 1977 until 1984. (Courtesy of Carlo Pisa.)

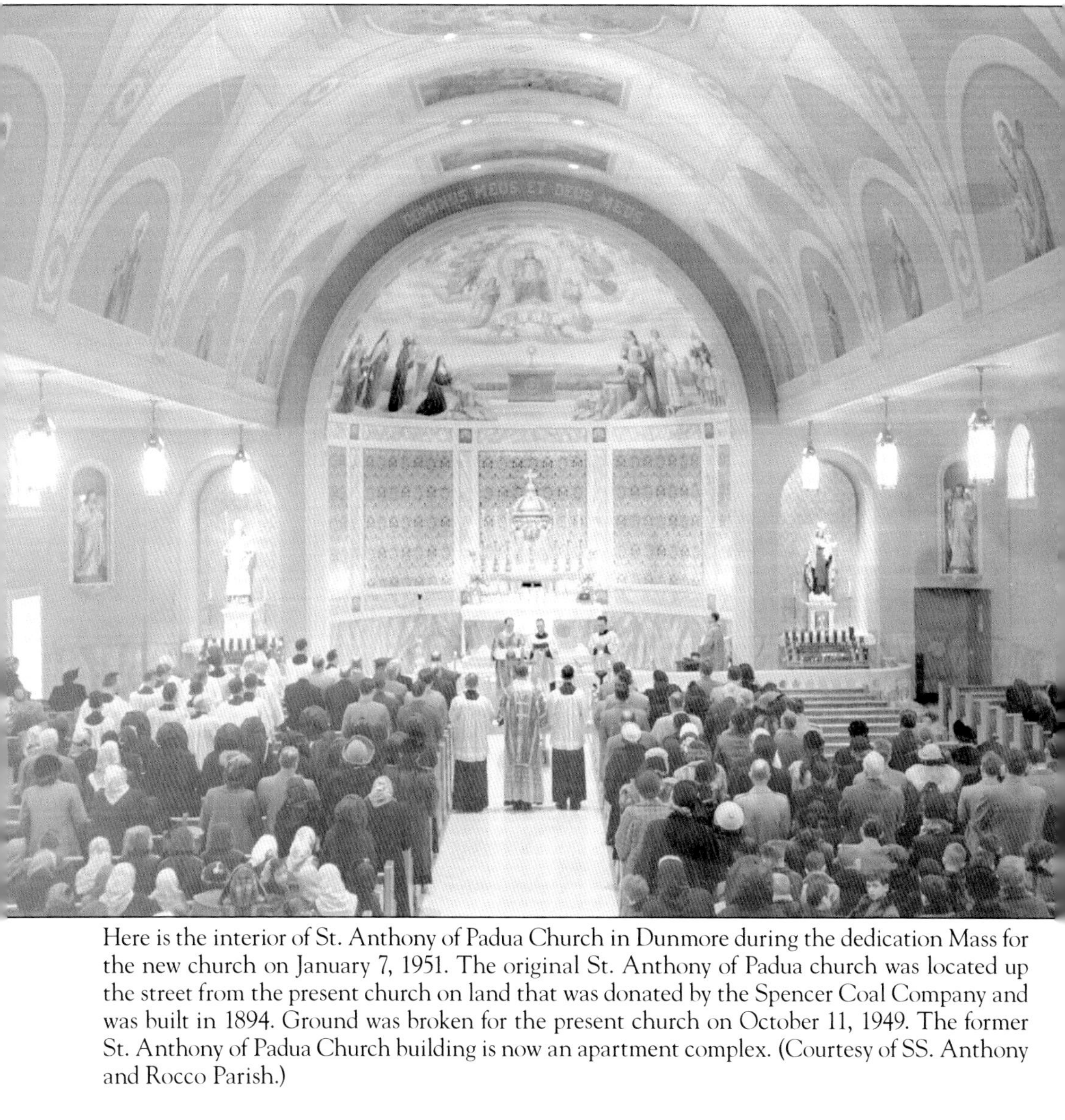

Here is the interior of St. Anthony of Padua Church in Dunmore during the dedication Mass for the new church on January 7, 1951. The original St. Anthony of Padua church was located up the street from the present church on land that was donated by the Spencer Coal Company and was built in 1894. Ground was broken for the present church on October 11, 1949. The former St. Anthony of Padua Church building is now an apartment complex. (Courtesy of SS. Anthony and Rocco Parish.)

St. Anthony of Padua Parish was the first Italian Catholic church to be founded in Dunmore in 1891 by the first 30 Italian immigrant families to settle in Dunmore. For a period of time, St. Rocco's Church in Bunker Hill was a mission of St. Anthony of Padua Church. The decision to construct a new church for the parish, pictured here, was made by Msgr. William Crotti, who was pastor of the parish from 1928 until 1973. (Courtesy of SS. Anthony and Rocco Parish.)

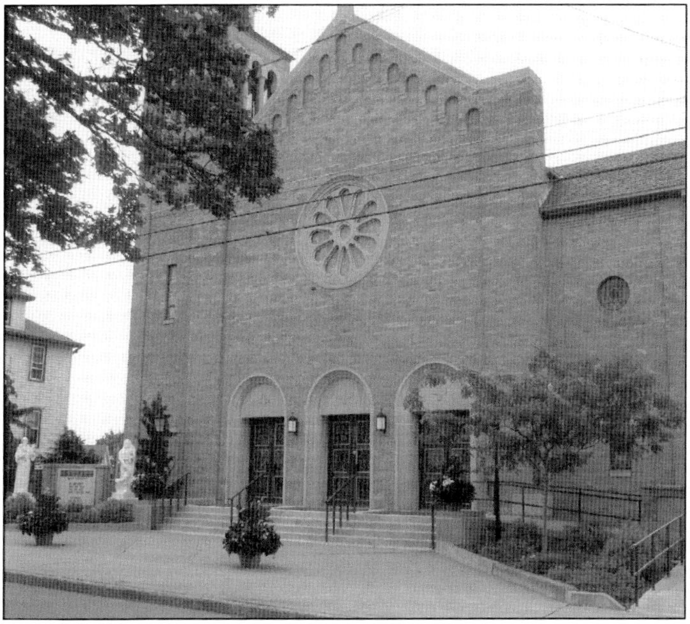

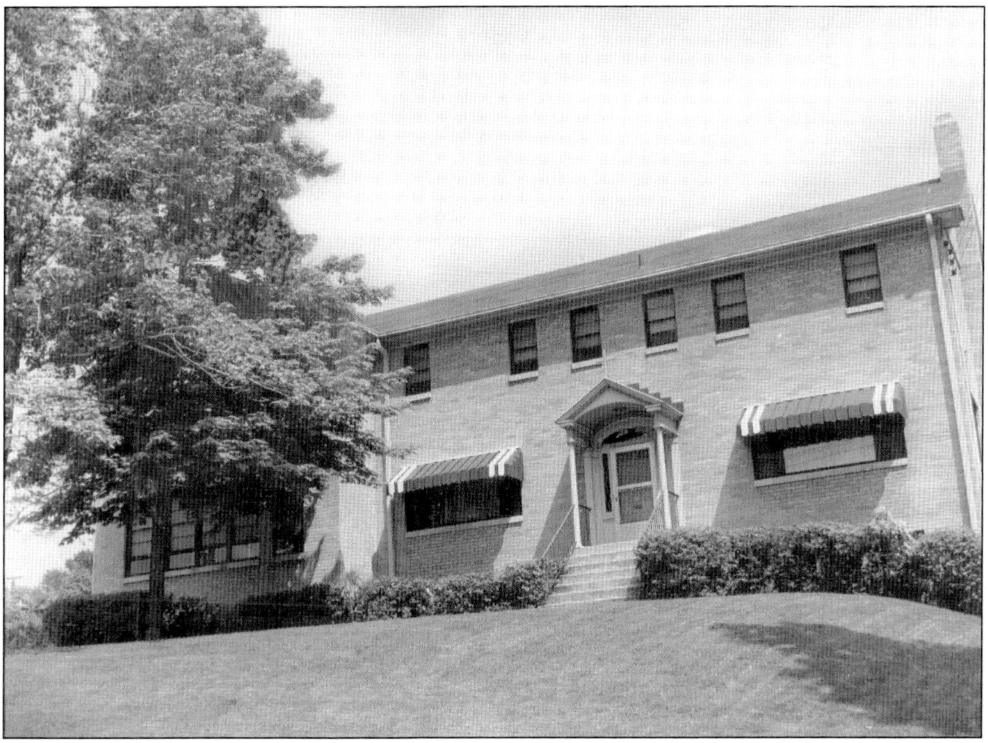

St. Anthony's Convent, home of the Religious Teachers Filippini, was built in 1940 on Franklin Street in Dunmore. The Religious Teachers Filippini is an order of nuns devoted to education. The convent was moved in 2008 to the former St. Rocco's Church rectory when the process of uniting the two parishes began as a part of the Diocese of Scranton's restructuring efforts. In 2011, the Religious Teachers Filippini order celebrated the 100th anniversary of their arrival in the United States from Italy. (Courtesy of SS. Anthony and Rocco Parish.)

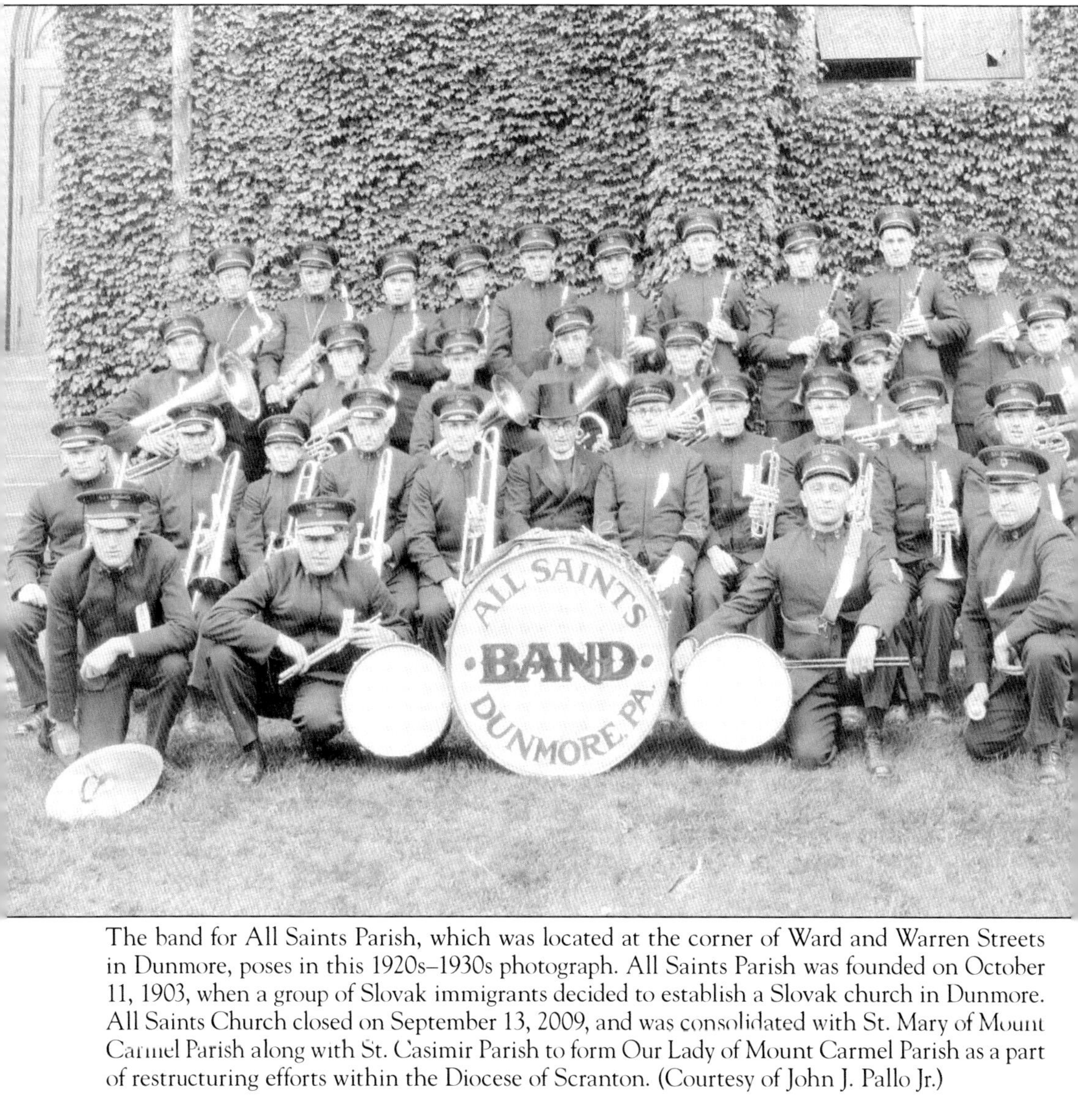

The band for All Saints Parish, which was located at the corner of Ward and Warren Streets in Dunmore, poses in this 1920s–1930s photograph. All Saints Parish was founded on October 11, 1903, when a group of Slovak immigrants decided to establish a Slovak church in Dunmore. All Saints Church closed on September 13, 2009, and was consolidated with St. Mary of Mount Carmel Parish along with St. Casimir Parish to form Our Lady of Mount Carmel Parish as a part of restructuring efforts within the Diocese of Scranton. (Courtesy of John J. Pallo Jr.)

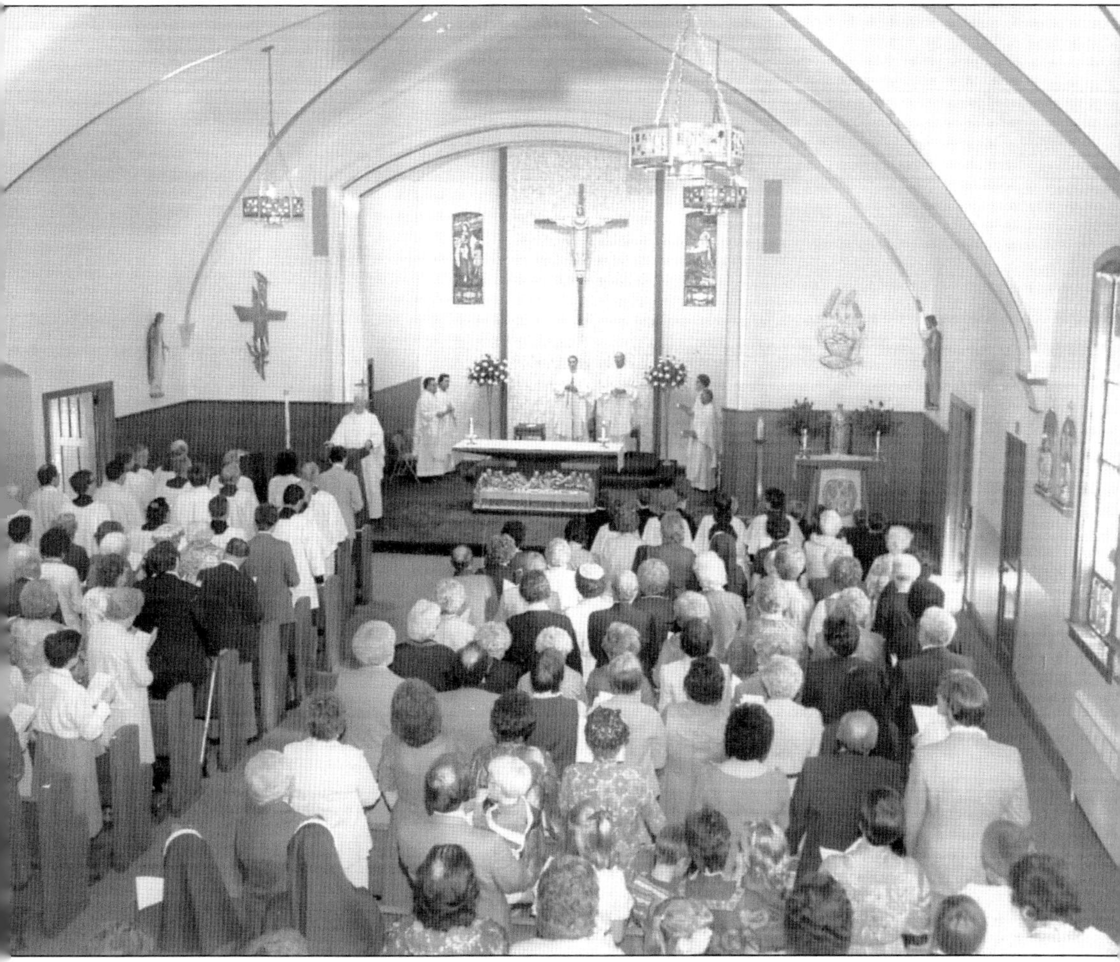

The dedication Mass for Christ the King Parish in Dunmore on December 16, 1951. Christ the King Parish was formed out of the parish communities of St. Peter's Cathedral in Scranton, St. Paul's in Scranton, and St. Mary of Mount Carmel in Dunmore. The church was closed on June 28, 2009, and consolidated with Immaculate Conception Parish in Scranton as a part of restructuring efforts within the Diocese of Scranton. (Courtesy of the Diocese of Scranton.)

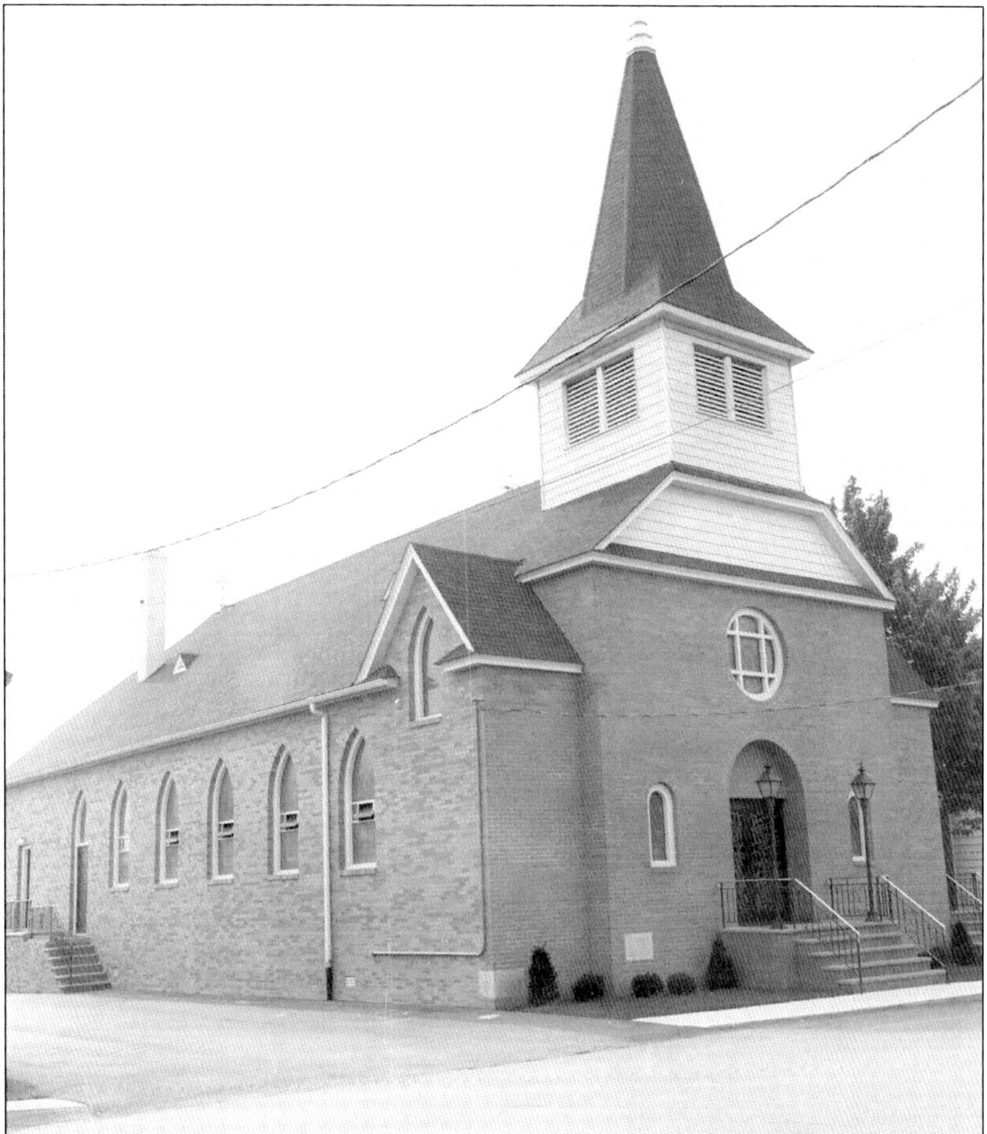

St. Casimir's Church, which served the Polish community of Dunmore, was built in 1929 following the fundraising efforts of the 93 Polish families residing in Dunmore. The church was originally a mission of Sacred Hearts of Jesus and Mary Church in Scranton but was declared a parish in 1939 by former Bishop of the Diocese of Scranton William Hafey. St. Casimir's closed on September 20, 2009, and was consolidated with St. Mary of Mount Carmel Parish along with All Saints Parish to form Our Lady of Mount Carmel Parish as a part of restructuring efforts within the Diocese of Scranton. (Courtesy of the Diocese of Scranton.)

Three

SCHOOL PRIDE

The growth of the education system in Dunmore also coincided with its becoming a borough as up until 1868 Dunmore only had ungraded schools that were small and poorly equipped. During 1868, the original "Old Brick" school was built at the corner of South Apple and Ambrose Streets in Dunmore. Although no photographs are known to exist of the "Old Brick" school, it was described as two stories in height and was 60 feet long and 40 feet wide. The decision to construct "Old Brick" was the direct result of the Pennsylvania Coal Company's influence on the borough's population.

As of June 7, 1869, records show that "Old Brick" had seven teachers, two men and five women. The average salary for men was $52 per month, while the women earned $28 per month. At the time, the school year lasted seven months, and the school's enrollment was 350 boys and 450 girls. For over 20 years, students attended "Old Brick," which was a graded school with three departments and 10 grades. The primary department had four grades, while the grammar and academic departments had six.

From the time of "Old Brick" up to the present, Dunmore School District has grown and expanded and has also been the witness of two local firsts: in 1900, Daisy L. MacCrory became the principal of the business department of Dunmore High School, making her the first female to reach such a high position in the district. MacCrory's accomplishment was surpassed in the 1960s when Eugenia DeFazio became the first female principal of all of Dunmore High School.

Besides the Dunmore School District, the Borough of Dunmore is also currently home to Holy Cross High School, which was once known as Dunmore Central Catholic High School and then Bishop O'Hara High School; St. Mary of Mount Carmel School; Marywood University; and the Pennsylvania State University's Worthington/Scranton Campus.

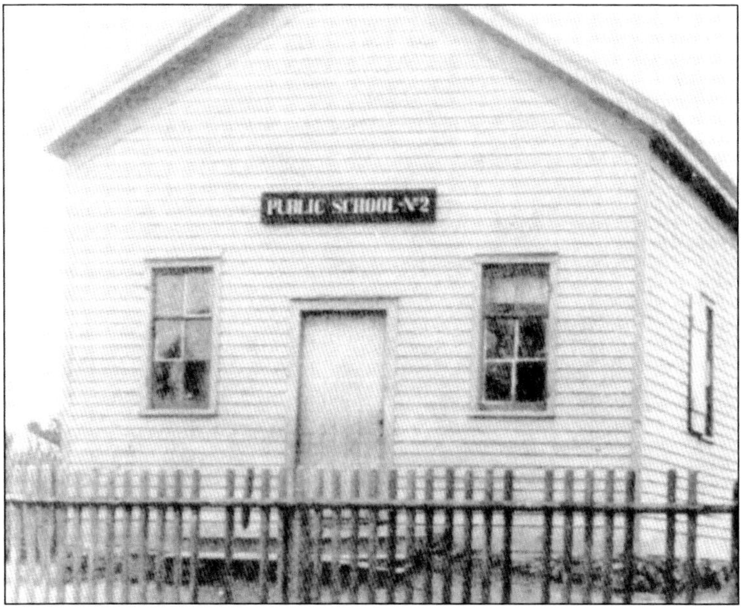

Dunmore's first school, the Public School No. 2, was a one-room schoolhouse on North Blakely Street, built in 1826. At the time, parents had to pay to send their children to school, yet there were no tuition charges at the Public School No. 2, which made it one of the few "free" schools in the Commonwealth of Pennsylvania. (Courtesy of Joe and Dolly Michalczyk.)

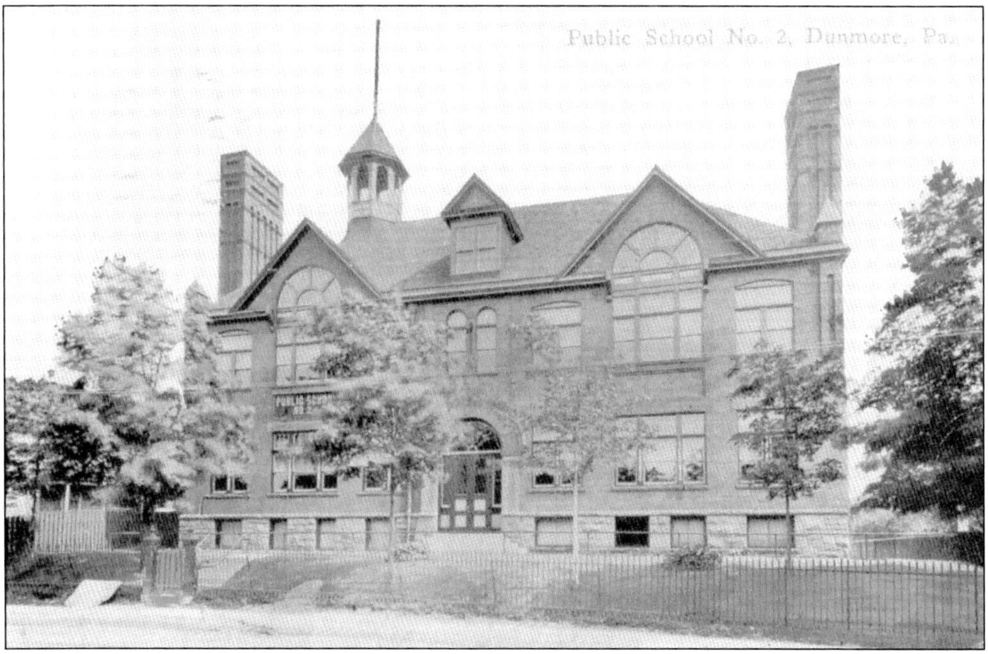

The Public School No. 2 eventually became known as the William Penn School. At one point, Dunmore had 10 elementary schools, but the number went down to four by 1962: William Penn (No. 2), George Washington (No. 3), Benjamin Franklin (No. 10), and Thomas Jefferson (No. 11). During the 1969–1970 school year, the Dunmore School District decided to consolidate all of the elementary schools and form the Dunmore Elementary Center. Today, the Robert E. Dougherty Senior High Rise stands on the site of the former William Penn School. (Courtesy of the Dunmore Historical Society.)

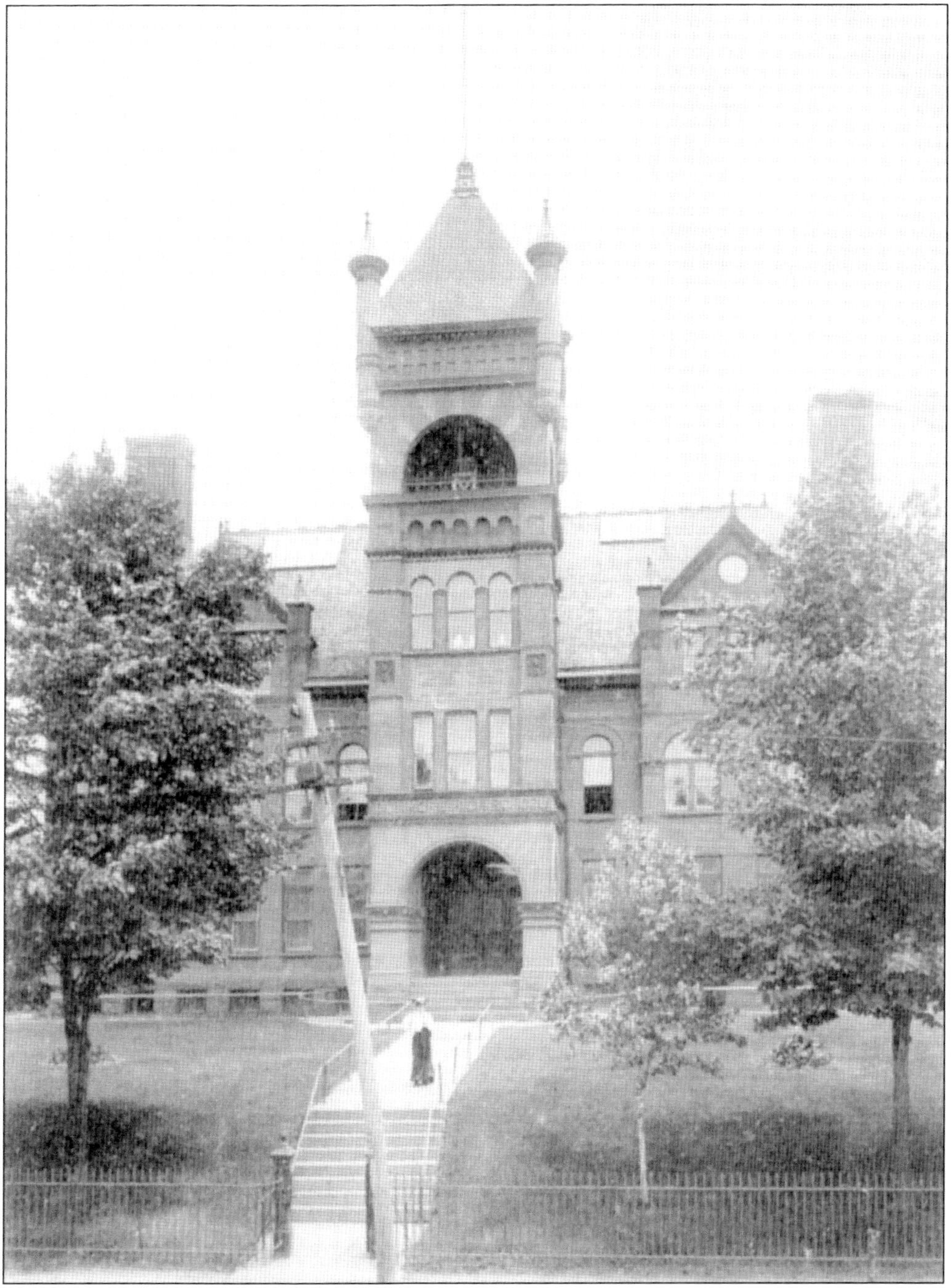

The first high school in Dunmore was built in 1868. Students attended classes there for 20 years until a newer, larger high school was built on South Apple Street. The "Central School" was opened in 1891, and its first class graduated in 1903. Unfortunately, a fire destroyed the building in 1908, and classes were held in the Dunmore Presbyterian Church. This image shows the rebuilt Central School, which served as Dunmore's high school until 1936. The old Central School then served as Dunmore's Junior High School until the late 1960s. (Courtesy of the Dunmore Historical Society.)

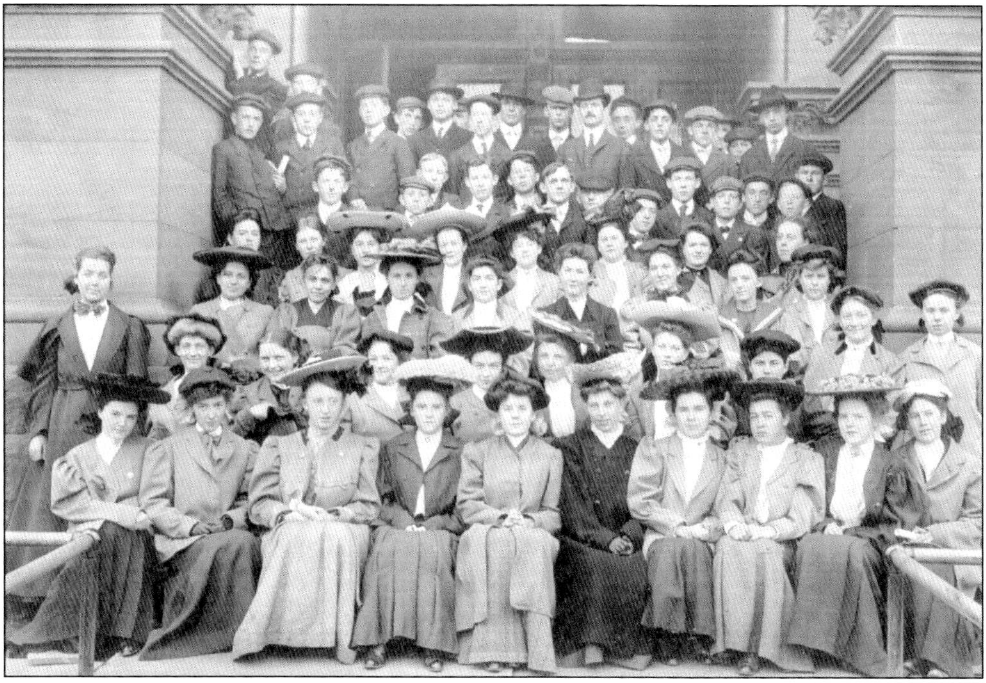

The Dunmore High School graduating class of June 1907 sits on the steps of the original Central School before it was destroyed by a fire. Until 1945, students at Dunmore High School could graduate in either January or June. (Courtesy of the Dunmore Historical Society.)

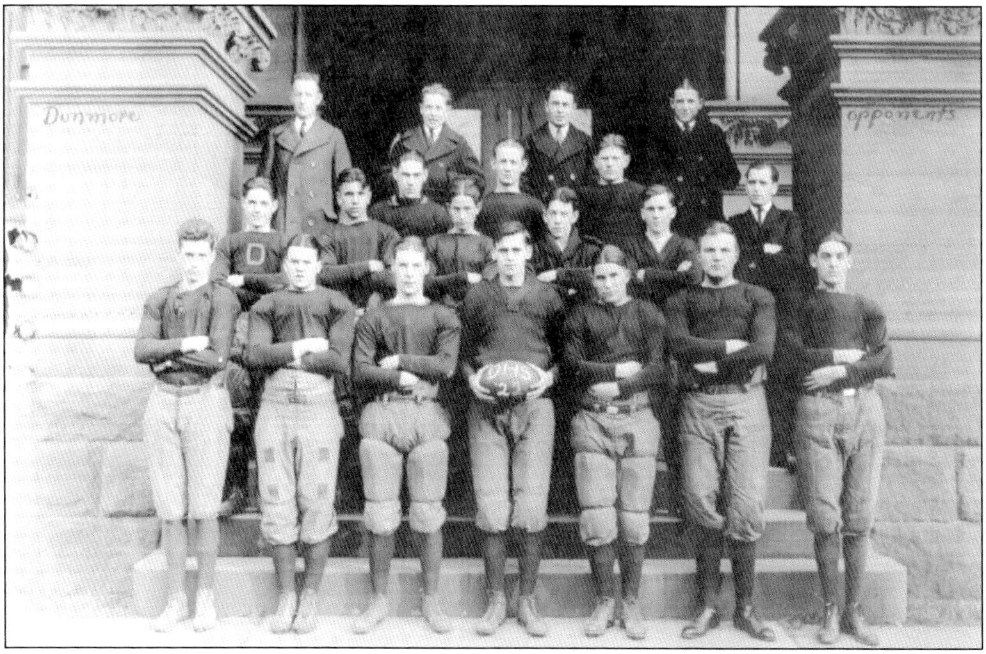

The Dunmore High School Bucks football team poses on the steps of the rebuilt Central School on South Apple Street in 1922. James P. Gilligan, who taught chemistry and physics for Dunmore High School until his death in 1950, can be seen in the top row at left. (Courtesy of Catherine G. Quinnan.)

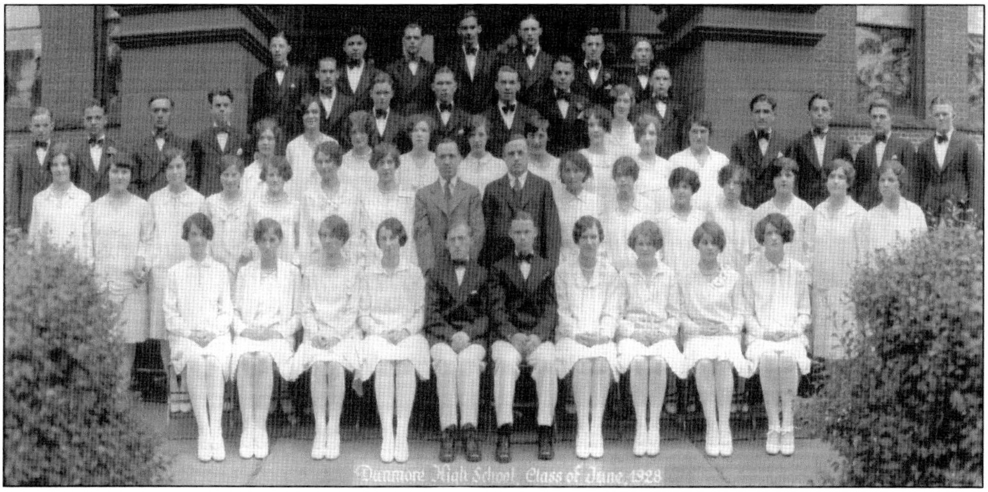

Members of the Dunmore High School graduating class of June 1928 sit on the steps of their alma mater on North Apple Street. (Courtesy of the Dunmore Historical Society.)

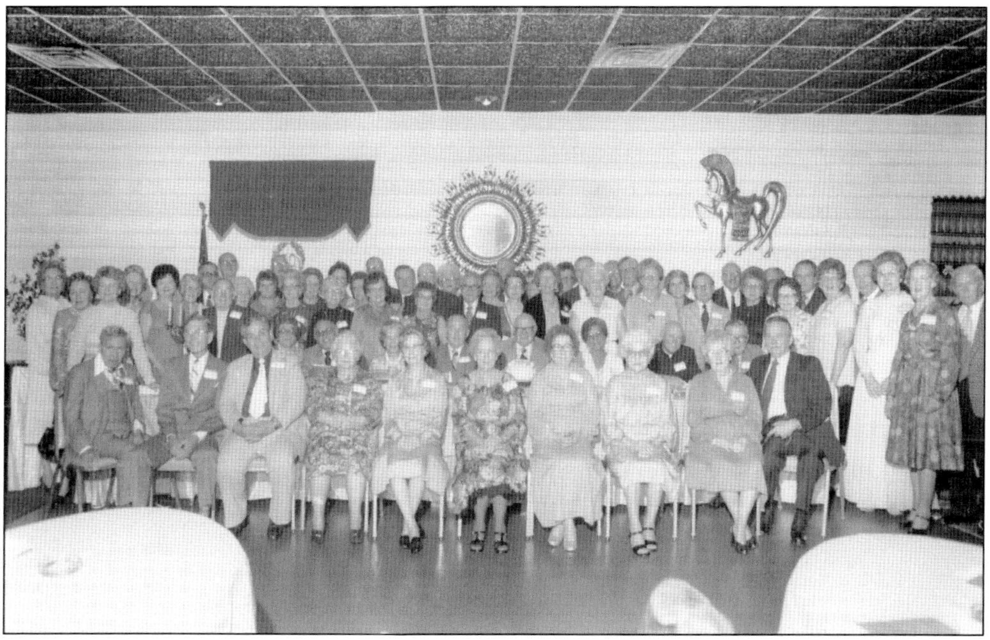

Fifty years later, on October 7, 1978, members of the Dunmore High School class of 1928 reunited in their hometown. This photograph was originally property of Frank Mangan, seated in the first row, second from the left. (Courtesy of Catherine G. Quinnan.)

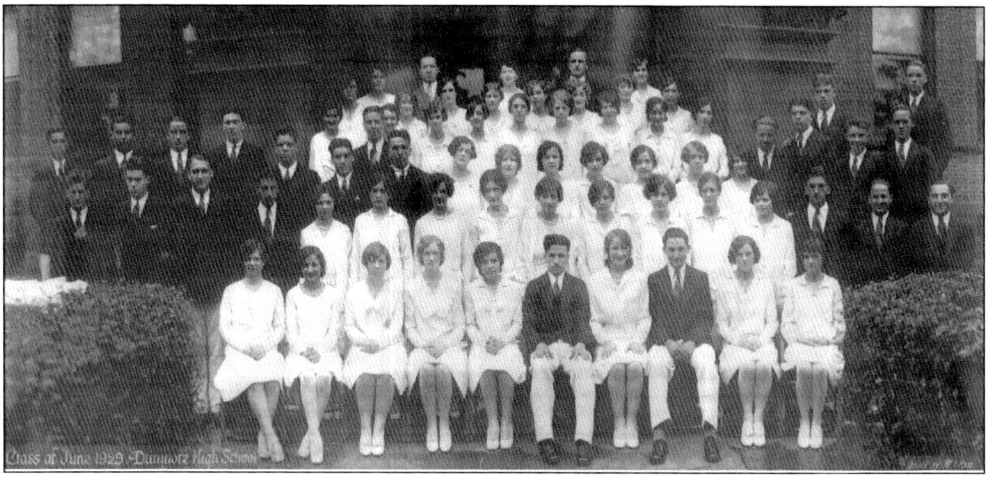

Eugenia Donato DeFazio, seated fifth from the left, was the valedictorian of her graduating class of June 1929. DeFazio received both a bachelor's and a master's degree from Marywood College and began her first teaching position for the Dunmore School District in 1935, teaching seventh and eighth grades at the Eugene Field School. (Courtesy of the Dunmore Historical Society.)

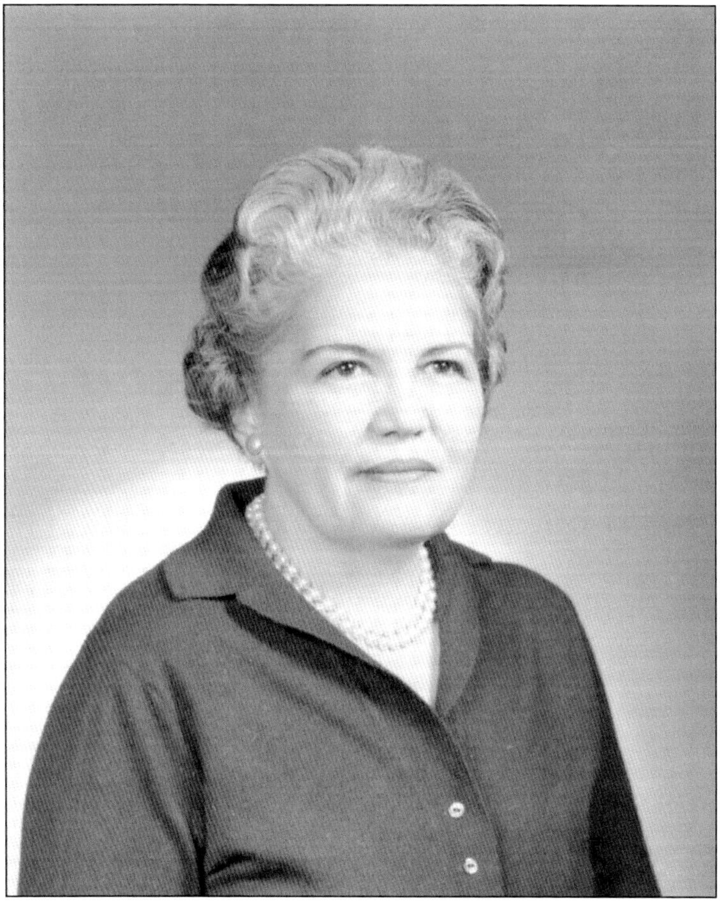

Eugenia DeFazio eventually became the first and only female principal of Dunmore High School in the 1960s after having served as its assistant principal as well as an English and Latin teacher for the district. She retired from Dunmore High School in the early 1980s. At the time of her passing in 2011, her former students remembered her as a stern but caring administrator. (Courtesy of the Dunmore School District.)

Here is the cover of the 1932 Dunmore High School football schedule. Frank Duffy coached the Bucks that year, and George Dwyer was the assistant coach. (Courtesy of Joella Moyes.)

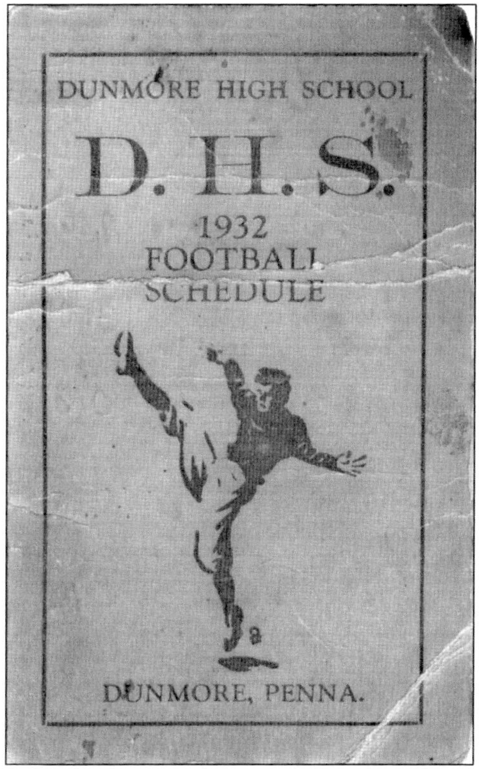

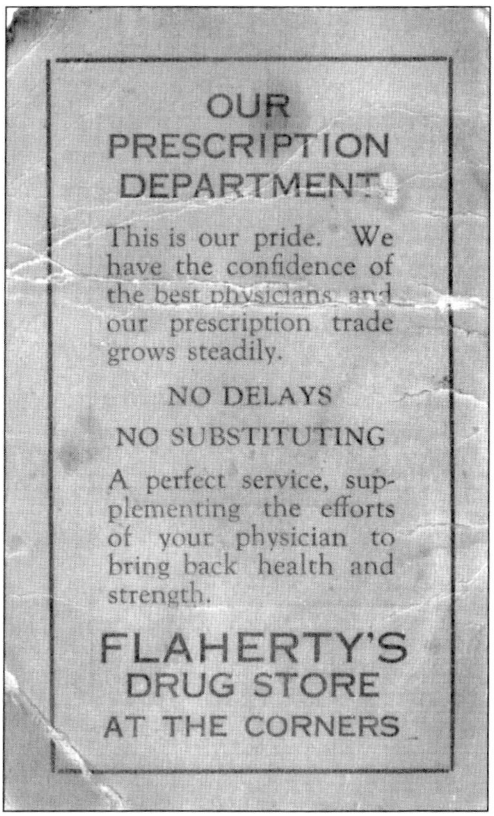

The 1932 Dunmore High School football schedule was sponsored by Flaherty's Drugstore, which was located at Dunmore Corners. (Courtesy of Joella Moyes.)

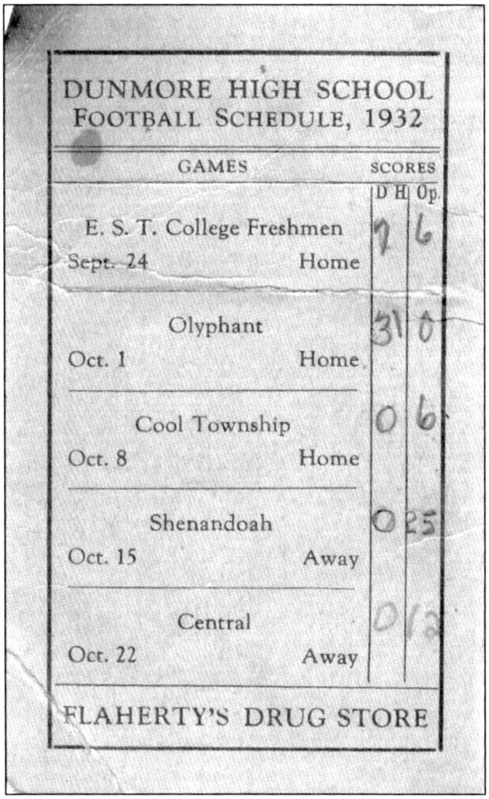
DUNMORE HIGH SCHOOL
FOOTBALL SCHEDULE, 1932

GAMES		SCORES D H	Op.
E. S. T. College Freshmen Sept. 24	Home	7	6
Olyphant Oct. 1	Home	31	0
Cool Township Oct. 8	Home	0	6
Shenandoah Oct. 15	Away	0	25
Central Oct. 22	Away	0	12

FLAHERTY'S DRUG STORE

School districts in Northeastern Pennsylvania were much different than what they are today; for example, Dunmore's best score in 1932 of 31-0 was against Olyphant High School. In 1969, the towns of Olyphant, Dickson City, and Throop consolidated their schools to form the Mid Valley School District. Mid Valley and Dunmore regularly play each other to this day. (Courtesy of Joella Moyes.)

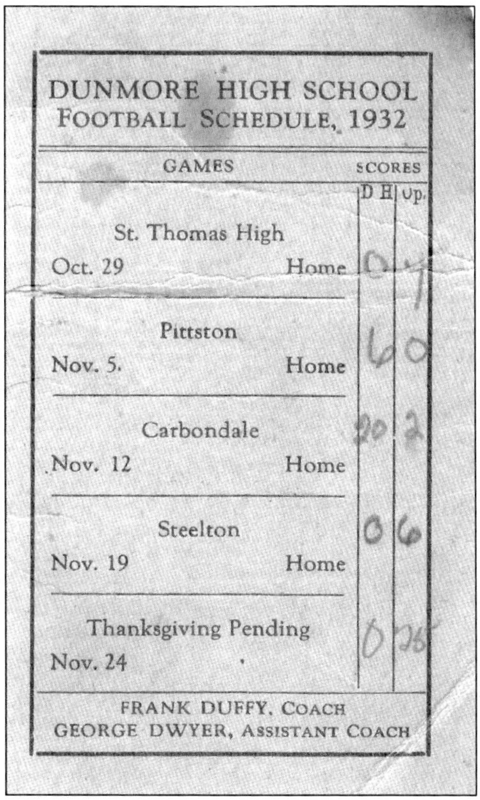
DUNMORE HIGH SCHOOL
FOOTBALL SCHEDULE, 1932

GAMES		SCORES D H	Op.
St. Thomas High Oct. 29	Home	0	7
Pittston Nov. 5.	Home	6	0
Carbondale Nov. 12	Home	20	2
Steelton Nov. 19	Home	0	6
Thanksgiving Pending Nov. 24		0	25

FRANK DUFFY, COACH
GEORGE DWYER, ASSISTANT COACH

Dunmore's opponents did not necessarily hail from the Northeastern Pennsylvania region. On this final page of the 1932 football schedule, Dunmore lost 0-6 to Steelton. The Steelton-Highspire School District is located in Dauphin County, just outside of the state capital of Harrisburg. (Courtesy of Joella Moyes.)

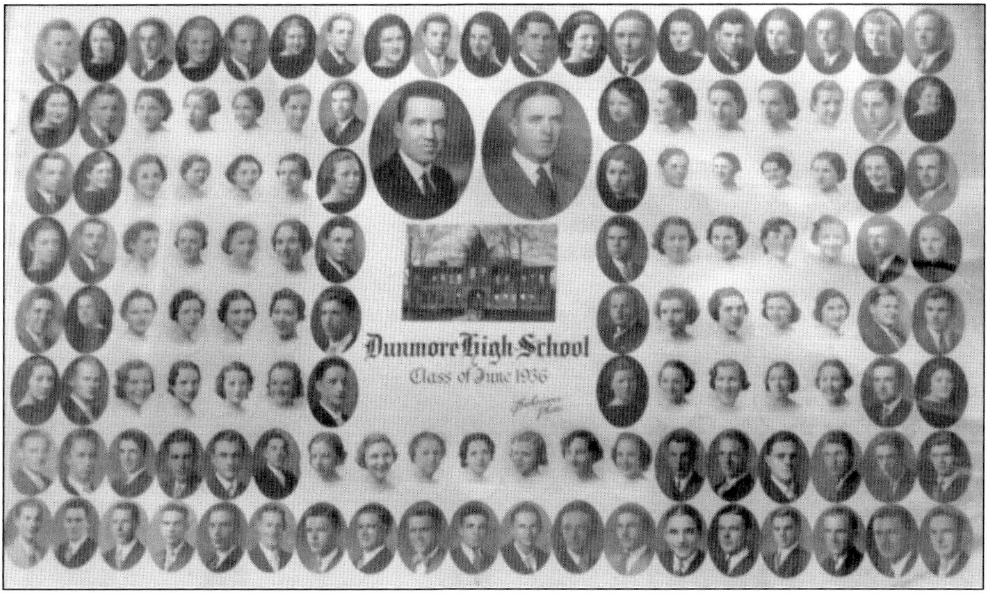

The Dunmore High School class of June 1936 was the final class to graduate from the Central School on South Apple Street. An image of the Central School at the time of its closing is inset in the center. (Courtesy of Joella Moyes.)

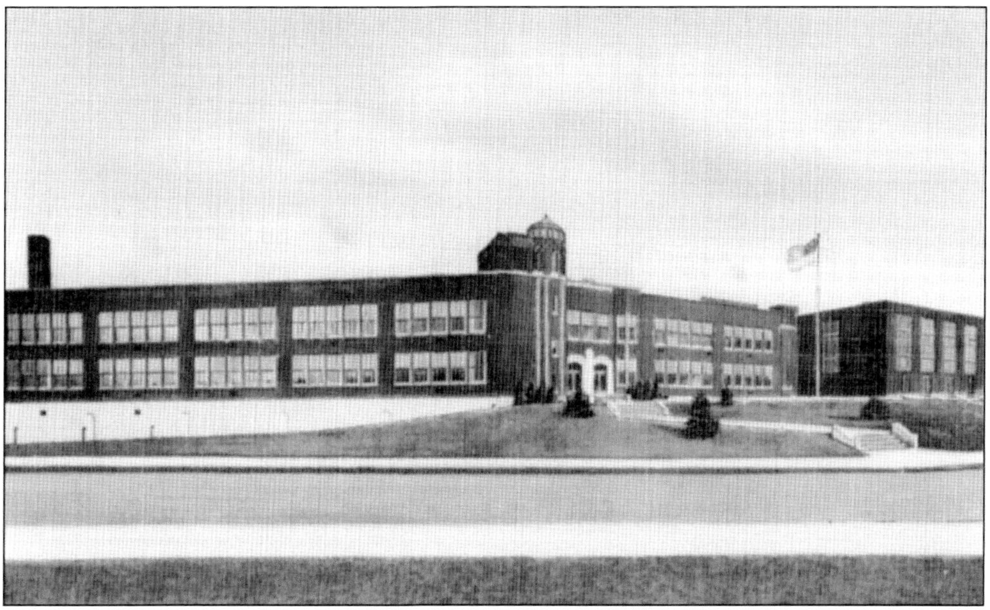

Because of overcrowding at the Central School, ground was broken for the present Dunmore High School on June 8, 1936, in a wooded area of the borough known as Bushnell's Woods. The Dunmore School District received a $266,727 grant from the federal government as well as a $326,000 loan from the Emergency Relief Appropriation Act of 1935 for its construction. The new high school was opened in September 1937. (Courtesy of the Dunmore Historical Society.)

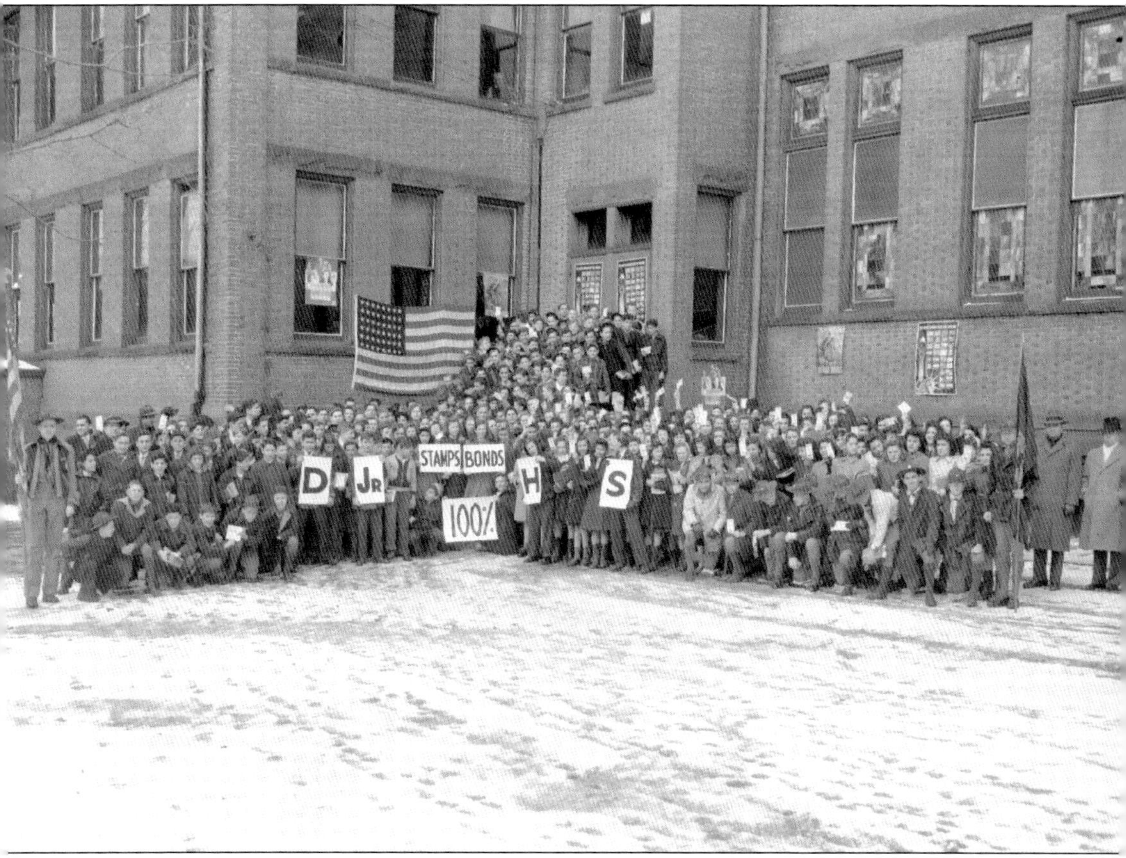

After the new Dunmore High School was opened, the Central School building on South Apple Street was used to house the Dunmore Junior High School until the late 1960s. In this photograph, students selling war bonds during World War II gather on the school's grounds to show support for American troops. (Courtesy of the Dunmore School District.)

The camera club at the new Dunmore High School was affectionately known as the "Film Foggers," as seen in this 1940s photograph. Club moderator James P. Gilligan, who taught chemistry and physics for Dunmore High School, is once again pictured in the top row at left. (Courtesy of Catherine G. Quinnan.)

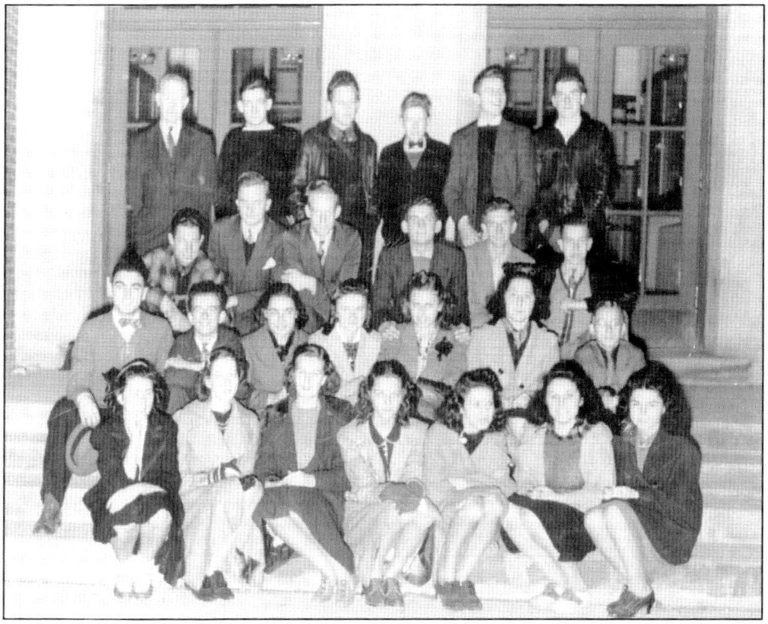

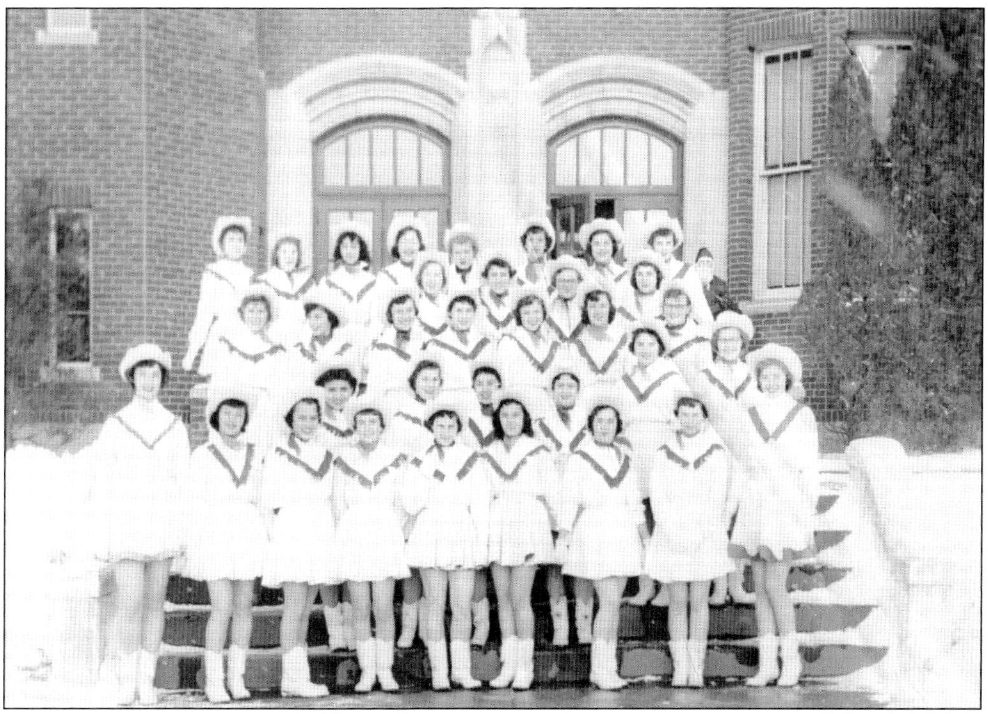

The Dunmore High School drill squad poses on the steps of Dunmore High School in November 1955. (Courtesy of Catherine G. Quinnan.)

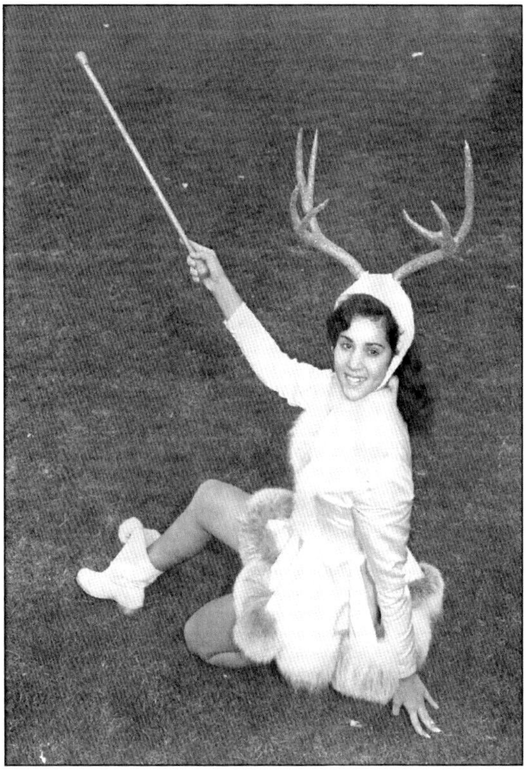

Every school year since the 1950s, one graduating cheerleader or member of the drill squad at Dunmore High School gets to be "Miss Buck." Jeanette Bardini Mellody, age 16 in this photograph, was Miss Buck in 1958. Her father, Victor Bardini, attached the antlers to a football helmet while her mother, Rose Bardini, gave her real fox fur from a coat for her costume. Mellody, along with her husband, the late Jim Mellody, also a Dunmore native, started the Beef O'Brady chain of restaurants in 1985. (Courtesy of Jeanette Bardini Mellody.)

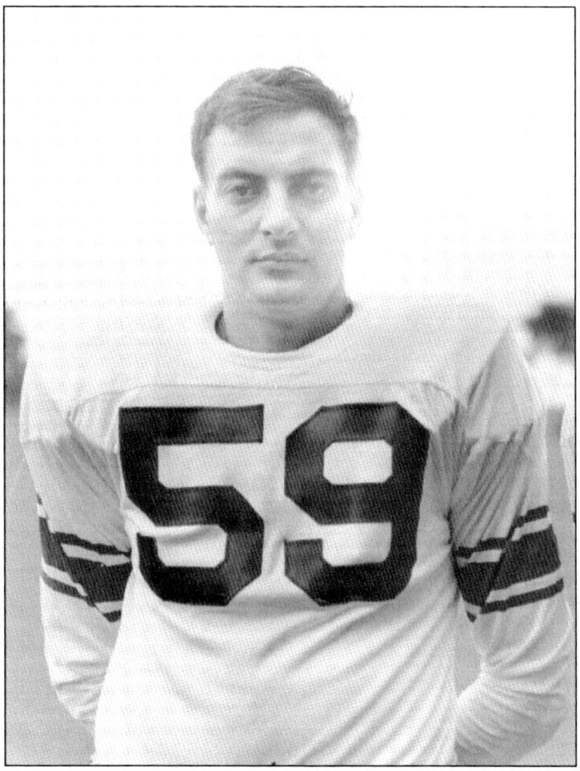

James Martinelli, a 1953 graduate of Dunmore High School, was one of the Dunmore Bucks' standout football players, even garnering national attention. After graduation, he eventually returned to Dunmore High School where he was a physical education and health teacher as well as coach for his former team. (Courtesy of the Dunmore Historical Society.)

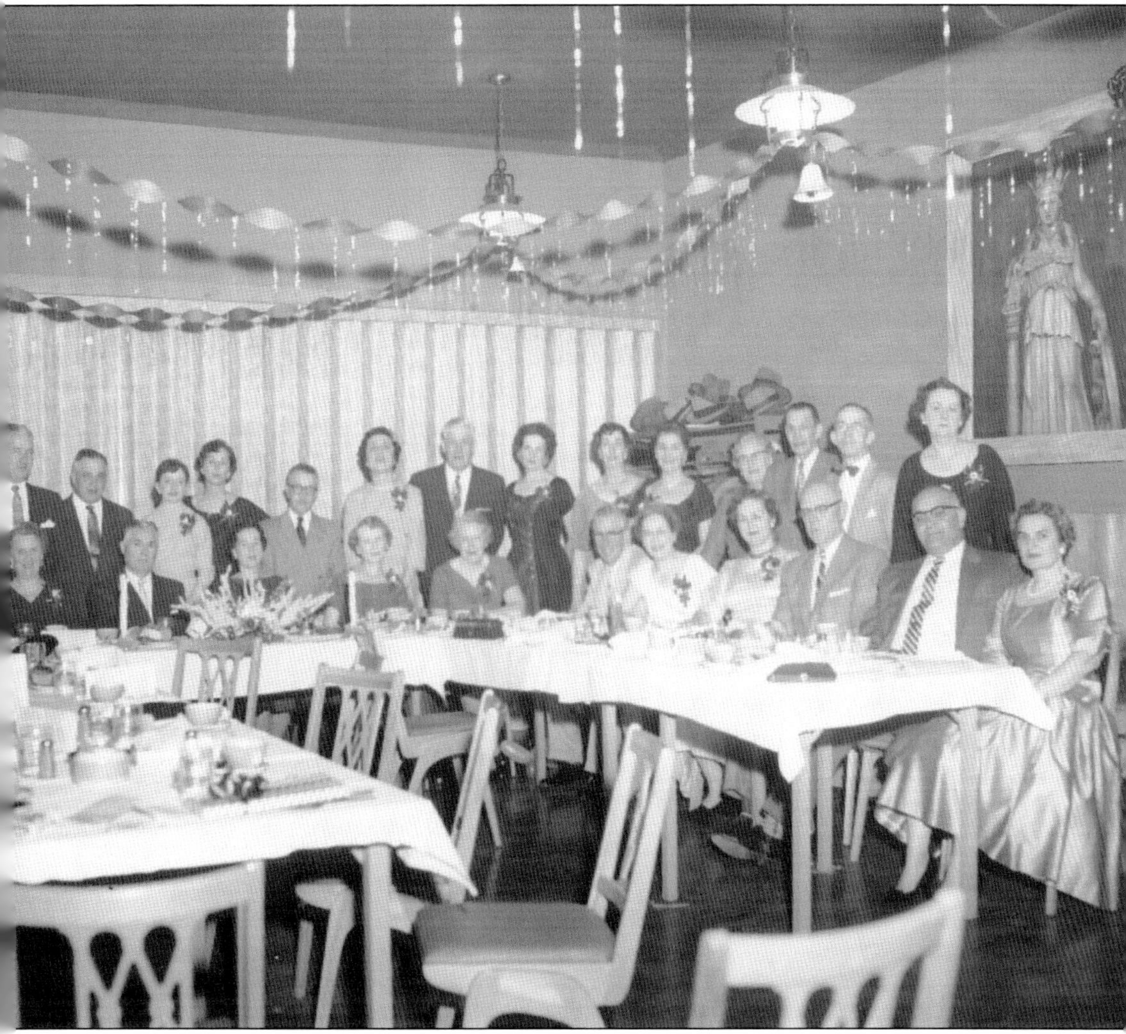

The faculty and staff of the Dunmore Junior High School are shown at a Christmas party on December 14, 1956. Pictured from left to right are (first row) Mary McDonnell, Albert Bradican, Mrs. Albert Bradican, Grace Gilmartin, Kit Haggerty, Leonard Doherty, Mrs. Leonard Doherty, Catherine M. Gilligan, James Casey, Arthur Gallo, and Mrs. Arthur Gallo; (second row) Frank McDonnell, Frank Summa, Vivienne Paskert, Mary Lucas, Joseph Durkin, Victoria Saponaro, Mr. Gillespie, Margaret Gillespie, Marguerite Kelly, Ellen Loughney, Mrs. Fox, Chris Fox, Albert Jordan, and Marian Morrison. (Courtesy of Catherine G. Quinnan.)

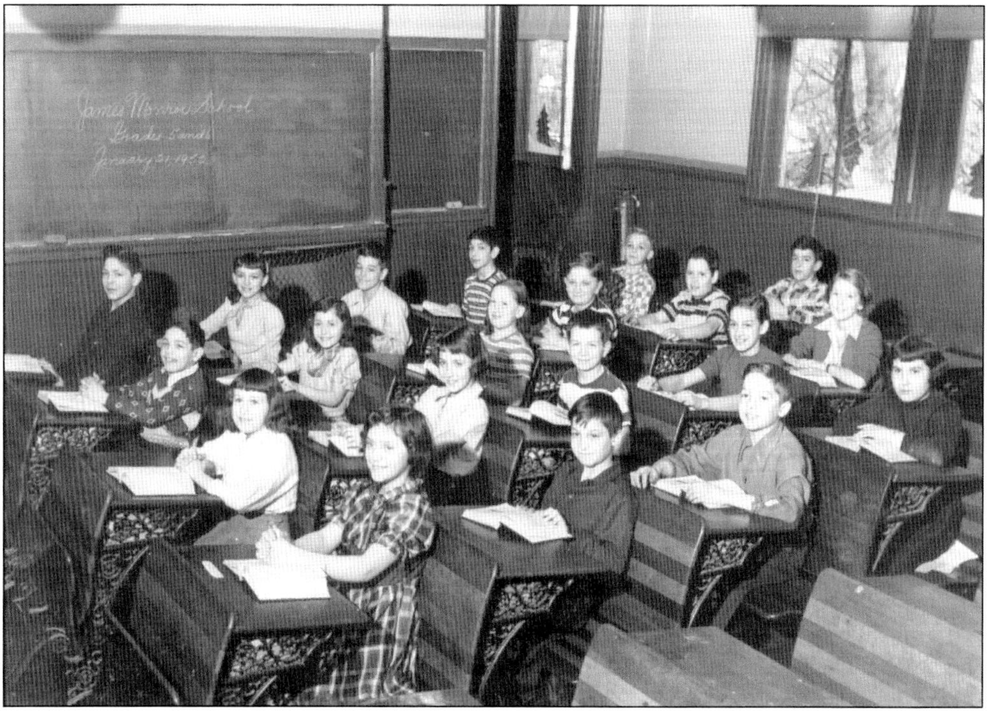

Fifth- and sixth-grade students at the James Monroe No. 5 elementary school pose for a class picture on January 21, 1952. From the front of the classroom to the back are, from left to right, (first row) Lucy Riccardo, P.J. DeNaples, Louie DeNaples, and Marian Genett; (second row) Mary Ellen Horvat, Carolyn Gillette, Eugene Horvat, Marie Castellano, and Marilyn Riccardo; (third row) Frank Genett, Lucille DeMarco, Jennie Coviello, Jimmy Finelli, Anthony Portanova, and Pat Montana; (fourth row) Frank DeMarco, Lou Furello, Bob Sestack, Francis De Sando, and Peter Castellano. (Courtesy of Finelli's Catering.)

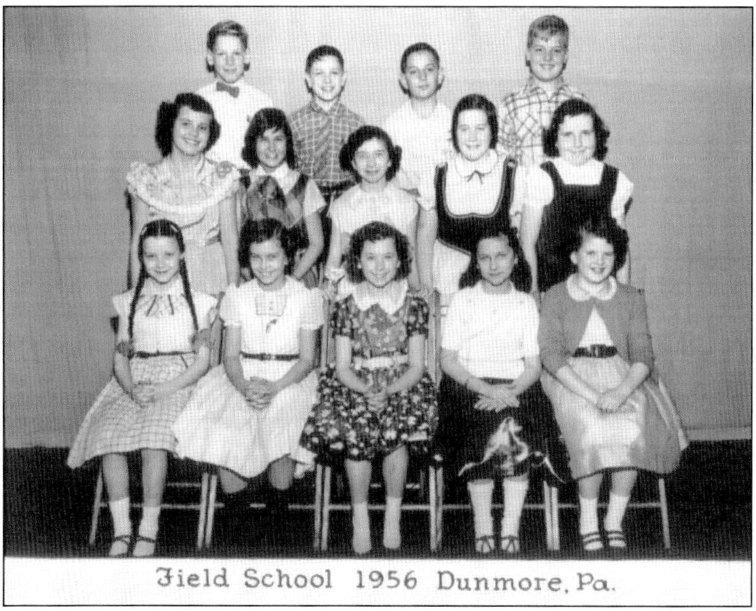

Pictured in 1956 are students of the Eugene Field School No. 8, one of several Dunmore elementary schools that ceased to exist by 1962. Other schools included Abraham Lincoln No. 4, James Monroe No. 5, Nay Aug No. 9, Henry Wadsworth Longfellow No. 12, and Dundell No. 13. (Courtesy of Karl Wegforth.)

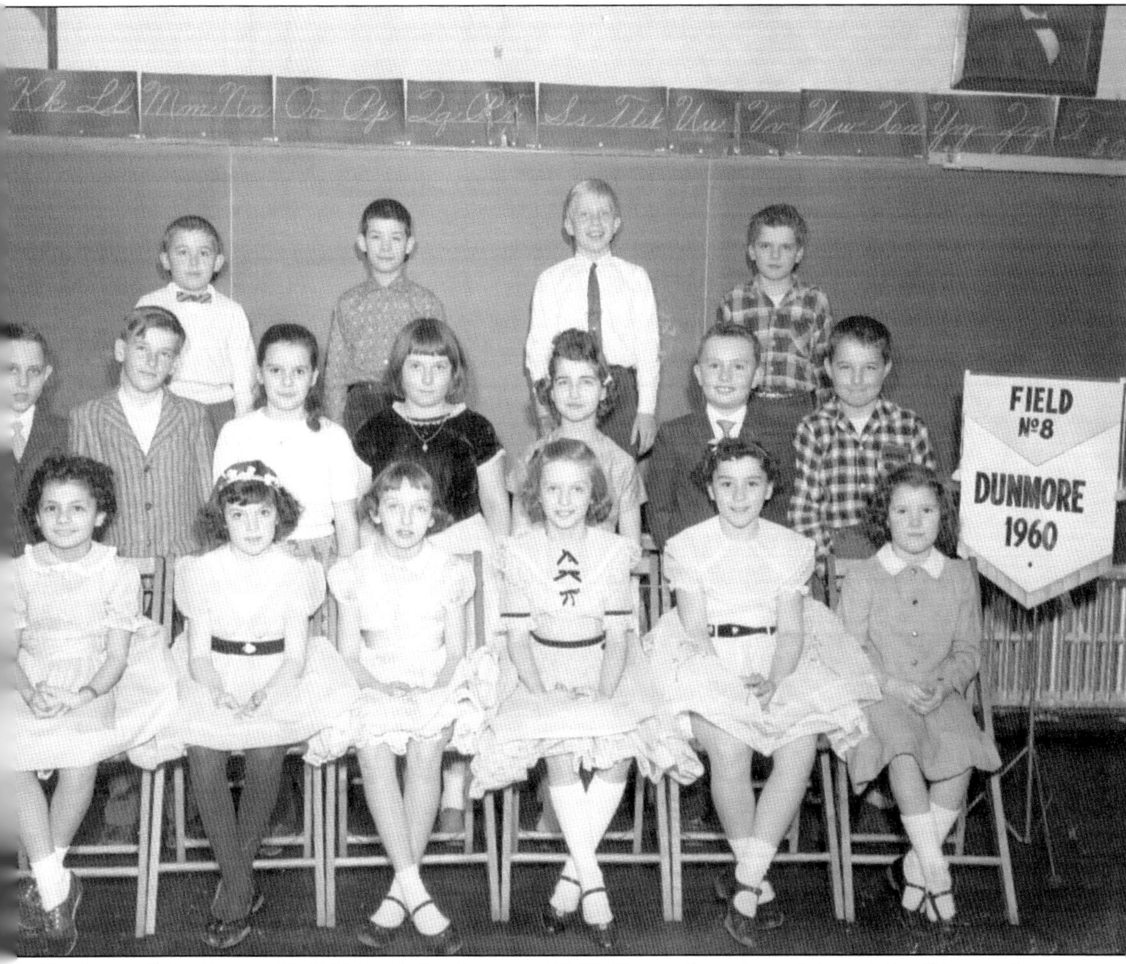

Students of the Eugene Field School No. 8 pose in 1960. Pictured are, from left to right, (first row) unidentified, Kathy Sabia, Suzanne Lucas, Bernadean Protroski, unidentified, and Carol Rabecs; (second row) Angelo Ceccarini, unidentified, Rose Gymory, unidentified, Suzanne Romanini, Jerry Piefier, and Frank Capowich; (third row) Louis Martarano, Tom Garvey, Noel Pidish, and Jesse Mills. (Courtesy of Karl Wegforth.)

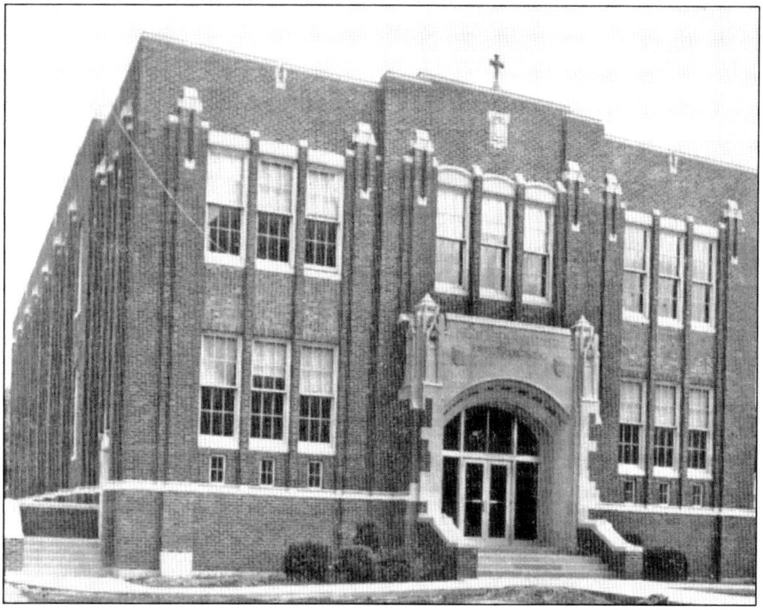

St. Mary of Mount Carmel School, located on Chestnut Street across from St. Mary of Mount Carmel Church, opened on September 4, 1935. (Courtesy of the Dunmore Historical Society.)

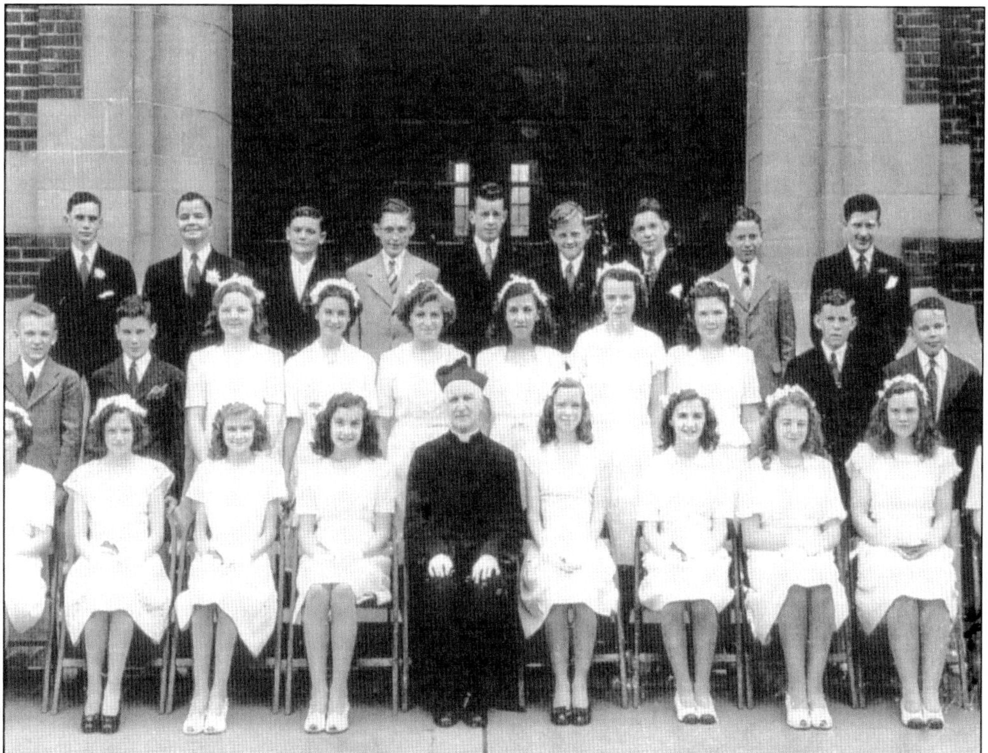

One of the classes of St. Mary of Mount Carmel School sits on the school's front steps with Msgr. Thomas McHugh, former pastor of St. Mary's Church, in the 1950s–1960s. (Courtesy of the Dunmore Historical Society.)

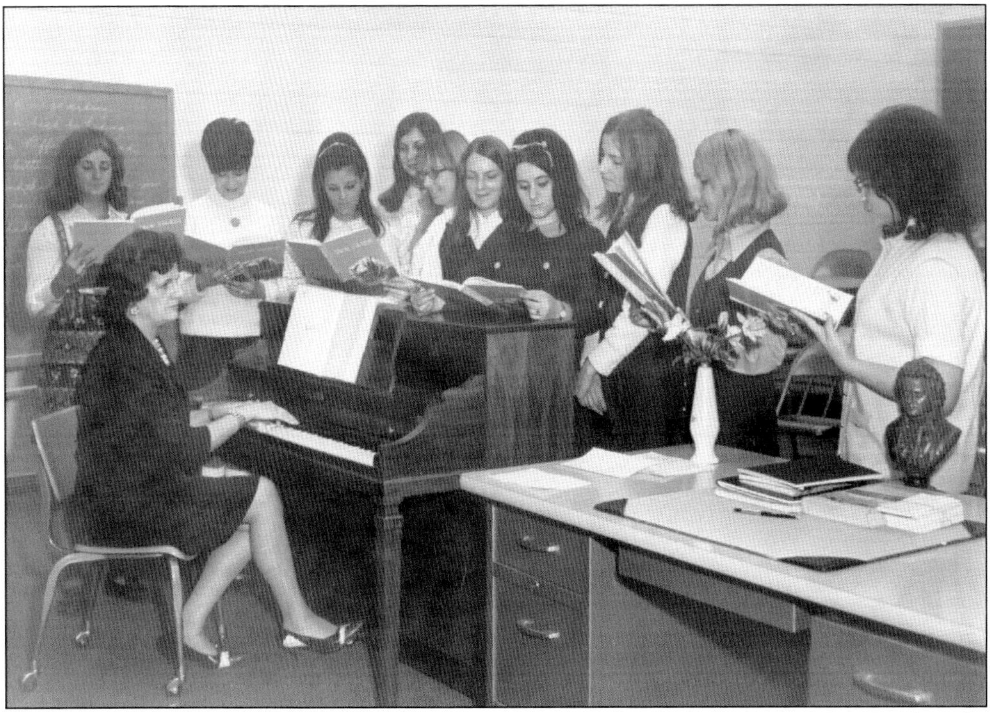

Margaret Gillespie, district music supervisor, instructs students at Dunmore High School in the 1960s. (Courtesy of the Dunmore School District.)

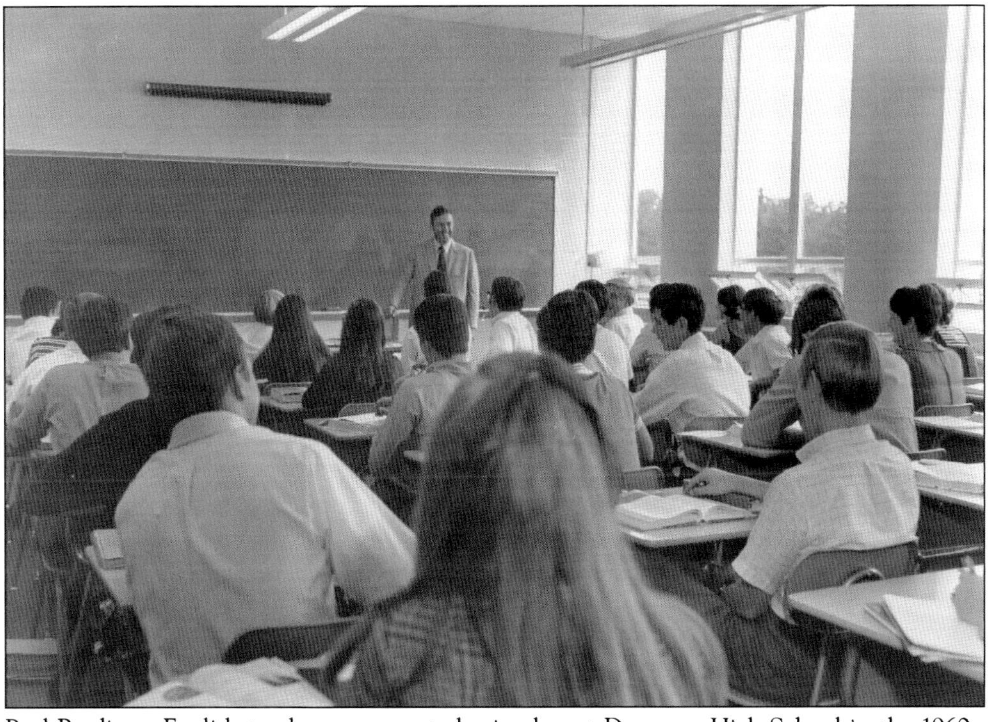

Paul Bradican, English teacher, prepares to begin class at Dunmore High School in the 1960s. (Courtesy of the Dunmore School District.)

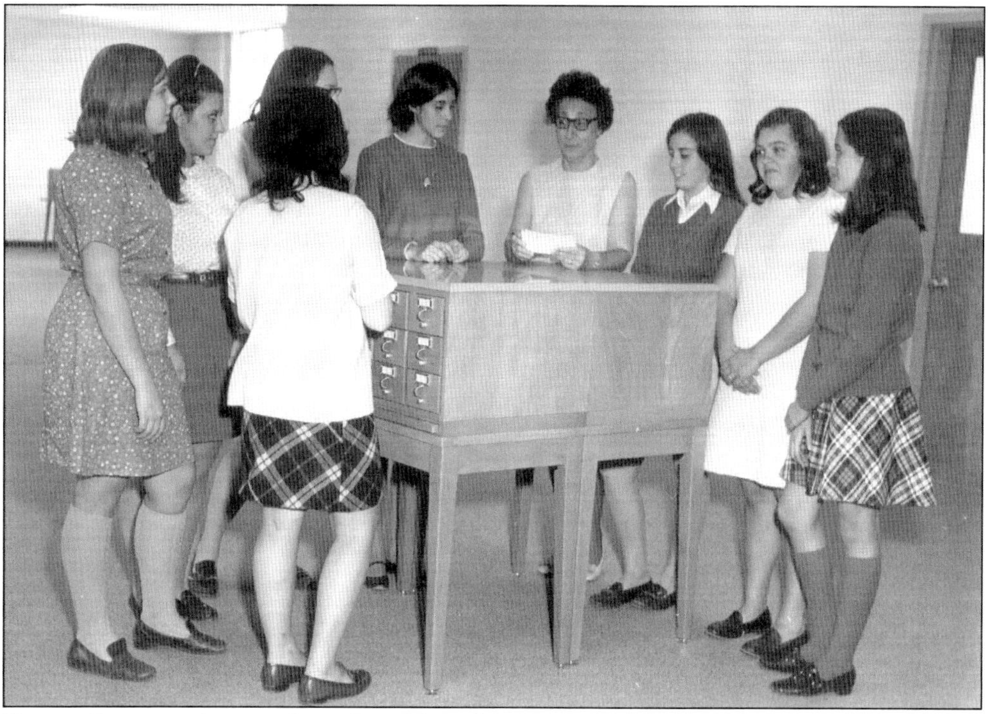
Victoria Saponaro shows students the card catalog in Dunmore High School's library in the 1960s. (Courtesy of the Dunmore School District.)

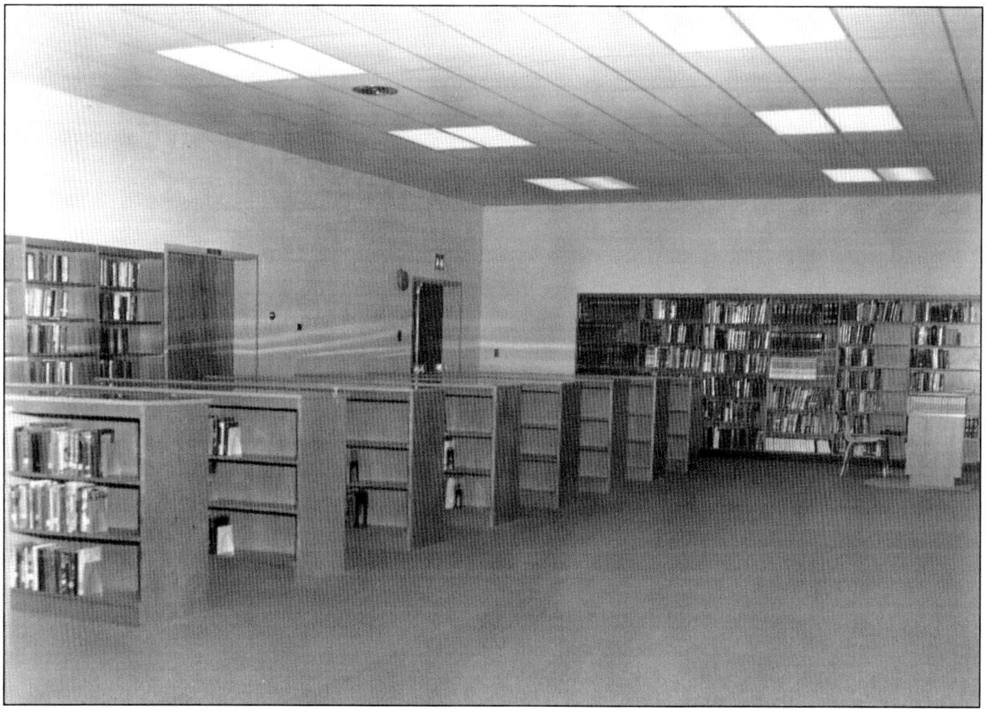
Here is a view of the Dunmore High School library in the 1960s. (Courtesy of the Dunmore School District.)

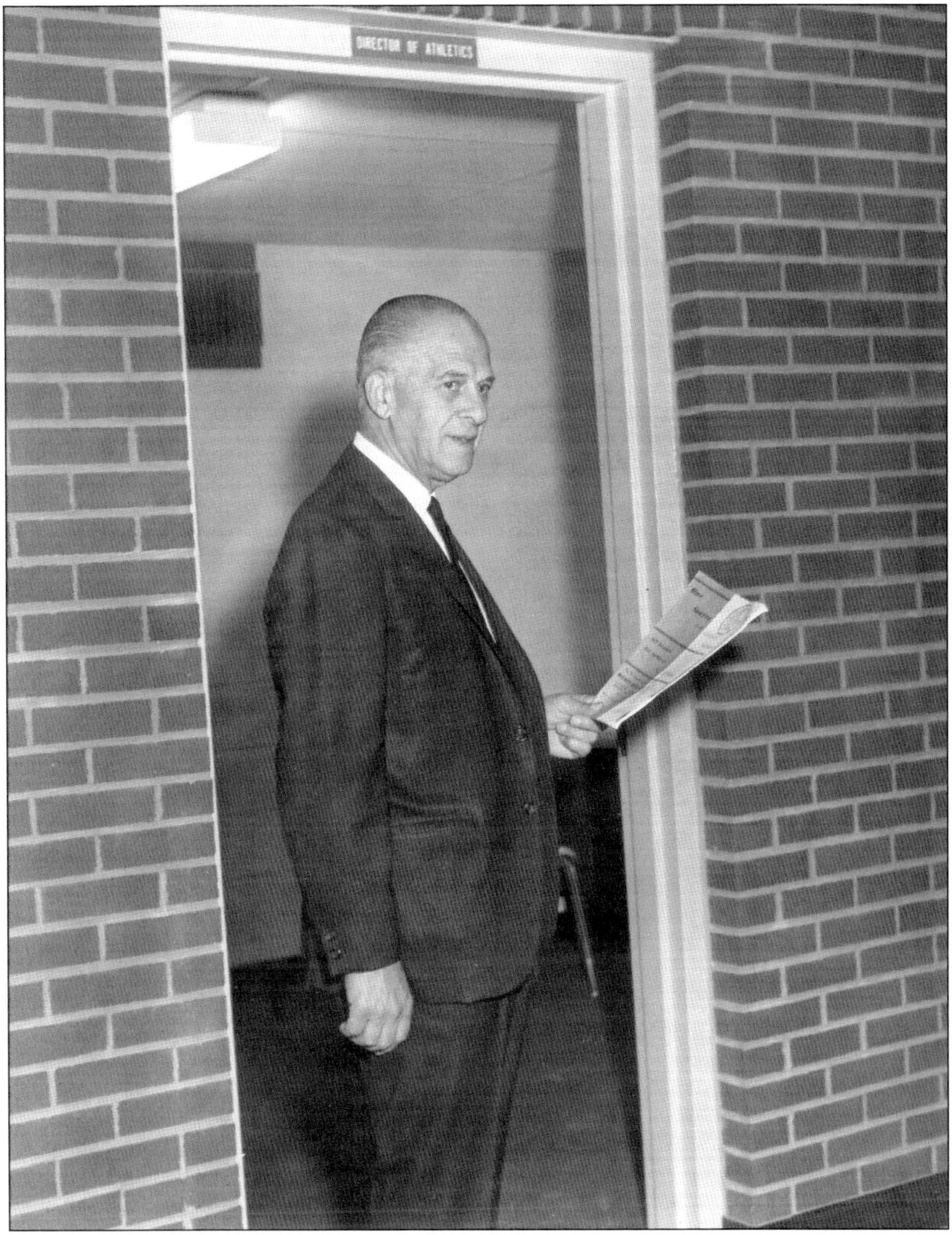

V. James Gatto was the director of athletics at Dunmore High School in the late 1960s as well as a teacher of government classes, including "Problems of Democracy." (Courtesy of the Dunmore School District.)

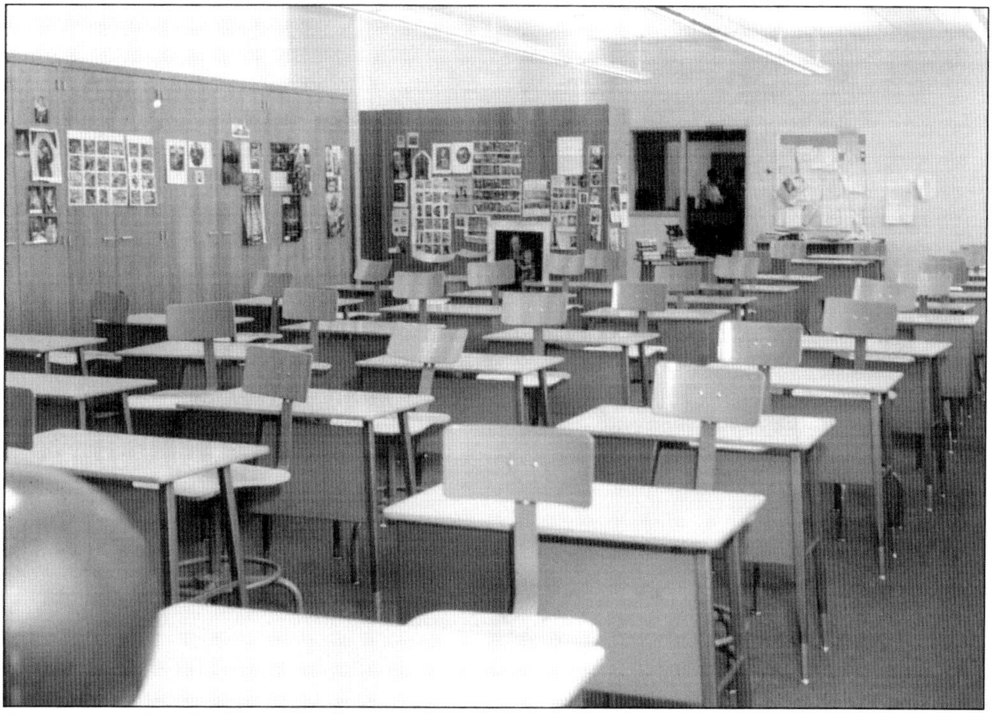

As it appeared in the late 1960s, here is a look inside the art classroom at Dunmore High School. (Courtesy of the Dunmore School District.)

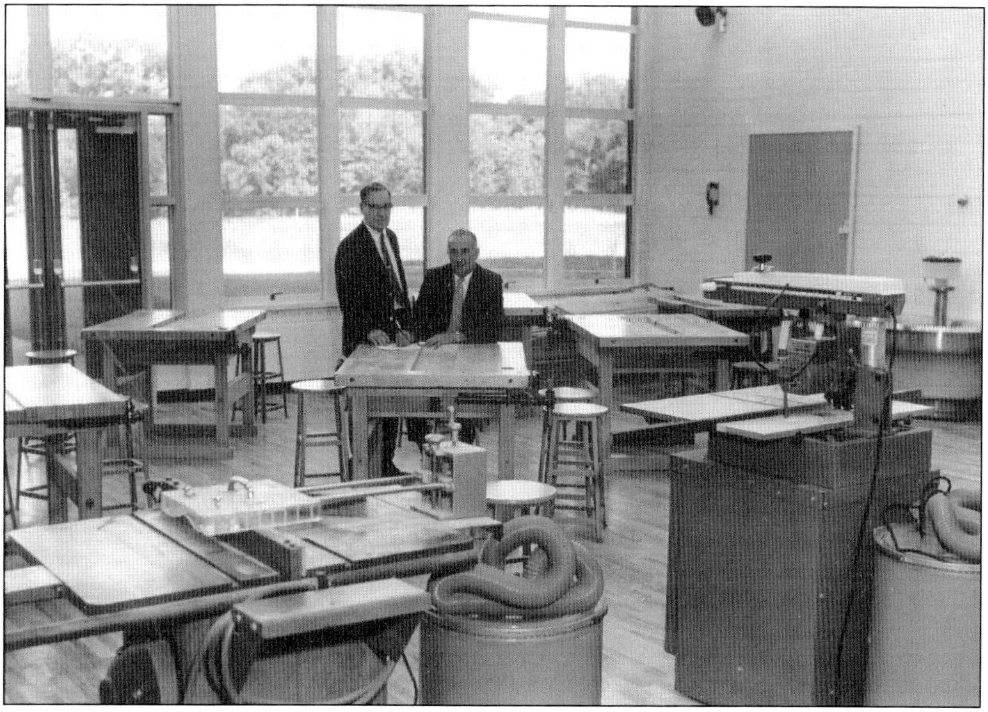

Faculty members of the Dunmore High School industrial arts department pose in the woodworking classroom in the late 1960s. (Courtesy of the Dunmore School District.)

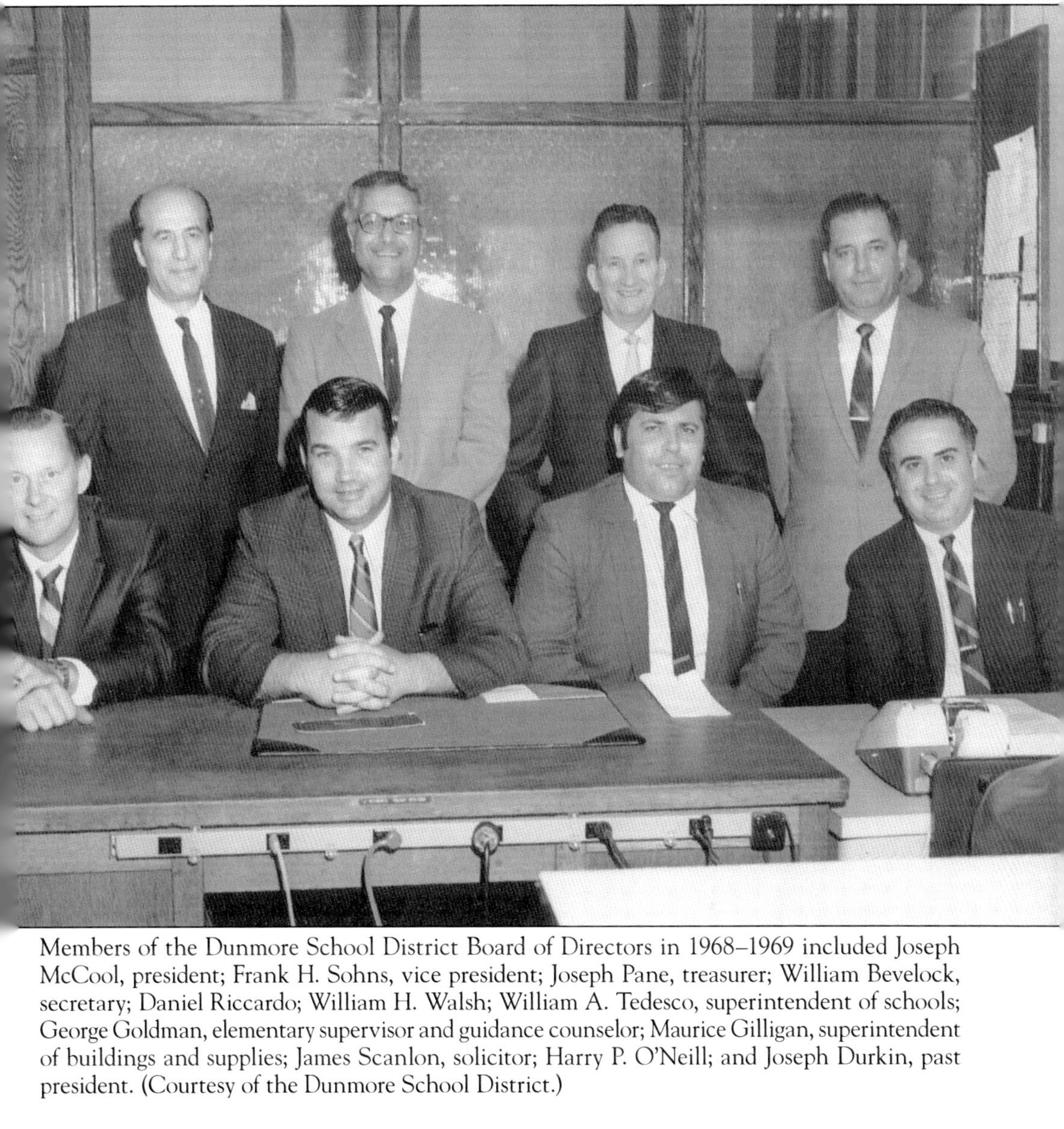

Members of the Dunmore School District Board of Directors in 1968–1969 included Joseph McCool, president; Frank H. Sohns, vice president; Joseph Pane, treasurer; William Bevelock, secretary; Daniel Riccardo; William H. Walsh; William A. Tedesco, superintendent of schools; George Goldman, elementary supervisor and guidance counselor; Maurice Gilligan, superintendent of buildings and supplies; James Scanlon, solicitor; Harry P. O'Neill; and Joseph Durkin, past president. (Courtesy of the Dunmore School District.)

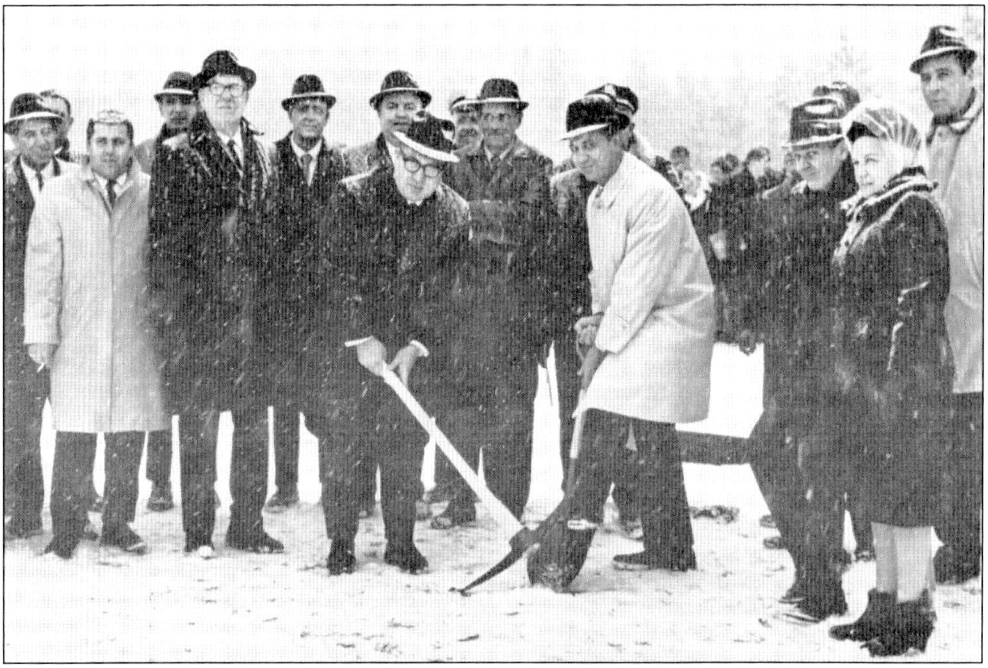

School board members and district administrators look on as ground was broken for the new Dunmore Junior-Senior High School during the winter of 1968. The junior-senior high school was an expansion of the existing Dunmore High School. (Courtesy of the Dunmore School District.)

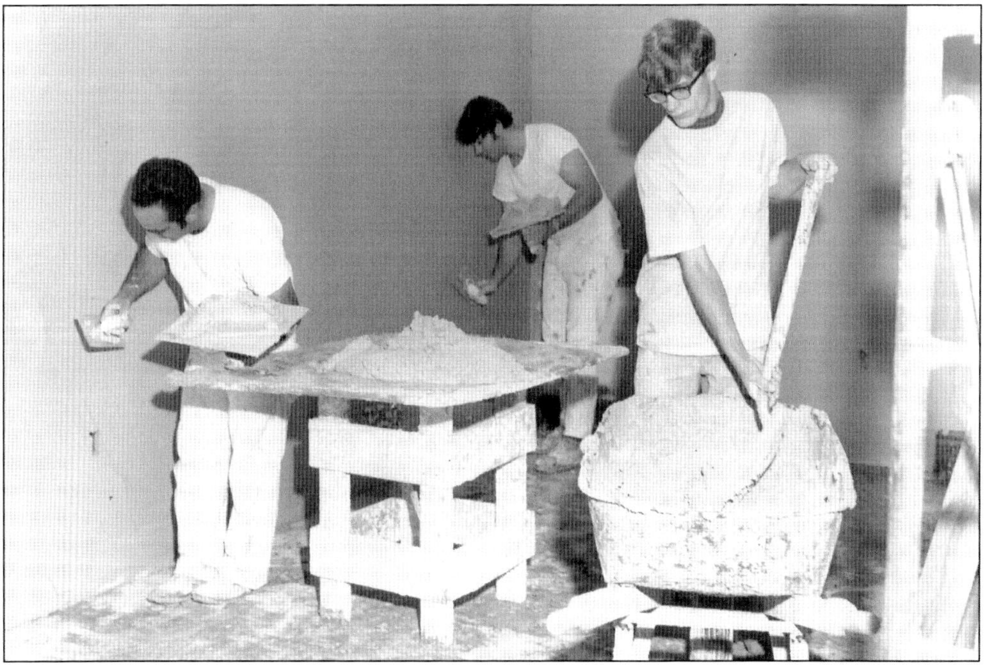

Construction workers work inside the new Dunmore Junior-Senior High School in 1969. After the opening of the new junior-senior high school, the old Central School building on South Apple Street was no longer used for instructional purposes. The Dunmore Junior-Senior High School was formally dedicated on December 14, 1969. (Courtesy of the Dunmore School District.)

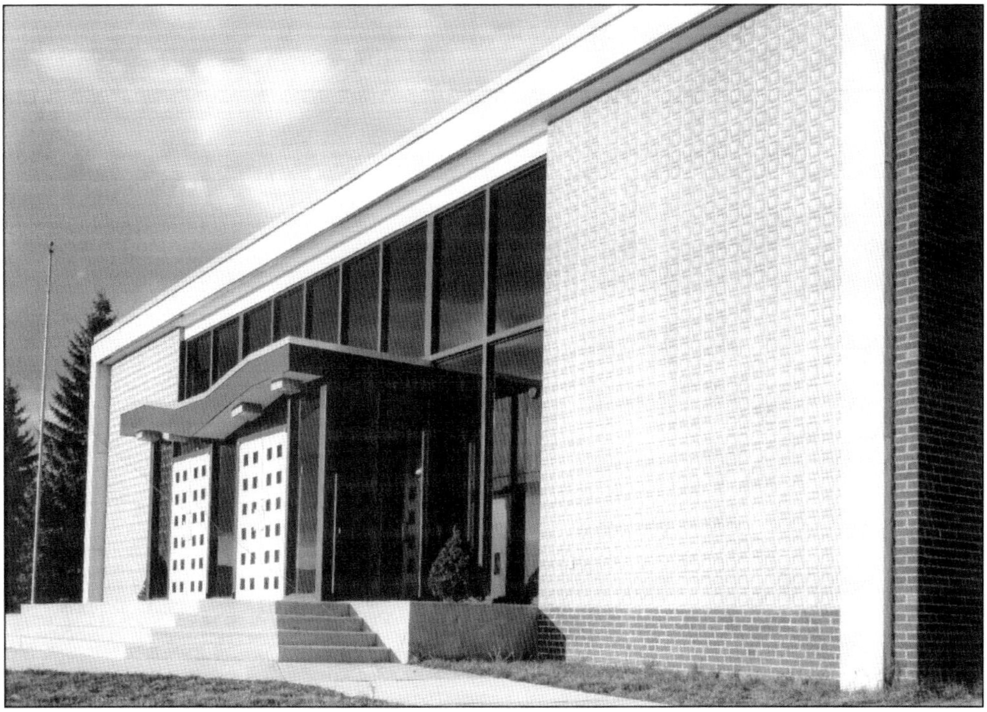

Here is an exterior view of the Dunmore Junior-Senior High School upon its opening in 1969. (Courtesy of the Dunmore School District.)

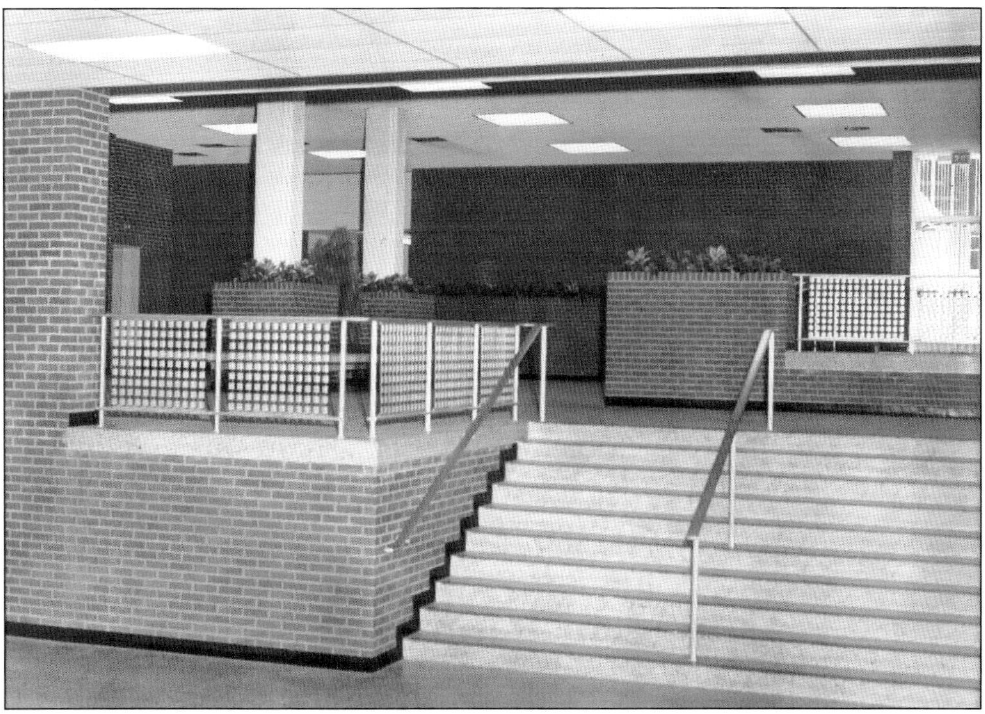

Here is the foyer of the Dunmore Junior-Senior High School in upon its opening in 1969. (Courtesy of the Dunmore School District.)

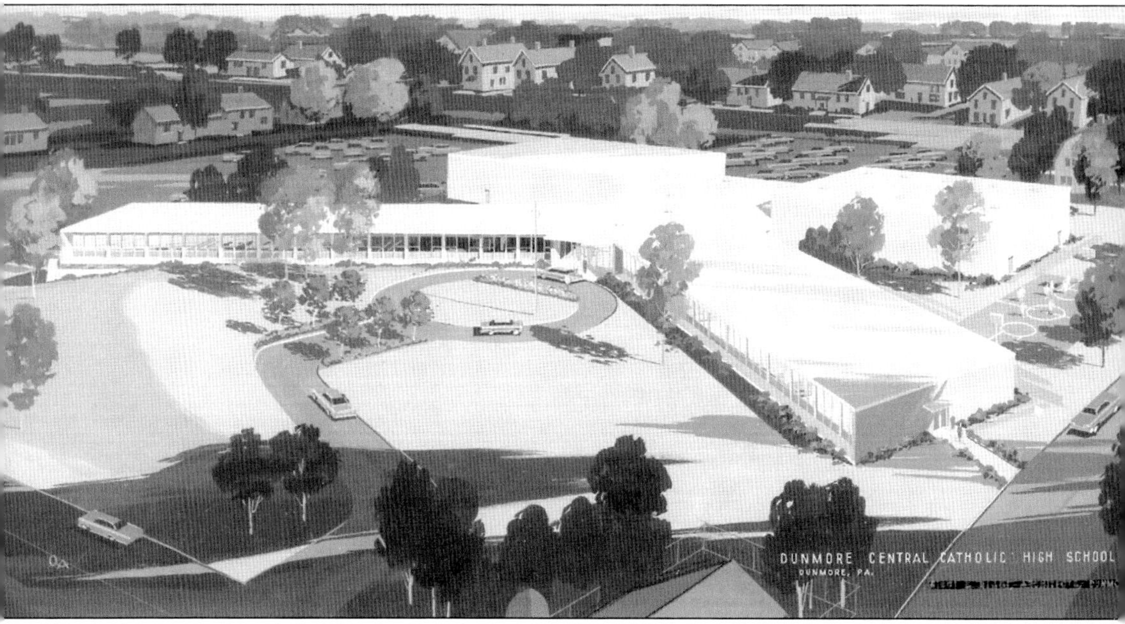

This artist's rendering by Riggi and Riggi Architects of Dunmore shows the proposed Dunmore Central Catholic High School on Drinker Street. The idea for the high school was conceived by the pastors of the Catholic parishes in Dunmore at the time of the early 1960s. They wanted to have a centralized Catholic high school in Dunmore rather than individual schools run by the parishes themselves. (Courtesy of the Diocese of Scranton.)

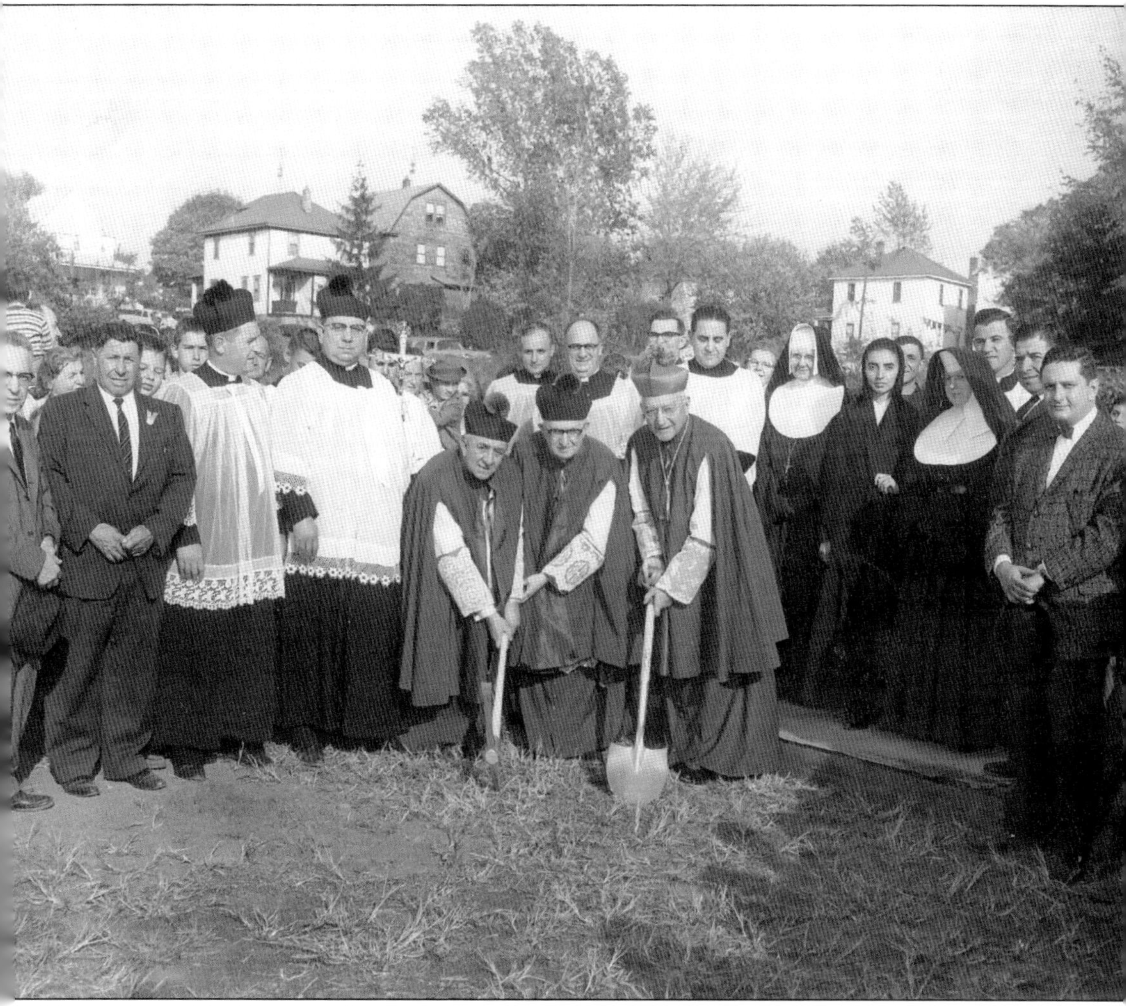

Then-bishop of the Diocese of Scranton Jerome D. Hannan holds the shovel to break ground on October 7, 1963, for the construction of Dunmore Central Catholic High School, which opened in the fall of 1964. Bishop Hannan is joined by Msgr. Raymond Larkin, center, then-pastor of St. Mary of Mount Carmel Parish in Dunmore, and Msgr. William Crotti, left, then-pastor of St. Anthony of Padua Parish in Dunmore. (Courtesy of the Diocese of Scranton.)

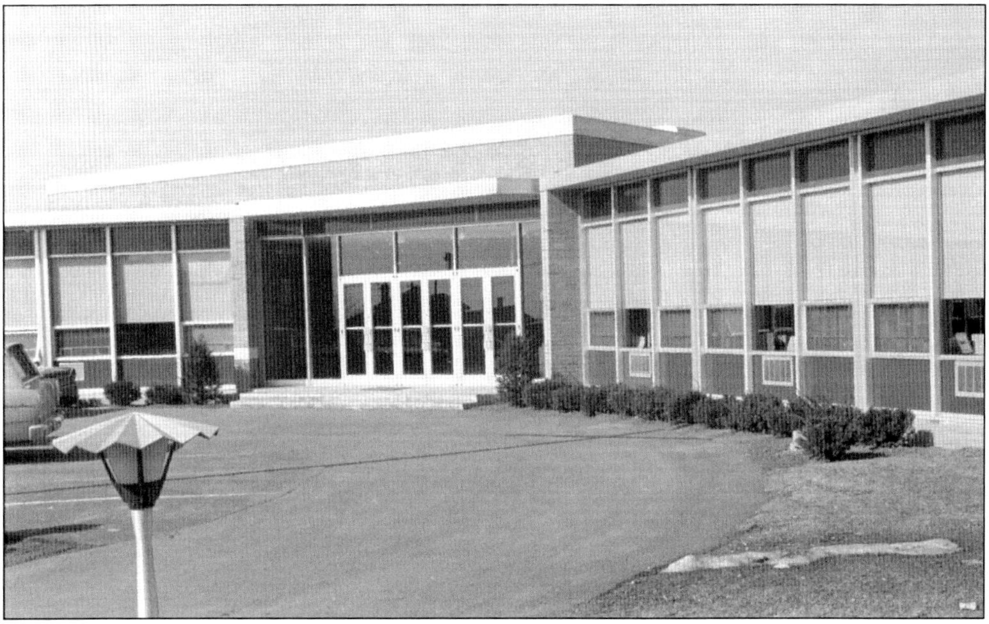

Here is an exterior view of Dunmore Central Catholic High School upon its opening in 1964. The school's first class graduated in 1968, and its last class graduated in 1973. In later years, the school was renamed Bishop O'Hara High School to include its growing population of students from outside of Dunmore. Bishop William O'Hara was the first bishop of the Diocese of Scranton. (Courtesy of the Diocese of Scranton.)

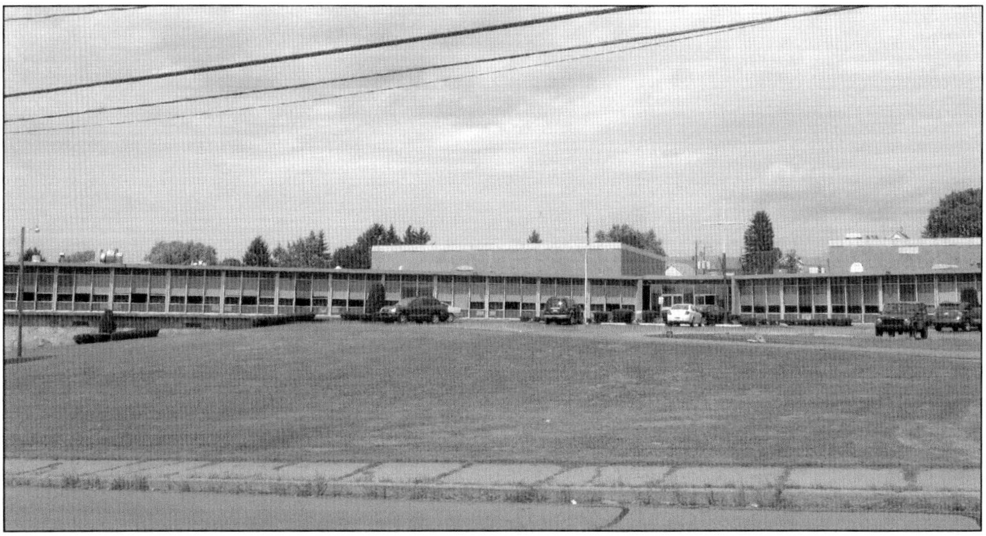

Bishop O'Hara High School remained in existence until 2007, when the Diocese of Scranton decided to unite Bishop O'Hara with Bishop Hannan High School in Scranton to form a Catholic high school to serve all of Lackawanna County. For one year, both school buildings remained open as the Dunmore and Scranton campuses of Holy Cross High School. In 2008, all students were moved to the former Dunmore Central Catholic/Bishop O'Hara High School building in Dunmore. The facade of the building remains largely unchanged since its opening in 1964, although modular classrooms were built behind the school to accommodate the larger student population since the formation of Holy Cross High School. (Courtesy of Holy Cross High School.)

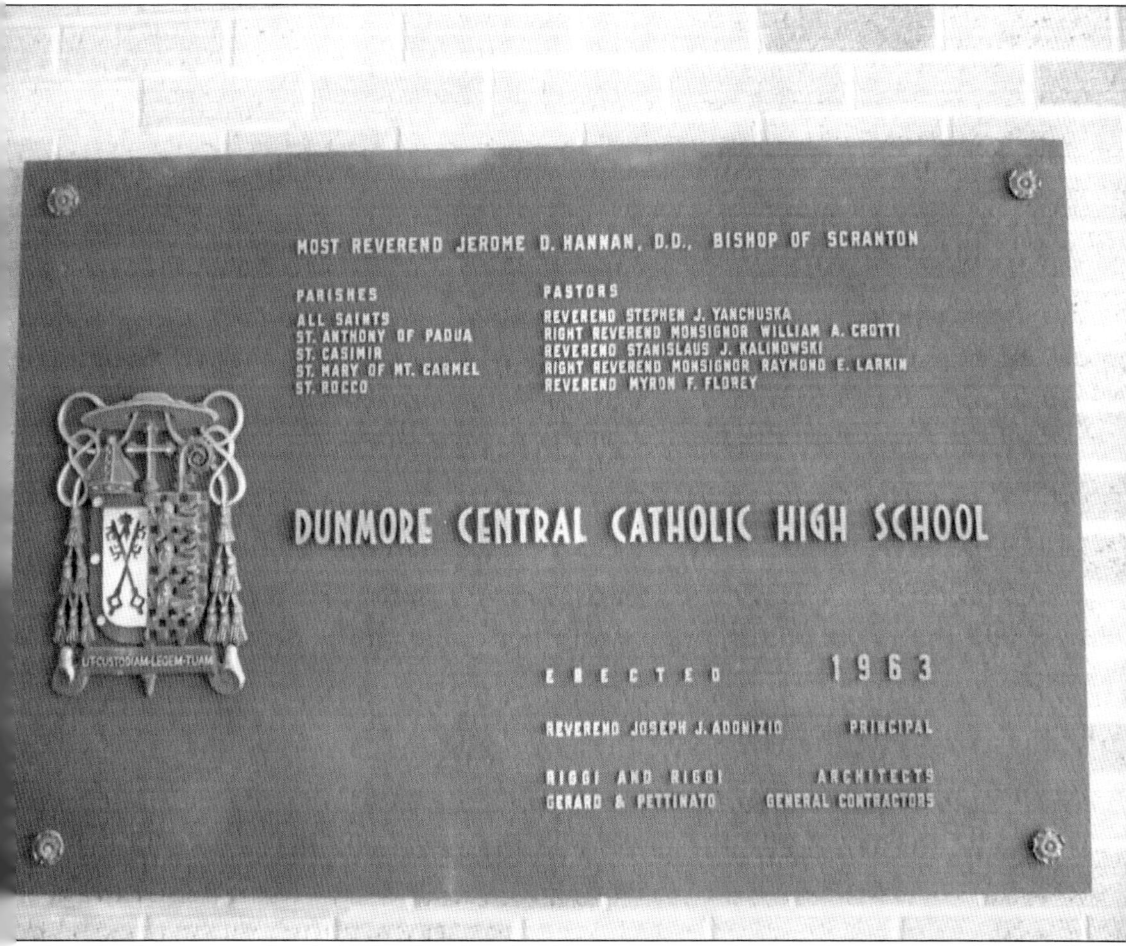

The original cornerstone of Dunmore Central Catholic High School from its construction in 1963 remains in place in the foyer of Holy Cross High School. The five original churches that formed Dunmore Central Catholic High School were All Saints Parish, St. Casimir's Parish, St. Mary of Mount Carmel Parish, St. Anthony of Padua Parish, and St. Rocco's Parish. Due to restructuring efforts in the Diocese of Scranton, both St. Casimir's Parish and All Saints Parish have been consolidated with St. Mary of Mount Carmel Parish and are now known as Our Lady of Mount Carmel Parish. St. Anthony of Padua Parish and St. Rocco's Parish have both united and have been renamed SS. Anthony and Rocco Parish. (Courtesy of Holy Cross High School.)

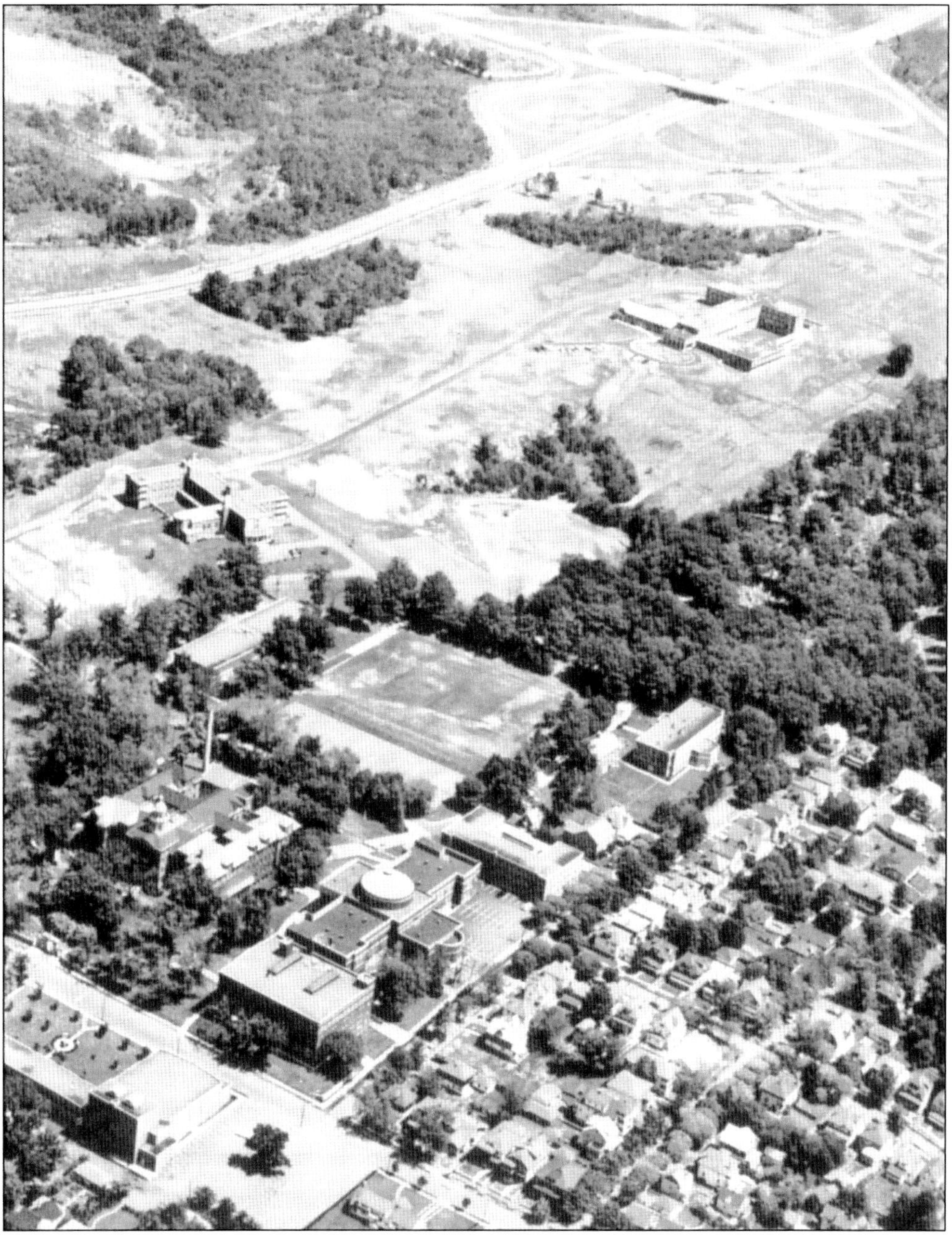

Here is an aerial view of the campus of Marywood College, including Dunmore's O'Neill Highway in the background, in the 1960s. Although mostly situated in the city of Scranton, parts of Marywood's campus reach into the borough of Dunmore. Marywood College was established by the Congregation of the Sisters, Servants of the Immaculate Heart of Mary, in 1915. In 1917, the college was incorporated under the laws of the Commonwealth of Pennsylvania, and in 1921 the approval of the Middle States Association of Colleges and Schools was secured. The college expanded to include graduate study in 1921, and the charter was extended on June 26, 1922, to include the master of arts degree. Marywood College became Marywood University in 1997. (Courtesy of Joe and Dolly Michalczyk.)

Four

The All-American Town

Like any other small town in America, Dunmore is proud of its citizens who have served in the US military. In 1919, Dunmore paid tribute to its returning World War I veterans with a "Welcome Home" parade as a part of its first Memorial Day services. In 1945, following World War II, Dunmore held another parade welcoming home returning soldiers. Images from both parades can be seen in this chapter as well as other military memories from residents.

In 1930, St. Mary of Mount Carmel Church donated ground in its cemetery to be used as a veterans' plot for the burial of veterans who were either poor or who had no family. Through the efforts of Dunmore's American Legion Post No. 13, a newsletter called the "Home Town News" was published during the 1950s and 1960s and delivered to Dunmore residents who served either at home or overseas. Msgr. William Crotti, pastor of St. Anthony of Padua Parish in Dunmore from 1928 until 1973, was even named permanent chaplain of the American Legion Post No. 13 and personally accompanied each group of Dunmore draftees to their point of departure during World War II, blessing them before they went off to serve.

On the national level, Dunmore is the hometown of 2nd Lt. Carol Ann Drazba, RN. Drazba was the first American enlisted woman to be killed in Vietnam when the helicopter she was riding in with six other people crashed after becoming entangled in high-tension wires.

Dunmore has two other memorials in honor of its veterans, a tank at the end of Blakely Street and a memorial listing the names of residents killed in World War I, World War II, and Vietnam on the grounds of the municipal building on Blakely Street.

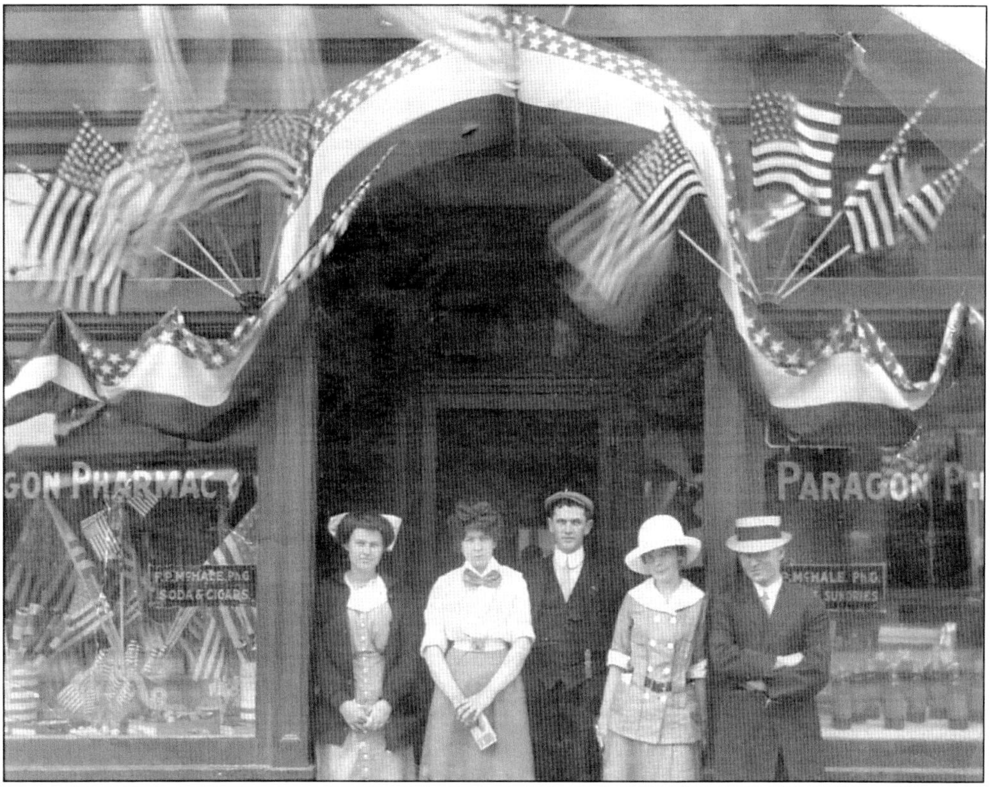

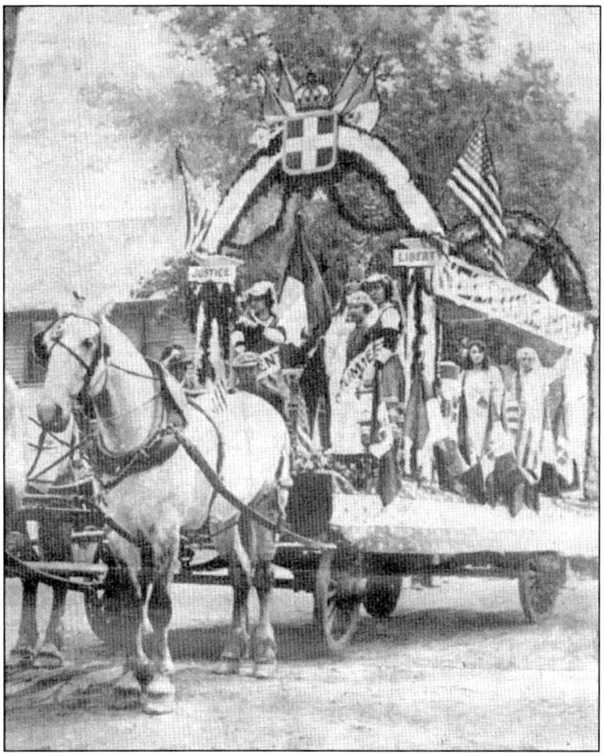

The Paragon Pharmacy, located on Drinker Street near Dunmore Corners, was owned by F.P. McHale. This picture shows the pharmacy during the Welcome Home Parade in 1919, which marked the first time Memorial Day was celebrated in Dunmore. (Courtesy of the Dunmore Historical Society.)

This photograph shows the float for Frank Pane's grocery store in Dunmore's Welcome Home Parade on May 30, 1919. The parade traveled down Green Ridge and Blakely Streets, crossing over to Drinker Street, and culminated in a celebration at Savage Field. The parade was a celebration to welcome home soldiers who fought in World War I. (Courtesy of the Dunmore Historical Society.)

Newly elected officers of the Dunmore American Legion Post No. 13 Junior Auxiliary are seen here on October 31, 1943. Pictured are, from left to right, (seated) Ann Marie McDonald, second vice president; Joanne Ferguson, past president; Marie Therese McDonald, president; and Antoinette Margotta, first vice president; (standing) Evelyn Barrett, secretary; Catherine Flynn, historian; Marie Margotta, chaplain; and Helen Engle, sergeant-at-arms. (Courtesy of the Dunmore Historical Society.)

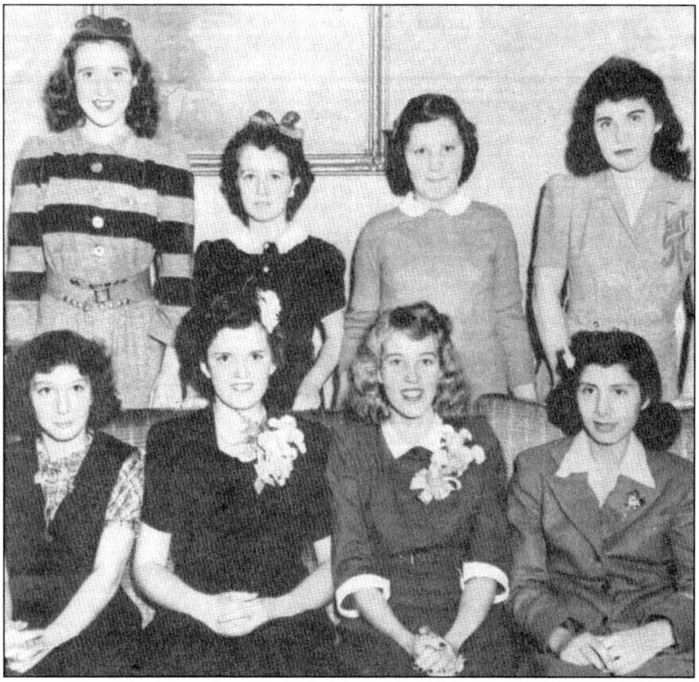

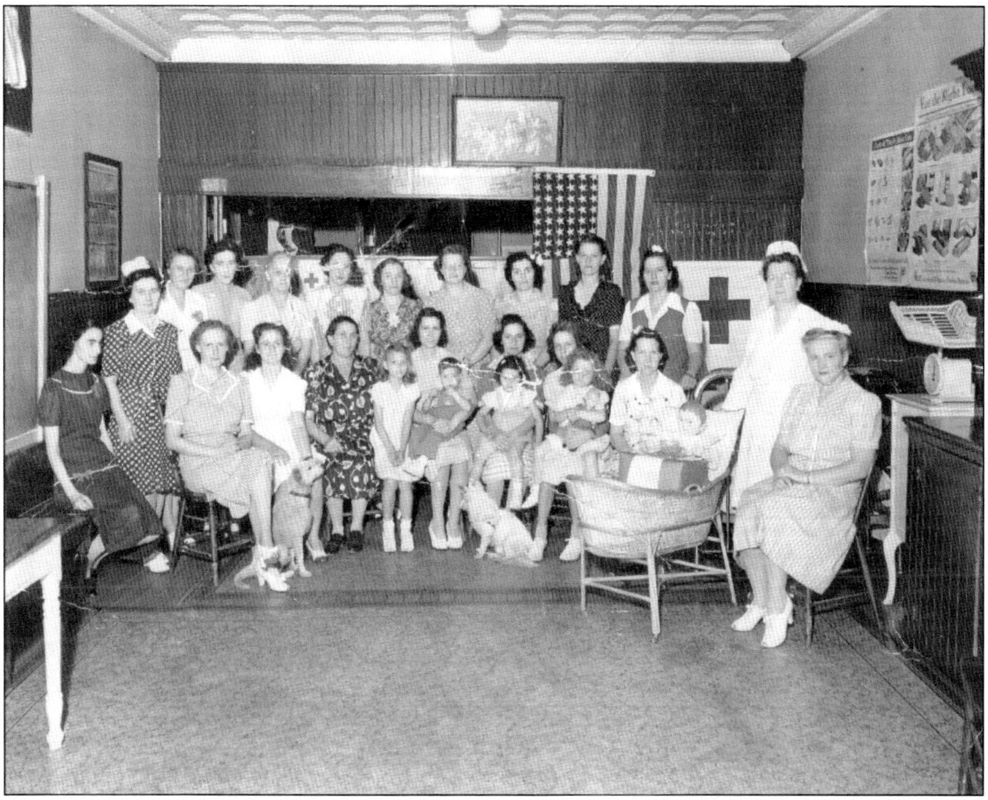

Dunmore women volunteered with the Red Cross during World War II, as seen in this photograph from about 1942. (Courtesy of Rosemary Summa.)

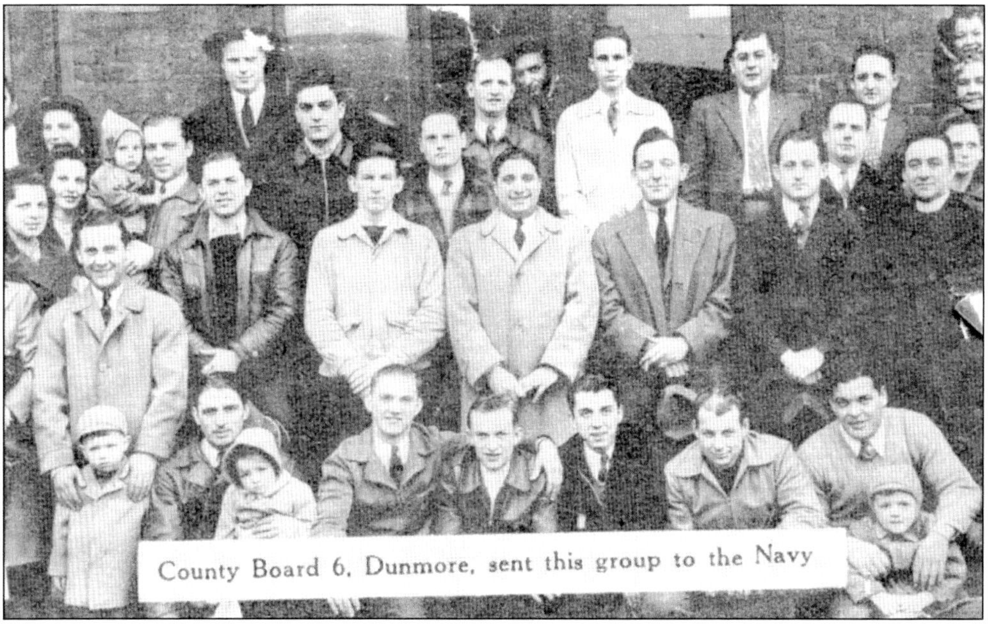

Dunmore residents leave for the US Navy in this early 1940s photograph. At the lower right is Frank F. Santarsiero with his son Bill. (Courtesy of Joseph Santarsiero.)

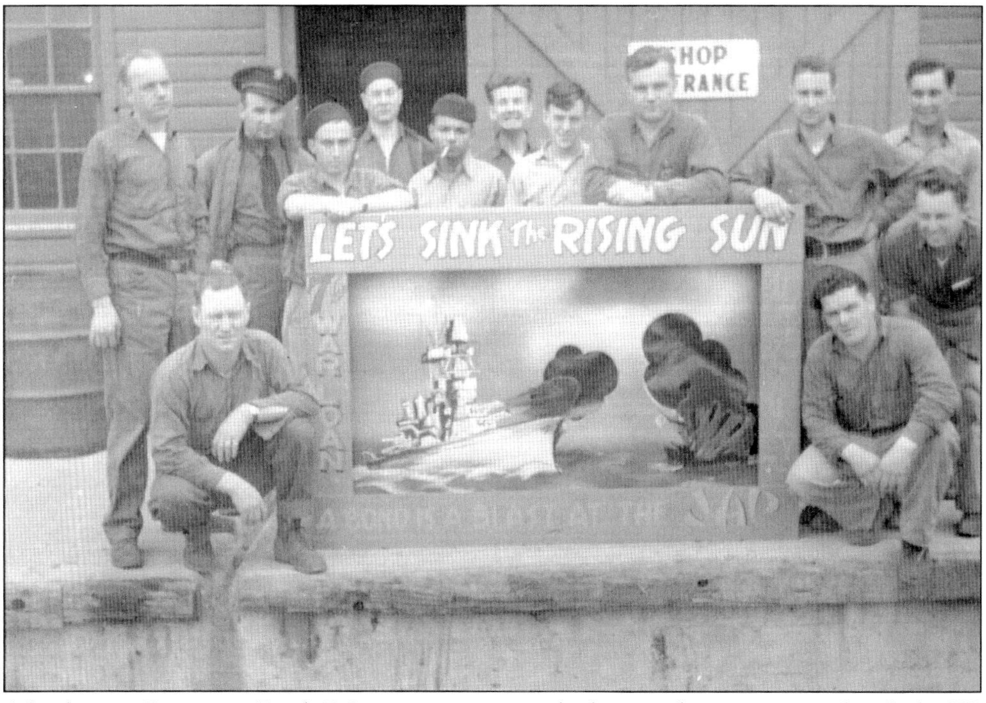

After leaving Dunmore, Frank F. Santarsiero, seen at the lower right, was stationed with the US Navy Sea Bees in the Aleutian Islands during World War II. (Courtesy of Joseph Santarsiero.)

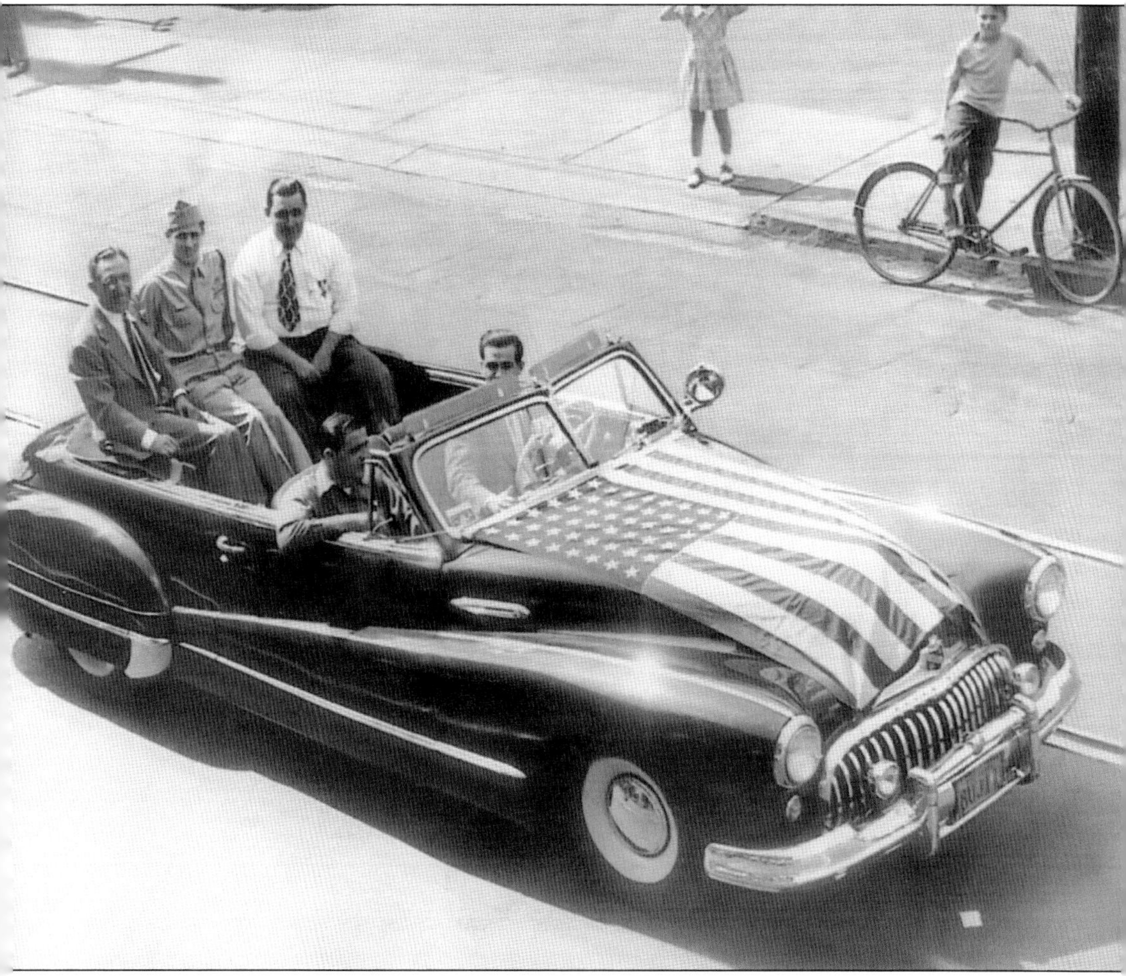

Gino Merli of Peckville, the center passenger in the back seat of this car, earned the Medal of Honor for his bravery during World War II at Sars-la-Bruyère, Belgium, by faking his death several times to defend against German forces. Merli is pictured here getting a hero's welcome during Dunmore's World War II victory parade in 1945. (Courtesy of the Dunmore Historical Society.)

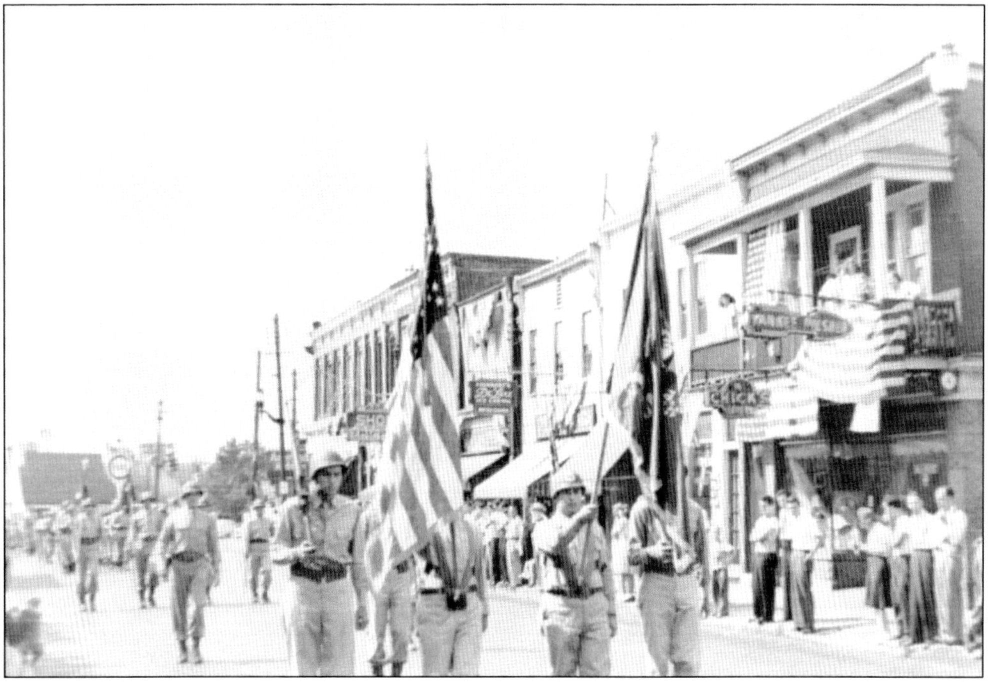

Returning World War II veterans carrying the American flag and the flag of the Commonwealth of Pennsylvania march down Drinker Street during the World War II victory parade in 1945. (Courtesy of Mary Riccardo.)

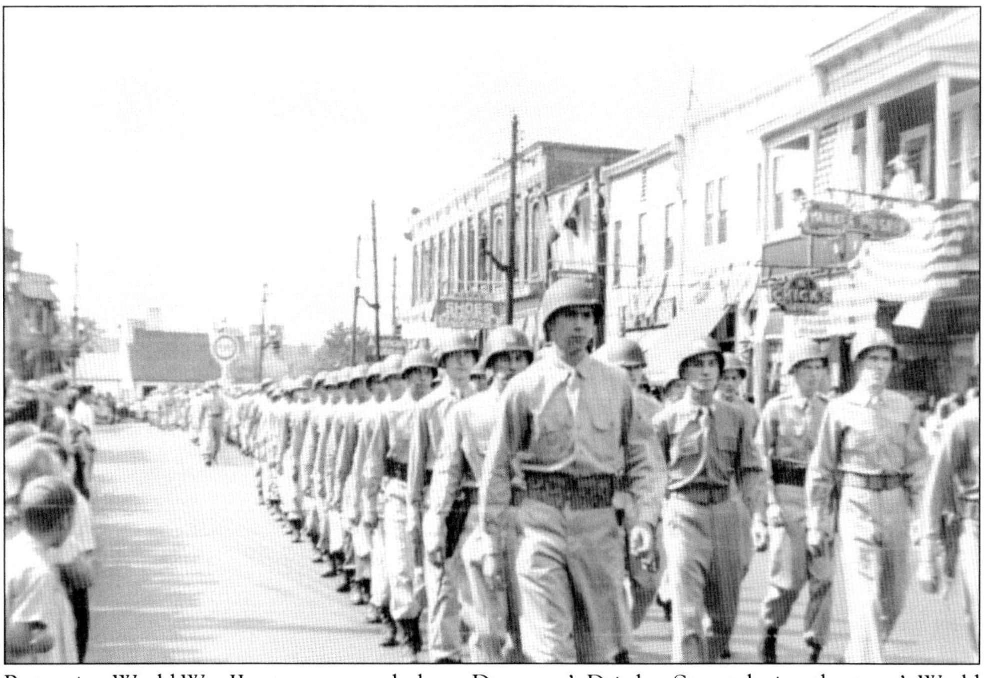

Returning World War II veterans march down Dunmore's Drinker Street during the town's World War II victory parade in 1945. (Courtesy of Mary Riccardo.)

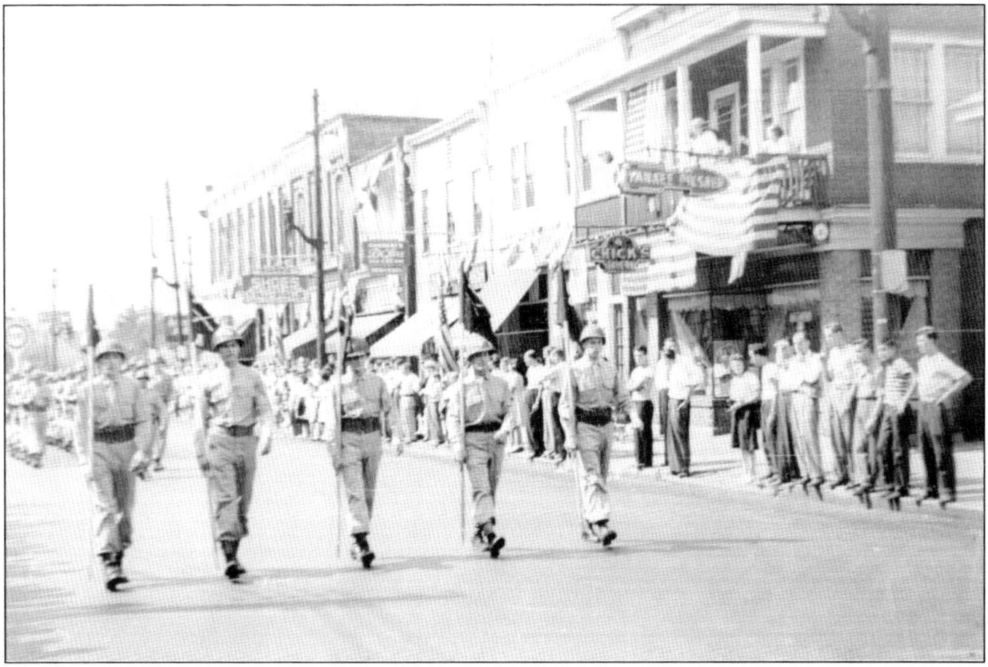

Returning World War II veterans are greeted by residents during Dunmore's World War II victory parade in 1945. (Courtesy of Mary Riccardo.)

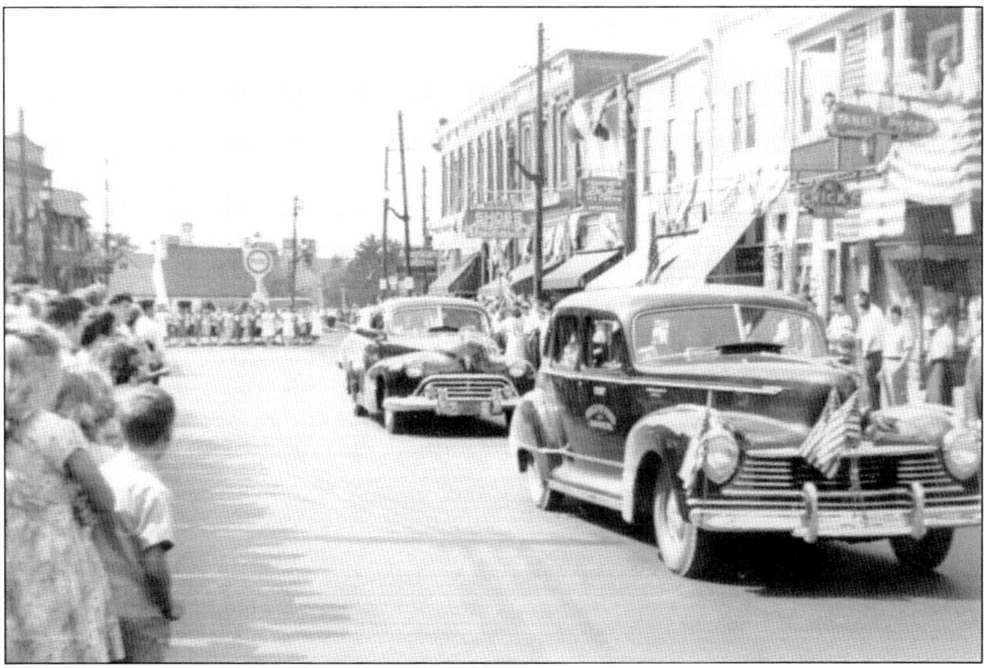

Cars from the Dunmore Borough Fire Department adorned with American flags travel down Drinker Street during the town's World War II victory parade in 1945. (Courtesy of Mary Riccardo.)

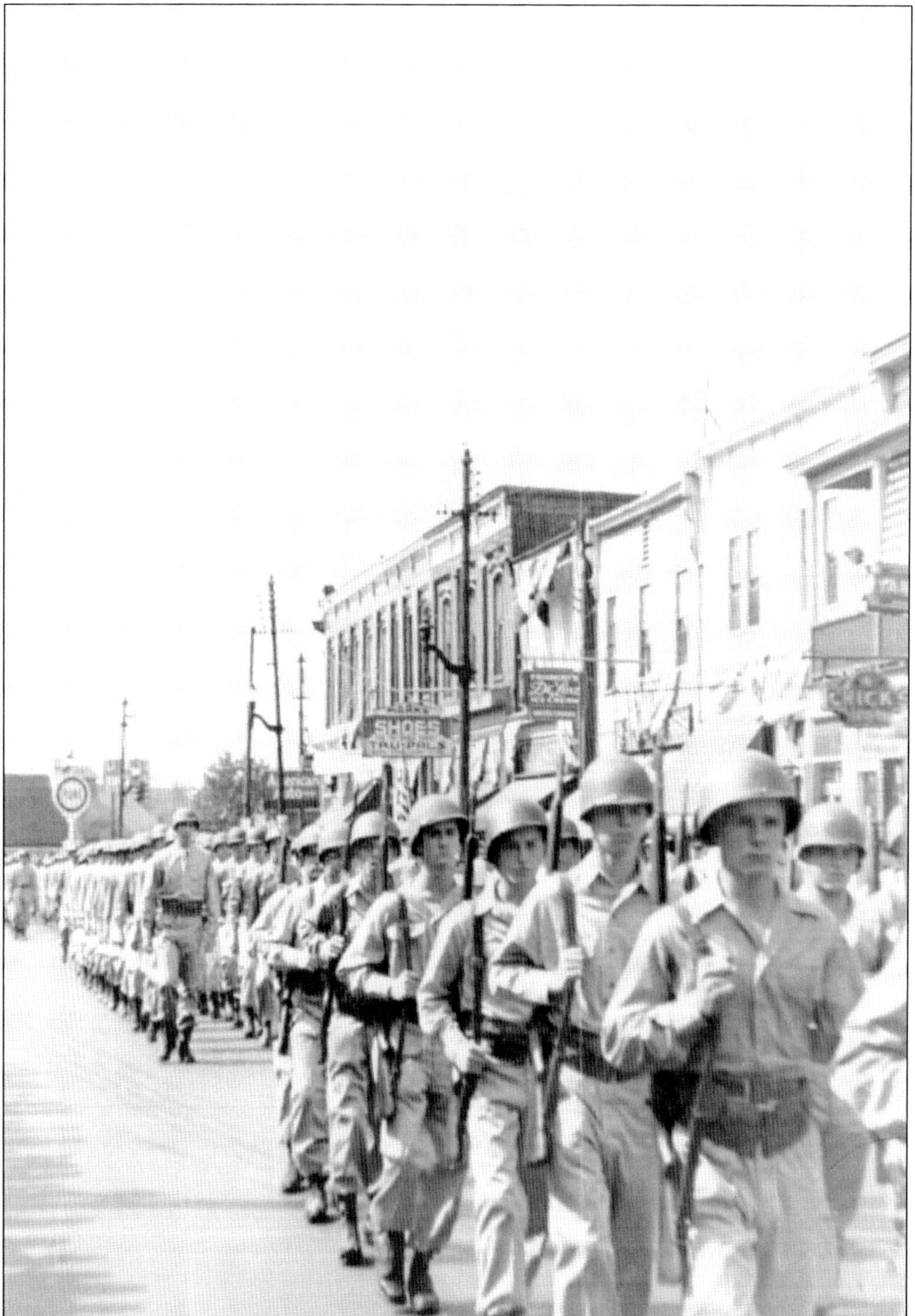

The World War II victory parade in Dunmore welcomed not only returning veterans who resided in the borough but also anyone who returned home from the war as a way to appreciate the soldiers for their sacrifices for the country. (Courtesy of Mary Riccardo.)

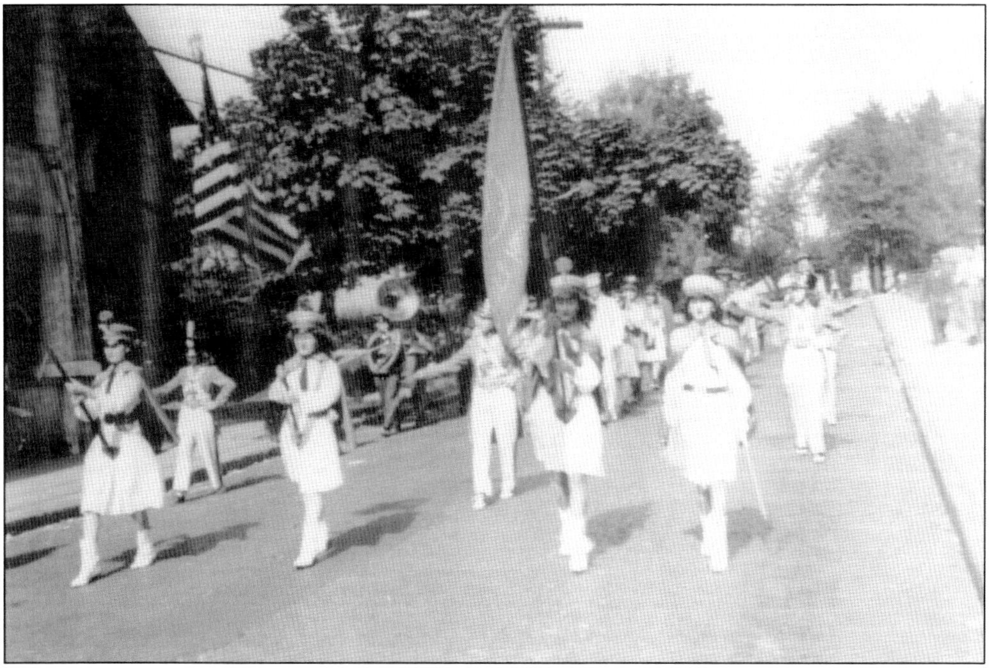

Members of the Dunmore High School drill squad participate in the town's World War II victory parade in 1945. (Courtesy of Mary Riccardo.)

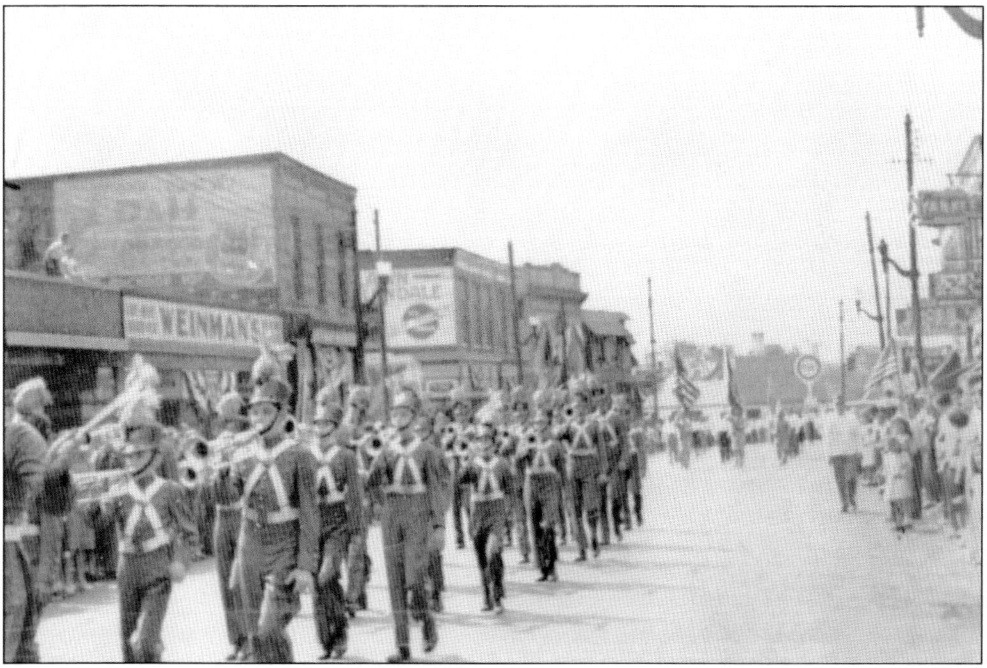

Members of the Dunmore High School marching band march down Drinker Street during the town's World War II victory parade in 1945. (Courtesy of Mary Riccardo.)

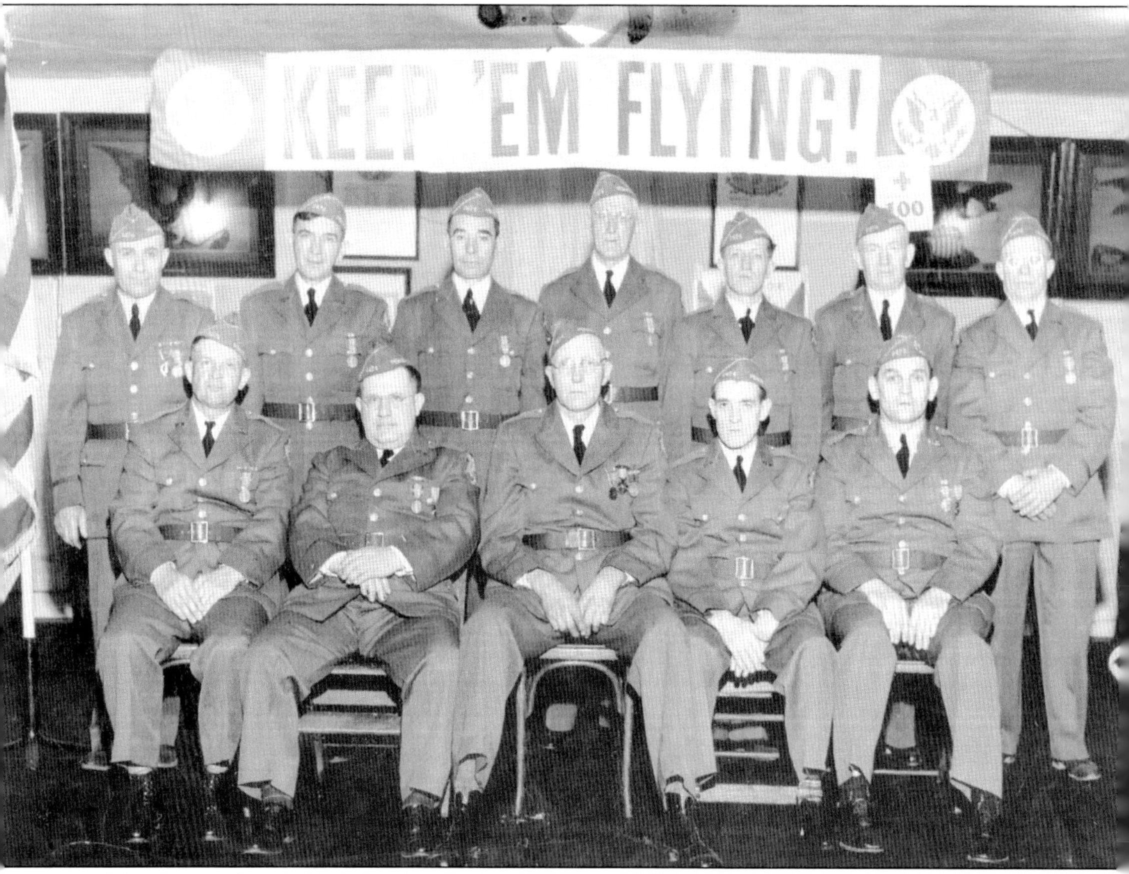

Members of the McHugh-Bushweller Post No. 3474 of the Veterans of Foreign Wars pose following the World War II victory parade. The McHugh-Bushweller Post is one of the oldest in Lackawanna County, having received its charter in 1936. The members met in various meeting rooms until they purchased their current meeting place on Chestnut Street in 1945. The McHugh-Bushweller Post was named in honor of John McHugh and Everett Bushweller, two Dunmore residents who were killed in World War I. (Courtesy of John J. Pallo Jr.)

One veteran who participated in the victory parade was Joseph Longo, seen here with his parents Salvatore and Nicoletta Luongo at their home in Dunmore's Bunker Hill neighborhood. Longo served as a cook for the Army and was stationed at Fort McClellan in Alabama. Longo arrived in the United States from Guardia dei Lombardi, Italy, in 1927 when he was 11 years old. Salvatore Luongo served in the Italian military in World War I before immigrating to the United States. (Courtesy of Ann Marie Longo.)

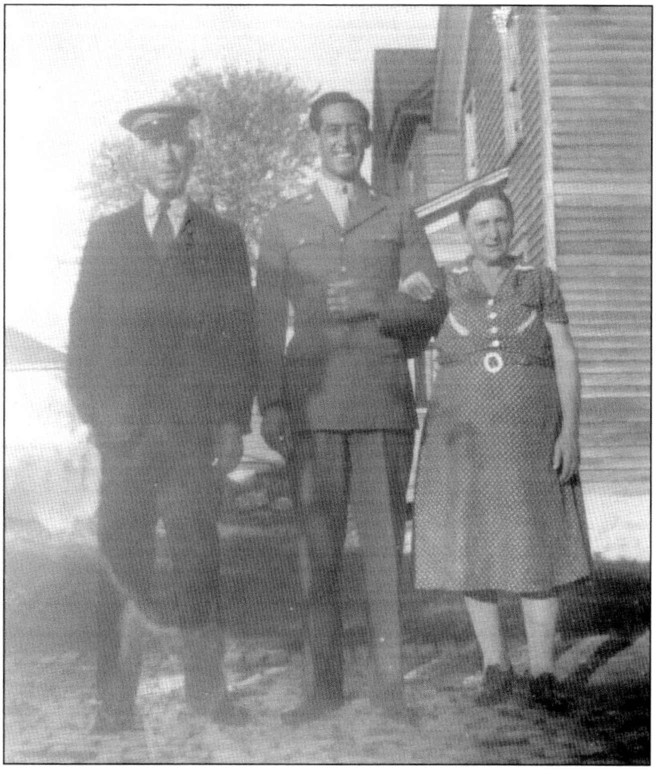

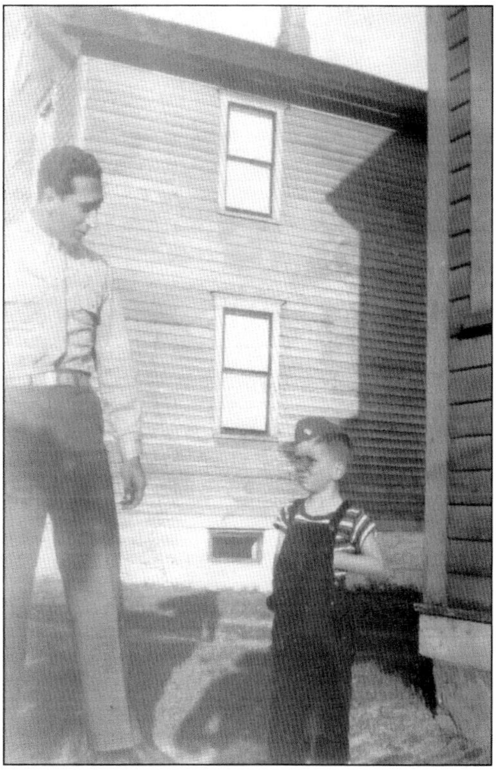

In later years, Joseph Longo became well known as a barber in Dunmore, having had a shop on Chestnut Street as well as a shop in the Bull's Head section of Scranton. Here, he is trying to teach his son Joseph how to salute the American flag. (Courtesy of Ann Marie Longo.)

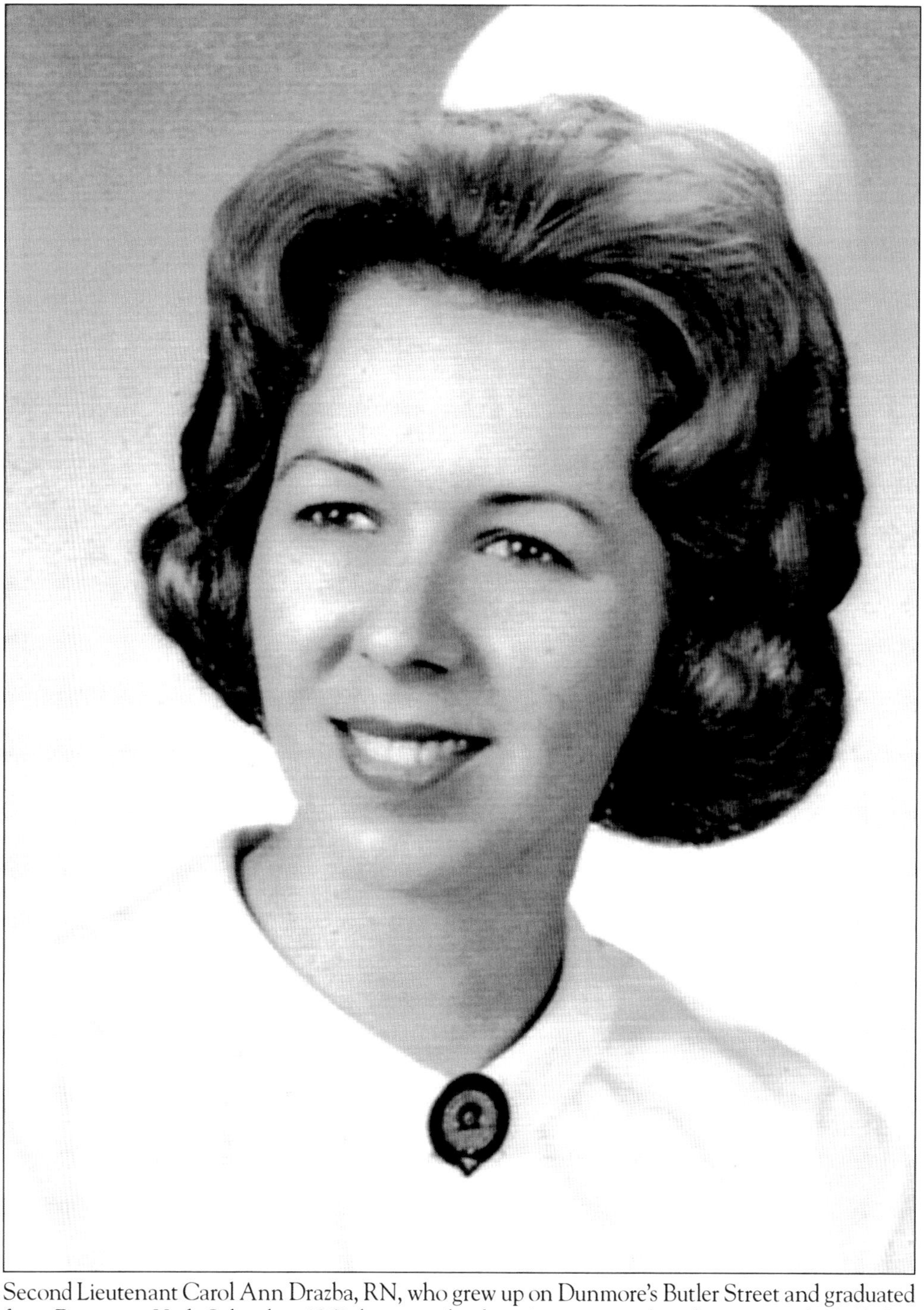

Second Lieutenant Carol Ann Drazba, RN, who grew up on Dunmore's Butler Street and graduated from Dunmore High School in 1961, became the first American enlisted woman to be killed in Vietnam on February 18, 1966, when the helicopter she was traveling in crashed into high-tension wires near Saigon. The other people killed with Drazba were Elizabeth Ann Jones, Charles M.M. Honour, Albert M. Smith Jr., Thomas Stasko, Gary Artman, and Christopher Lantz. (Courtesy of Anne Domin.)

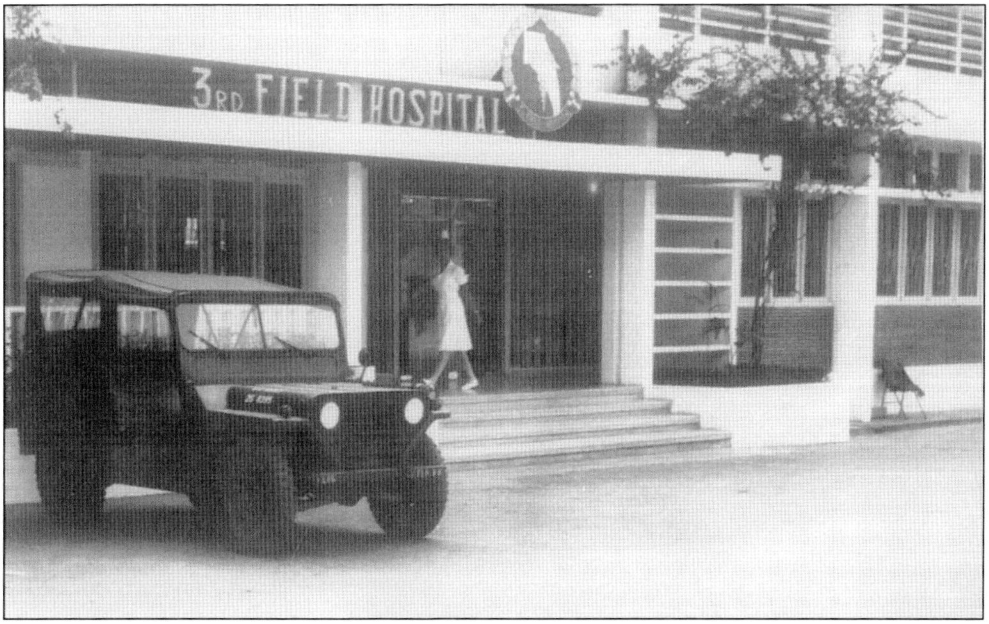

Drazba is pictured entering the Third Field Hospital in Saigon, where she was stationed. In her 1961 Dunmore High School yearbook, Drazba was described as "rolling out sunbeams and fun by the barrel" and, upon entering nursing school at the Scranton State General Hospital School of Nursing, expressed a desire to go over to Vietnam to help sick and wounded soldiers. (Courtesy of Anne Domin.)

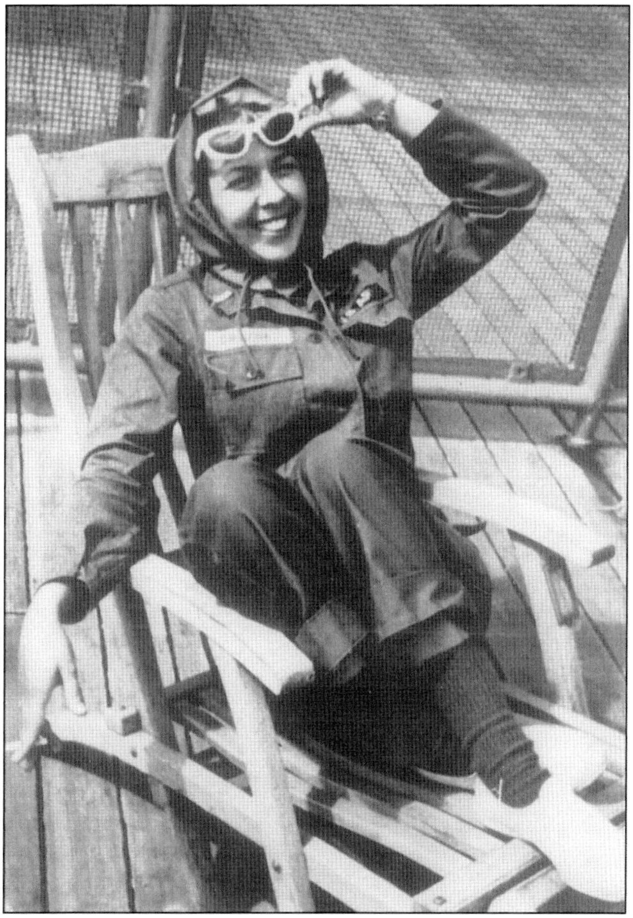

Drazba, seen on board the USS *Upshur* en route to Vietnam, began her tour of duty on October 13, 1965, and had worked nonstop until her death on February 18, 1966. At the time of her death, Drazba was on her way to Nha Trang, Vietnam, for a period of rest and rehabilitation. (Courtesy of Anne Domin.)

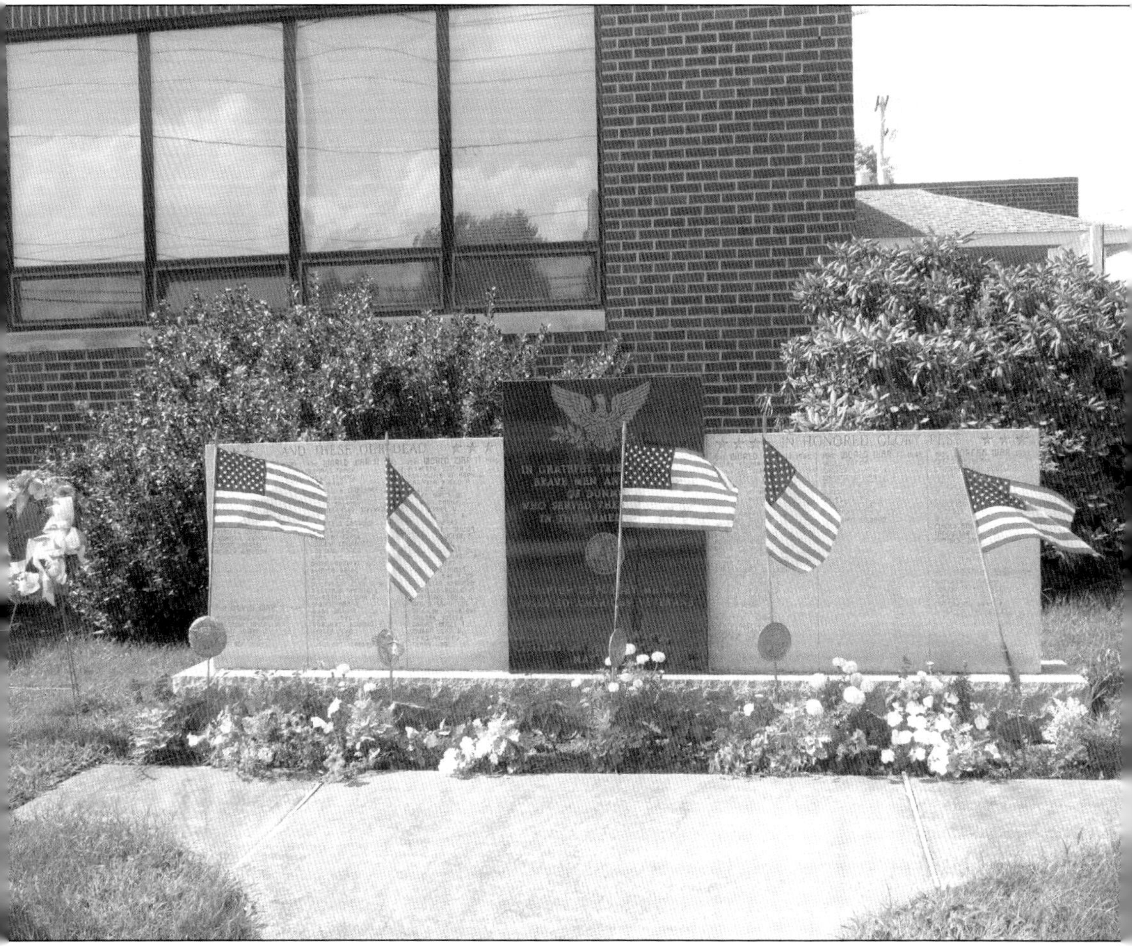

The Dunmore war memorial outside of the borough building on Blakely Street has the name of every town resident killed from World War I, World War II, the Korean War, and Vietnam. Chapter No. 23 of Forget Me Not Disabled Veterans erected the monument in 1983. (Author.)

Five

100 Years and Beyond

Dunmore's Centennial Celebration in 1962 was, literally, a party 100 years in the making for the borough. Residents decided to don costumes reminiscent of the 1860s, and men in the borough grew beards and moustaches.

The yearlong celebration fittingly began on April 10, 1962, with a "Charter Night" ceremony. There, the then-council members reenacted the first council meeting of April 10, 1862, based on the minutes from that meeting that were found in borough archives. Then-solicitor attorney Daniel Penetar converted the minutes into a script that was then acted out at Dunmore High School.

According to the script, the first Dunmore Borough Council meeting contained the swearing in of Burgess Calvin Spencer by Justice of the Peace Thomas Collins. Burgess Spencer then swore in the first council: Peter W. Widener; John Duffy; Peter Burschell, who became president of council; Henry Brennan; James Kennedy; and Henry Sommers.

During the public comment portion of that first meeting, audience members at the reenactment were asked to portray borough residents who had complaints for council, such as Luther Smith, who complained that stray cows were damaging his property. Also at the first meeting, Councilman James Kennedy asked for the creation of an ordinance to prevent hogs from running at large on borough streets.

Obviously, Dunmore has come a long way from the days of stray hogs and cows and horse-drawn carriages, trains, and trolleys. As Bucktown readies itself to celebrate its 150th anniversary, this chapter is meant to remember the love that went into the 1962 centennial celebration—a celebration that many borough residents today are too young to remember. The one thing that does remain true, whether it be 1862, 1962, or 2012, is that anyone who has lived a day in Dunmore has an overwhelming amount of pride for it.

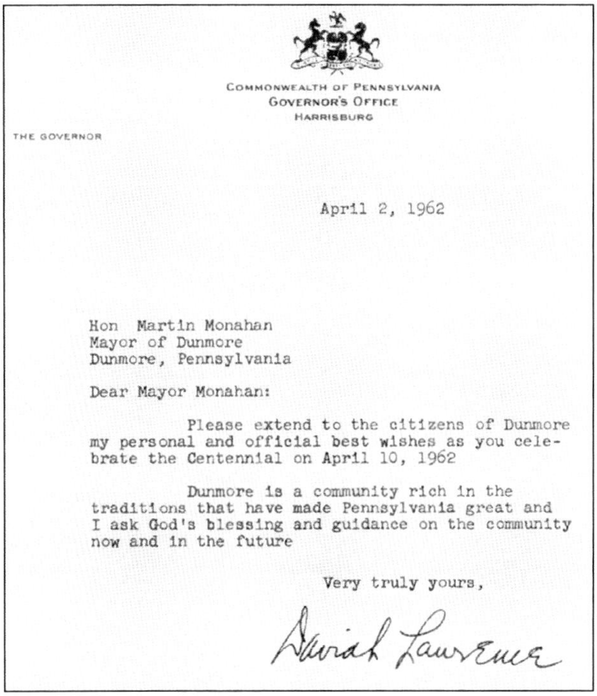

COMMONWEALTH OF PENNSYLVANIA
GOVERNOR'S OFFICE
HARRISBURG

THE GOVERNOR

April 2, 1962

Hon Martin Monahan
Mayor of Dunmore
Dunmore, Pennsylvania

Dear Mayor Monahan:

Please extend to the citizens of Dunmore my personal and official best wishes as you celebrate the Centennial on April 10, 1962

Dunmore is a community rich in the traditions that have made Pennsylvania great and I ask God's blessing and guidance on the community now and in the future

Very truly yours,

David Lawrence

One of the first people to congratulate Dunmore on its centennial was Pennsylvania governor David L. Lawrence, who attended the centennial parade and festivities in the borough in August 1962. Active in politics since his youth, the former mayor of Pittsburgh was known as the "maker of presidents," having helped both Franklin Delano Roosevelt and John F. Kennedy secure the Democratic nomination for president of the United States. As governor, Lawrence was known for antidiscrimination legislation, expanding Pennsylvania's library system, passing the state's fair housing law, and advocating historic preservation. Lawrence sent this letter to Dunmore mayor Martin Monahan on April 2, 1962. (Courtesy of Dunmore Borough.)

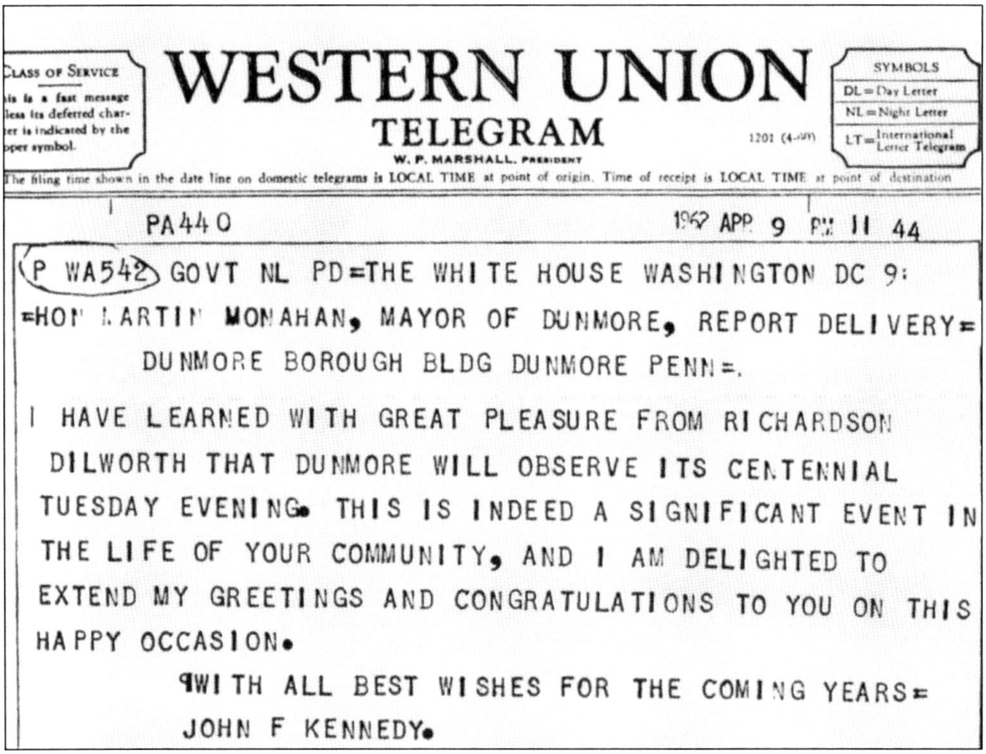

WESTERN UNION
TELEGRAM
W. P. MARSHALL, PRESIDENT

CLASS OF SERVICE
...is is a fast message
...less its deferred char-
...er is indicated by the
...oper symbol.

SYMBOLS
DL = Day Letter
NL = Night Letter
LT = International Letter Telegram

1201 (4-...)

The filing time shown in the date line on domestic telegrams is LOCAL TIME at point of origin. Time of receipt is LOCAL TIME at point of destination

PA440 1962 APR 9 PM 11 44

P WA542 GOVT NL PD=THE WHITE HOUSE WASHINGTON DC 9:
=HON MARTIN MONAHAN, MAYOR OF DUNMORE, REPORT DELIVERY=
DUNMORE BOROUGH BLDG DUNMORE PENN=.

I HAVE LEARNED WITH GREAT PLEASURE FROM RICHARDSON DILWORTH THAT DUNMORE WILL OBSERVE ITS CENTENNIAL TUESDAY EVENING. THIS IS INDEED A SIGNIFICANT EVENT IN THE LIFE OF YOUR COMMUNITY, AND I AM DELIGHTED TO EXTEND MY GREETINGS AND CONGRATULATIONS TO YOU ON THIS HAPPY OCCASION.

WITH ALL BEST WISHES FOR THE COMING YEARS=
JOHN F KENNEDY.

A few days after receiving Governor Lawrence's letter, Pres. John F. Kennedy sent this telegram at 11:44 p.m. on Monday, April 9, 1962, to congratulate Dunmore on its centennial celebration, set to begin the next day. (Courtesy of Dunmore Borough.)

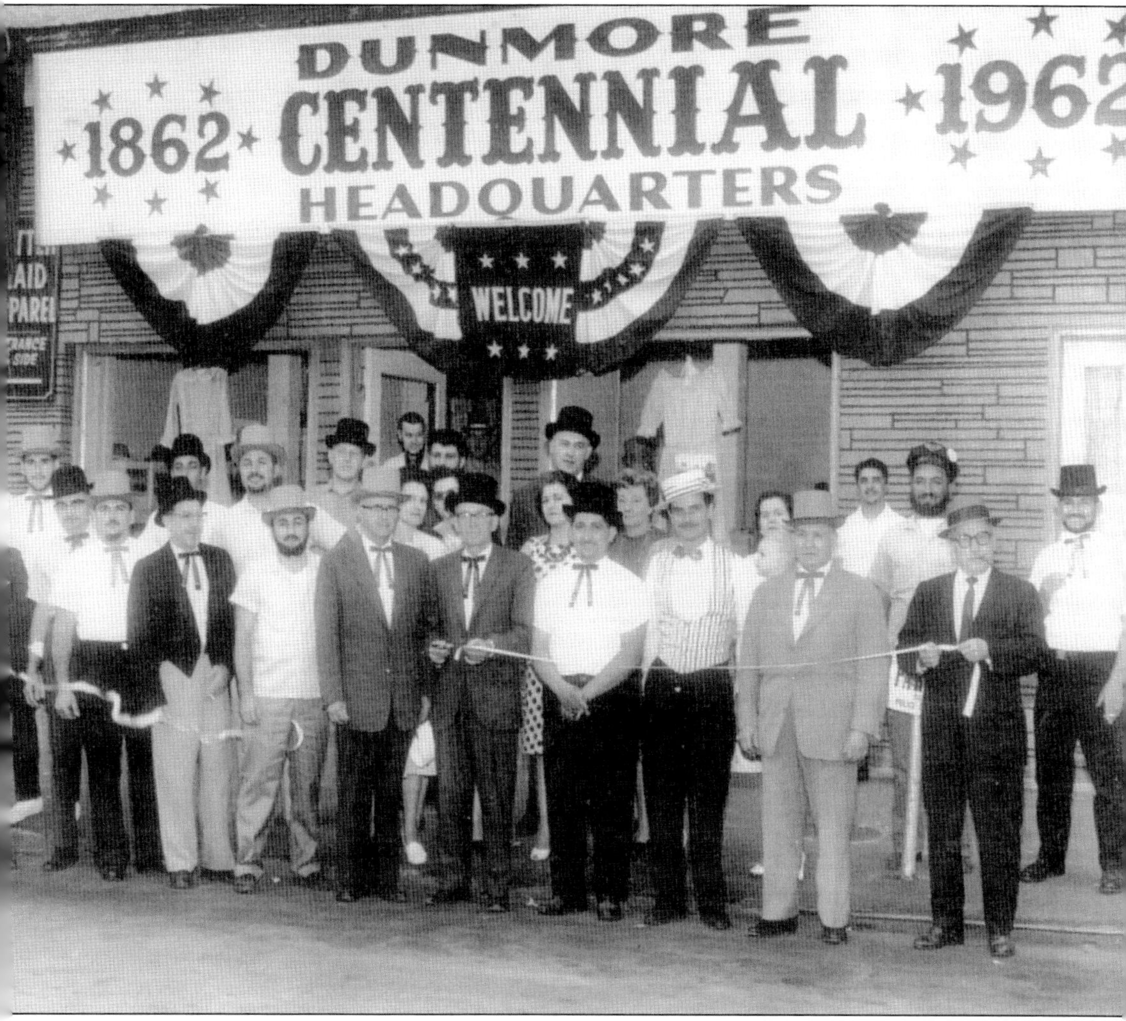

Dunmore mayor Martin Monahan (center, holding ribbon) officially opened the Dunmore Centennial Headquarters on June 23, 1962. The headquarters was located at 108 East Drinker Street and was the center for planning and coordinating all centennial festivities. It was also where residents could purchase centennial souvenirs, including wooden nickels, stock in the centennial committee, bow ties, flags, and coasters. (Courtesy of the Dunmore Historical Society.)

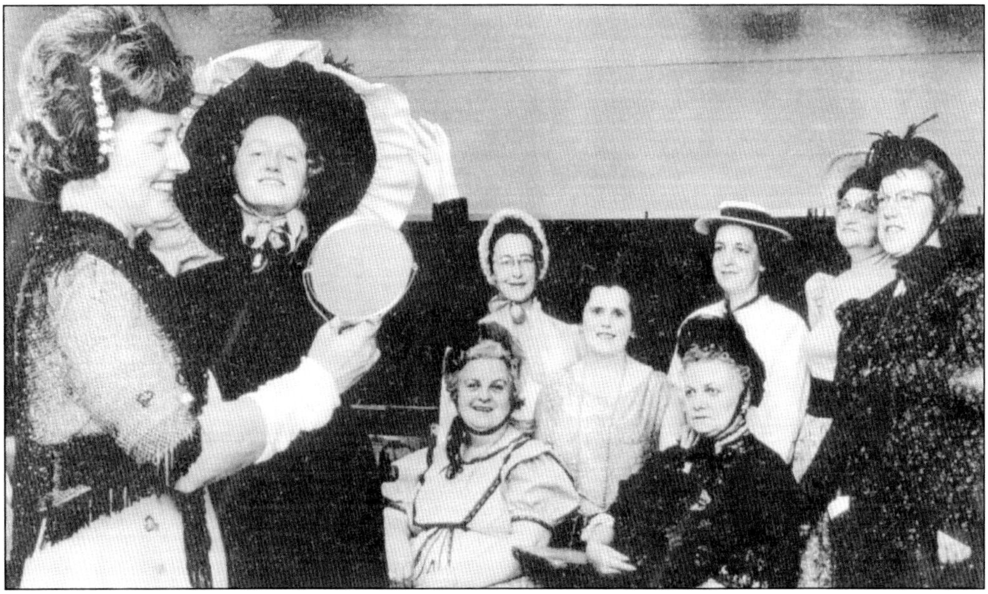

One way that Dunmoreans celebrated the town's 1962 centennial was by donning fashions that would have been popular when the borough was established in 1862. In this picture, local women show off some of their costumes at a fashion show held on June 27, 1962, at the Dunmore High School Gymnasium. Mrs. Jerome Higgins, the general chairman of the women's division for the centennial, holds a mirror for Jane Gilroy, who is wearing a dress once worn by her great-great grandmother. (Courtesy of the Dunmore Historical Society.)

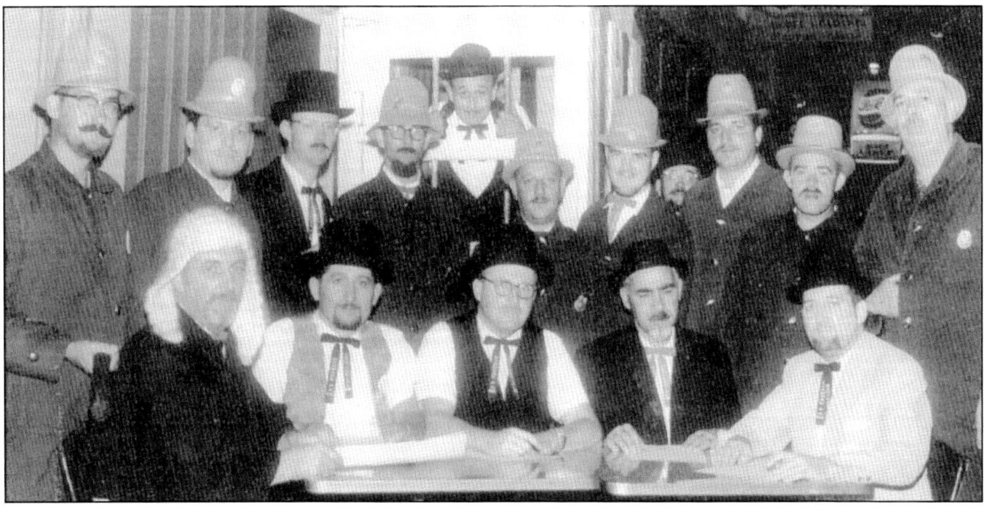

On August 2, 1962, the Dunmore Centennial's men's division began holding a series of kangaroo courts, where volunteer "defendants" were brought before the court and convicted and sentenced to a series of "penalties." Program planners included, from left to right, (seated) John "Buster" Jenkins, the presiding judge; Leonard Verrastro, Brothers of the Brush chairman; Frank Flannelly, the men's participation chairman; Anthony Calabro; and Thomas Hunt, kangaroo court cochairmen; (standing) Gene Quinn, James D'Andrea, Robert A. Kreis, Vito Carlucci, Edward DeSando, William Matticks, Thomas Dougherty, James Halpin, and Thomas Tonnetti, who were all deputy sheriffs. Locked in the court's "jail" was Anthony Constable. (Courtesy of the Dunmore Historical Society.)

One unfortunate resident to be sentenced by the kangaroo court was Russ Cordaro, seen here receiving his sentence to stay in medieval-style stocks during one of the nights of the centennial celebration, which took place throughout the month of August 1962. (Courtesy of the Dunmore Historical Society.)

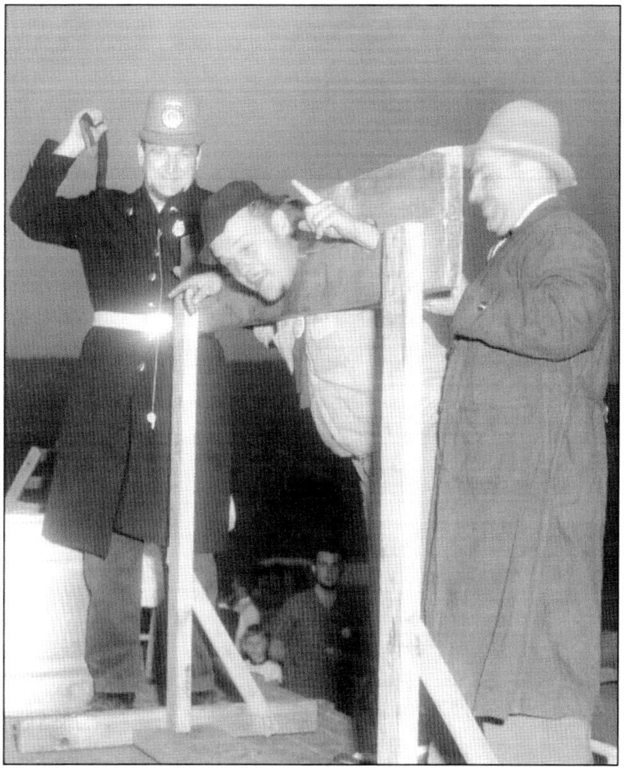

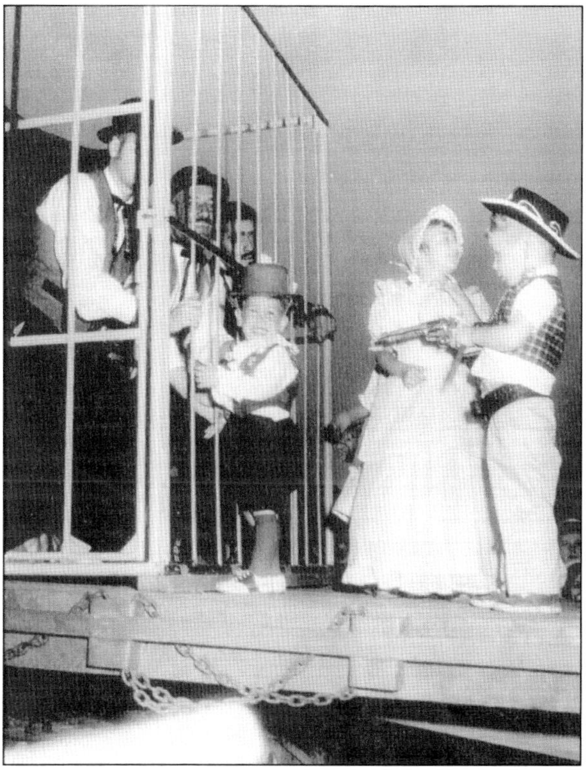

Even children got in on the act, as seen here in this August 17, 1962, photograph. Matthew Dillon holds a toy gun to keep his "prisoners" behind bars in the "jail" located at St. Anthony's Field in Dunmore. (Courtesy of the Dunmore Historical Society.)

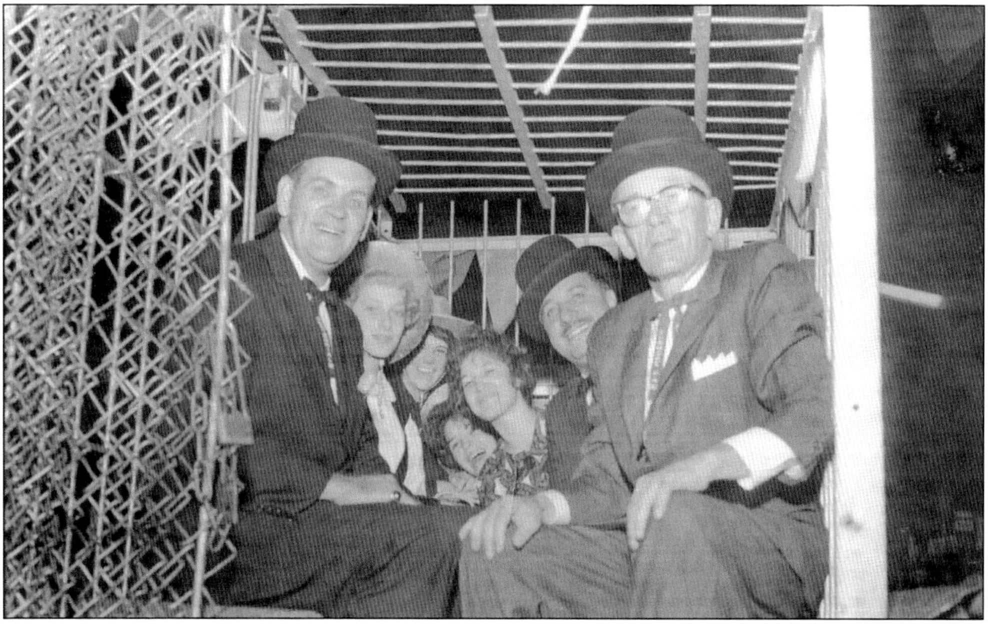

Dunmore mayor Martin Monahan, seated in the front with glasses, and Dunmore councilman Sam Cali, seated next to him, take a ride with other Dunmore residents on their way to Scranton on August 21, 1962. The purpose of the "centennial caravan" was to invite Scrantonians to participate in the centennial festivities since Dunmore is one of Scranton's larger suburbs. (Courtesy of the Dunmore Historical Society.)

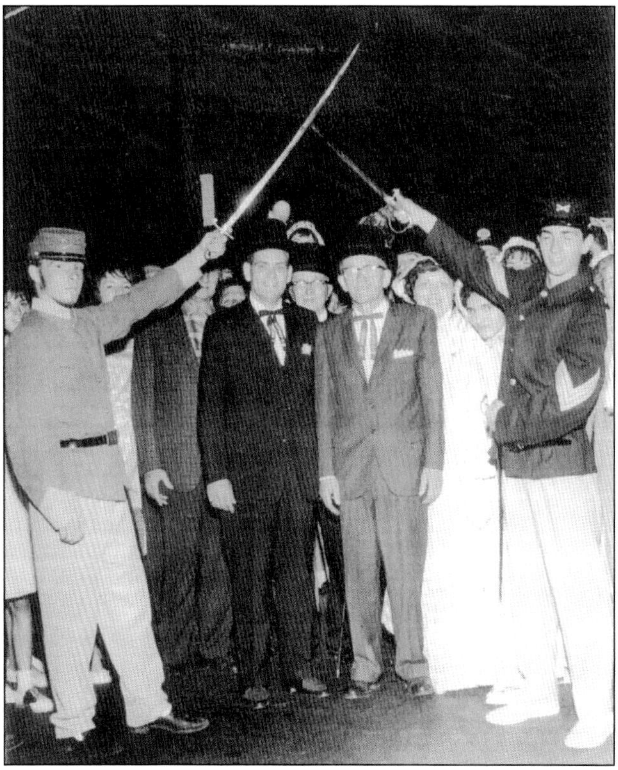

Scranton mayor William T. Schmidt, center left, and Dunmore mayor Martin Monahan, center right, wear their centennial garb as they meet at the intersection of Wyoming and Lackawanna Avenues in downtown Scranton at the conclusion of the centennial caravan. Crossing the swords over the two mayors were Frank Pendel (left) and Charles Mecca (right). (Courtesy of the Dunmore Historical Society.)

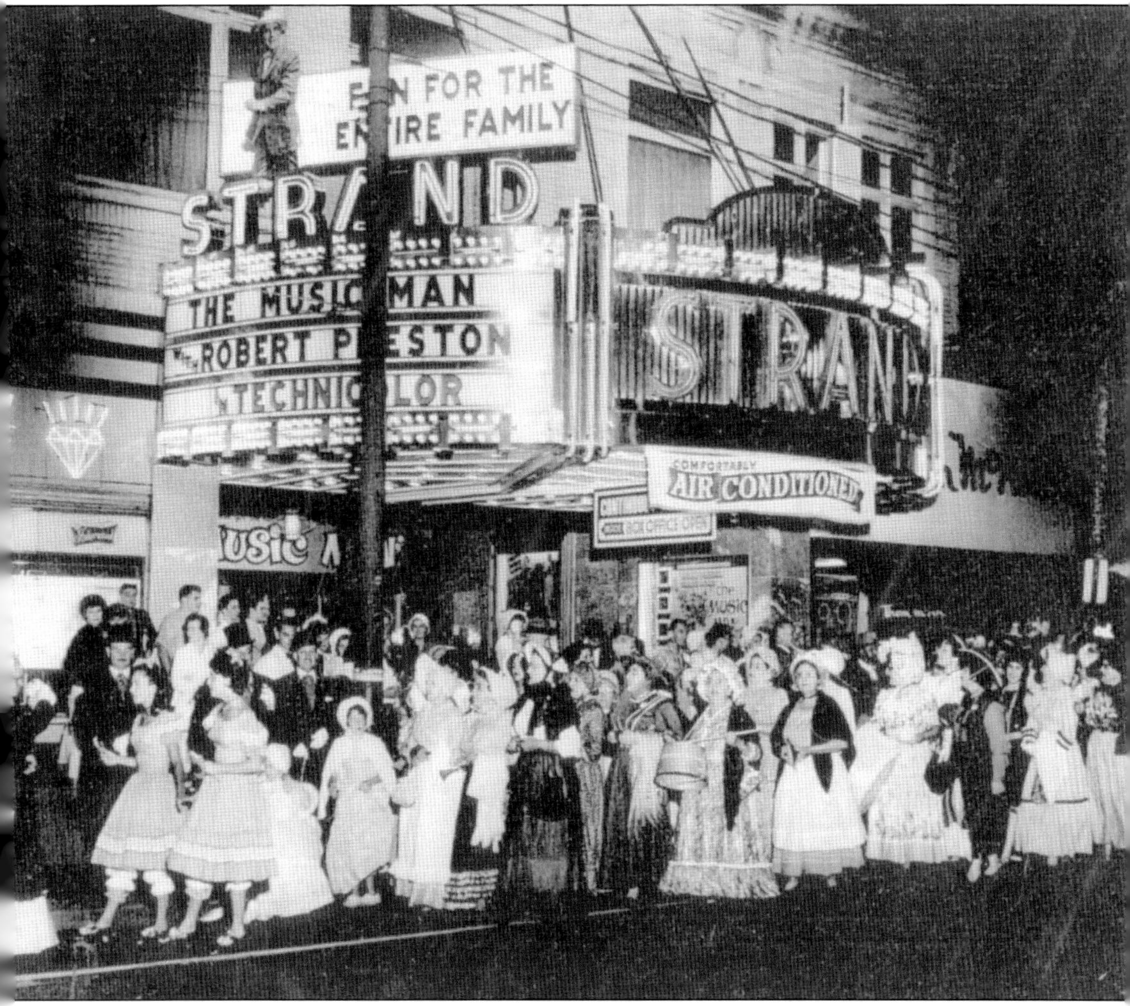

Another stop on the centennial caravan was a special screening of *The Music Man* at the Strand movie theater, which was located on Spruce Street in downtown Scranton. Dunmoreans dressed in centennial costumes are seen entering the movie theater to see the musical, which was set in 1912, Dunmore's 50th anniversary year. (Courtesy of the Dunmore Historical Society.)

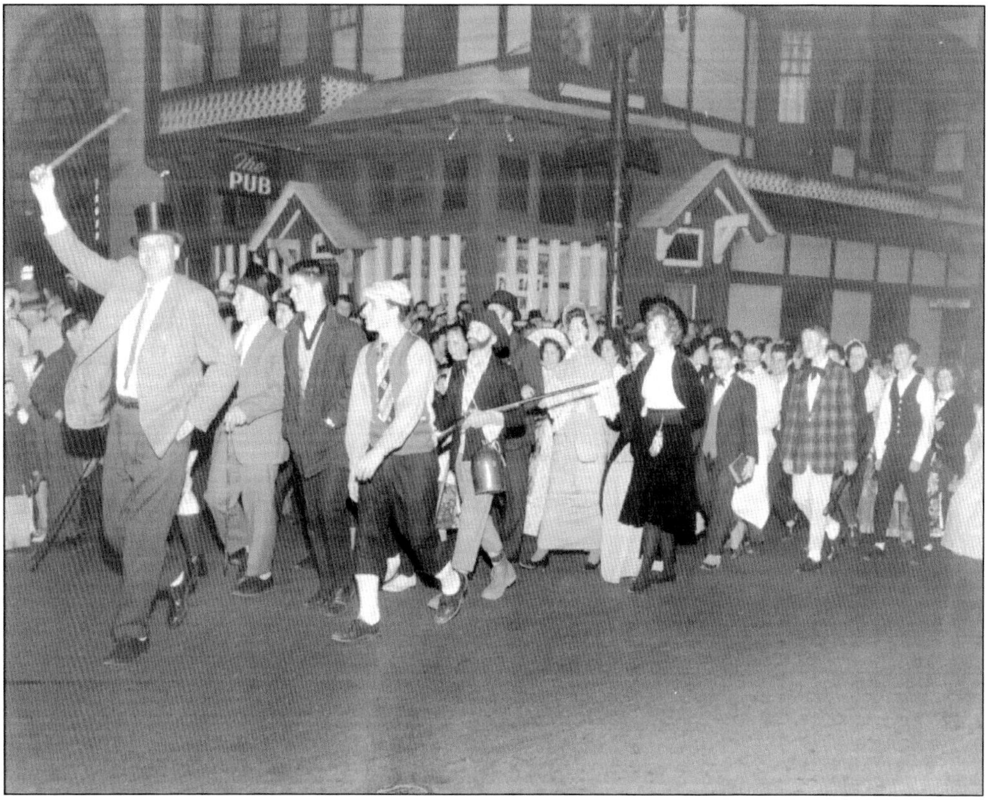

Former Dunmore High School football coach James Martinelli leads residents through Dunmore Corners as a part of the "Open Door" pageant that told the tale of how Dunmore was settled and eventually grew to become a borough. (Courtesy of the Dunmore Historical Society.)

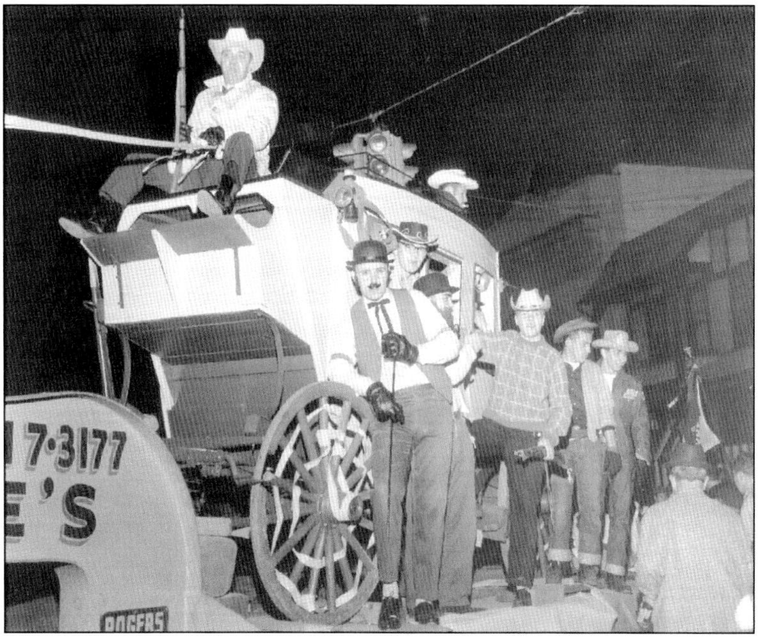

Residents ride through Dunmore Corners on their way to Dunmore High School in coaches to take part in the "Open Door" pageant on August 30, 1962. (Courtesy of the Dunmore Historical Society.)

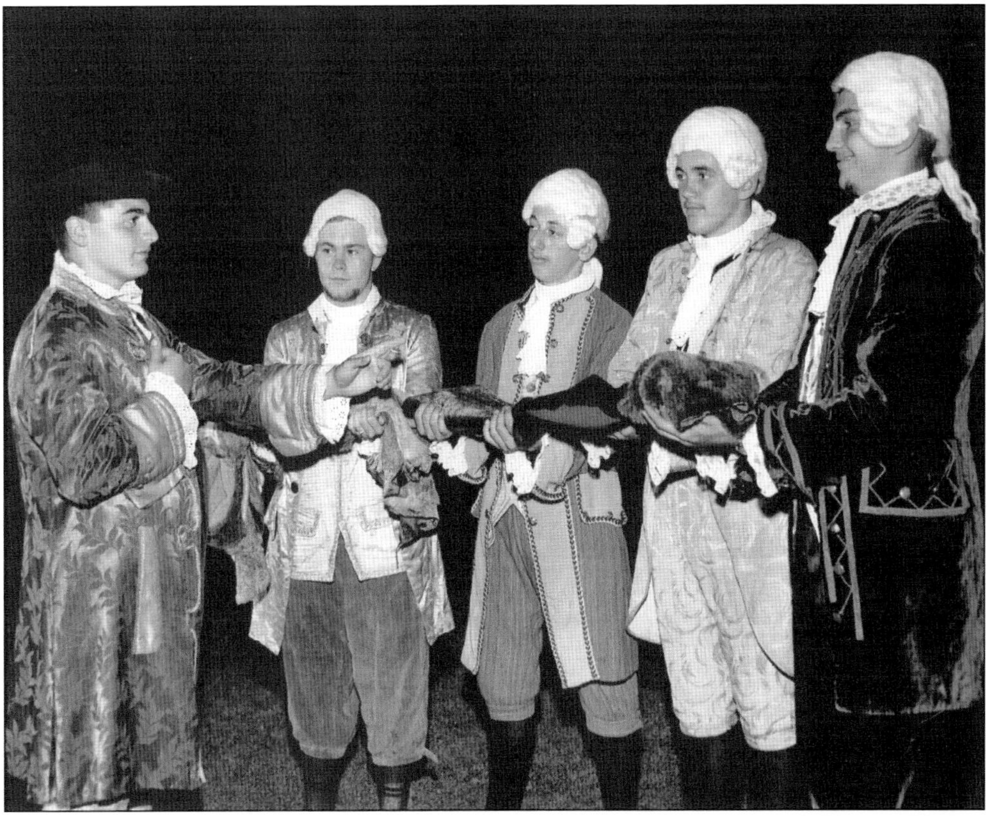

This scene from the "Open Door" pageant depicts colonial officers receiving instructions on how to deal with Native American tribes from William Penn, portrayed by Ernest Gregory. Pictured are, from left to right, Ernest Gregory, Gerald Durkin, Canio Cianci, William Lyons, and Michael Giumento. (Courtesy of the Dunmore Historical Society.)

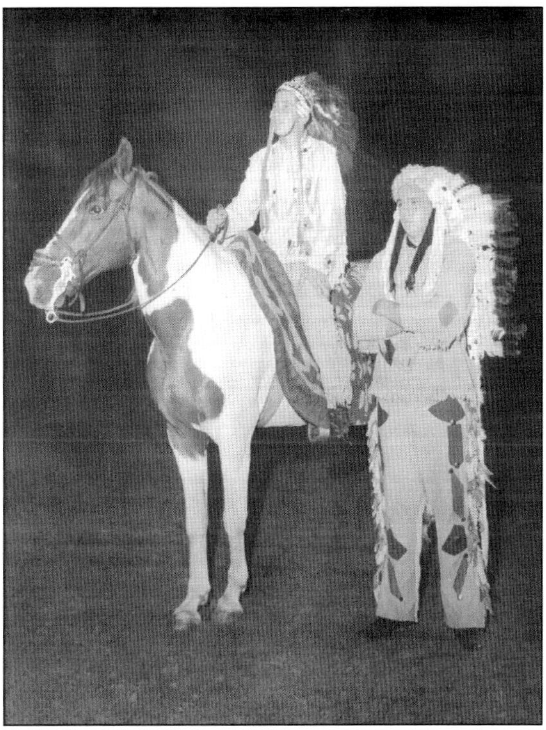

Other scenes from the pageant included the various Native American tribes that occupied the territory that eventually became Dunmore, Pennsylvania. In this photograph, residents are dressed as members of the Delaware tribe, from which Dunmore's Delaware Street received its name. (Courtesy of the Dunmore Historical Society.)

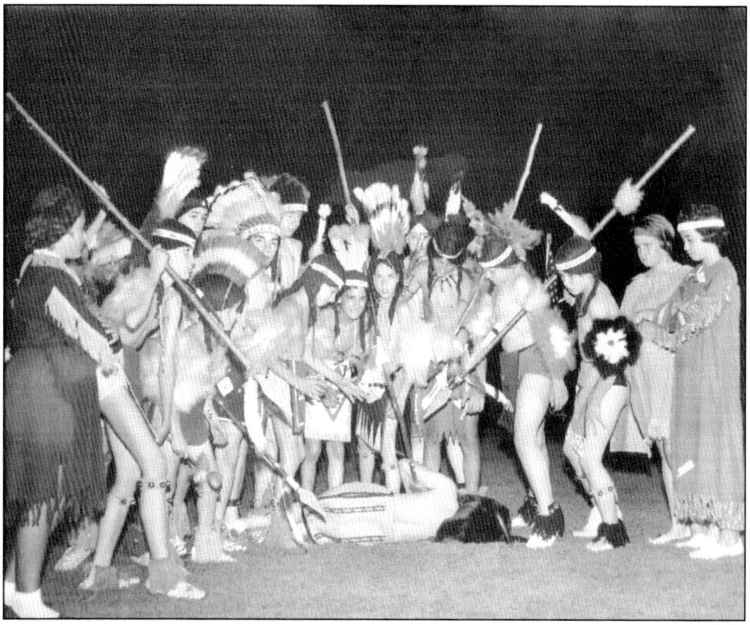

Members of Boy Scout Troop No. 80, which was located at Dunmore's Christ the King Church, represent members of the Delaware tribe as they hunt buffalo during the "Open Door" pageant, held on August 30, 1962, at the Dunmore High School Stadium. (Courtesy of the Dunmore Historical Society.)

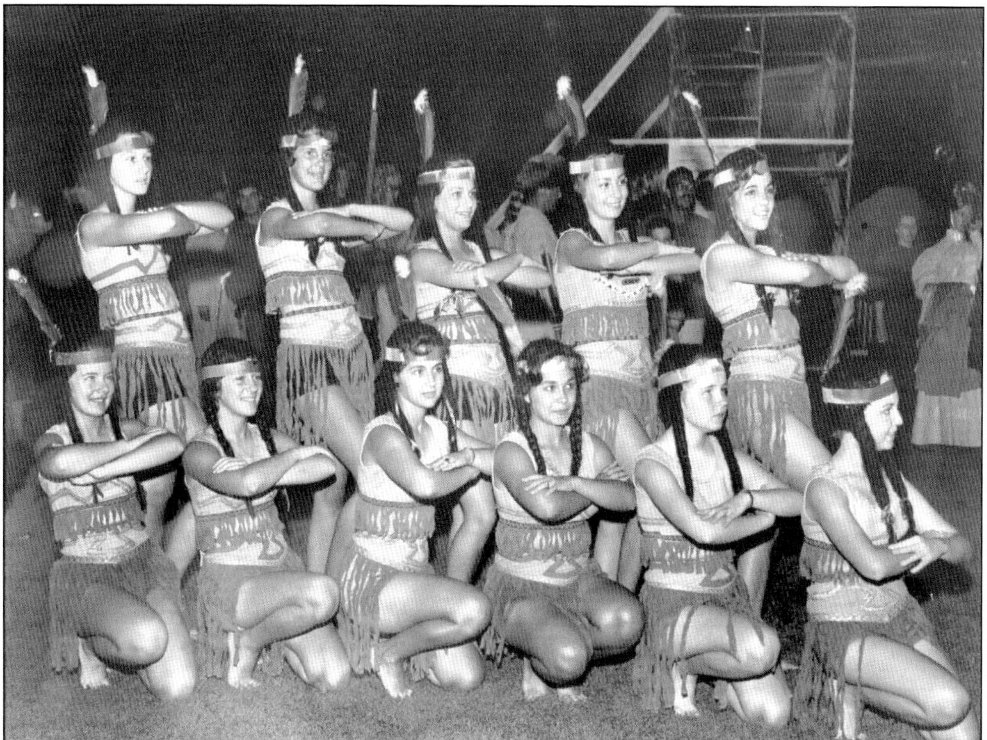

Native American princesses take part in the "Open Door" pageant at the Dunmore High School Stadium. Pictured from left to right are (kneeling) Linda McDonnell, Carol McDonnell, Roseann Verrastro, Johanna Nicastro, Trudy McDermott, and Donna Prall; (standing) Mary Ann Gianoni, Gail Moyer, Kathy Bordi, Laura Sandone, and Marietta Palumbo. (Courtesy of the Dunmore Historical Society.)

Former Dunmore High School teacher Al Evans, center, speaks to his tribe during the "Open Door" pageant. (Courtesy of the Dunmore Historical Society.)

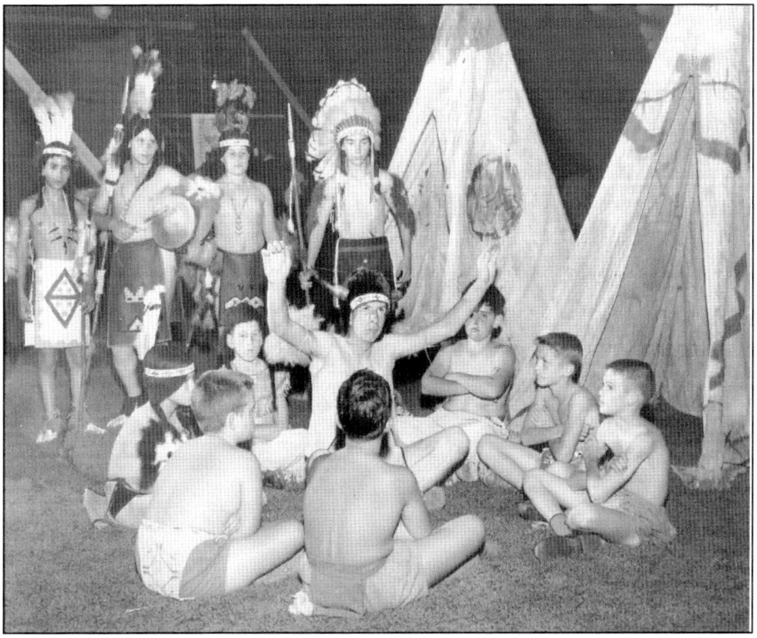

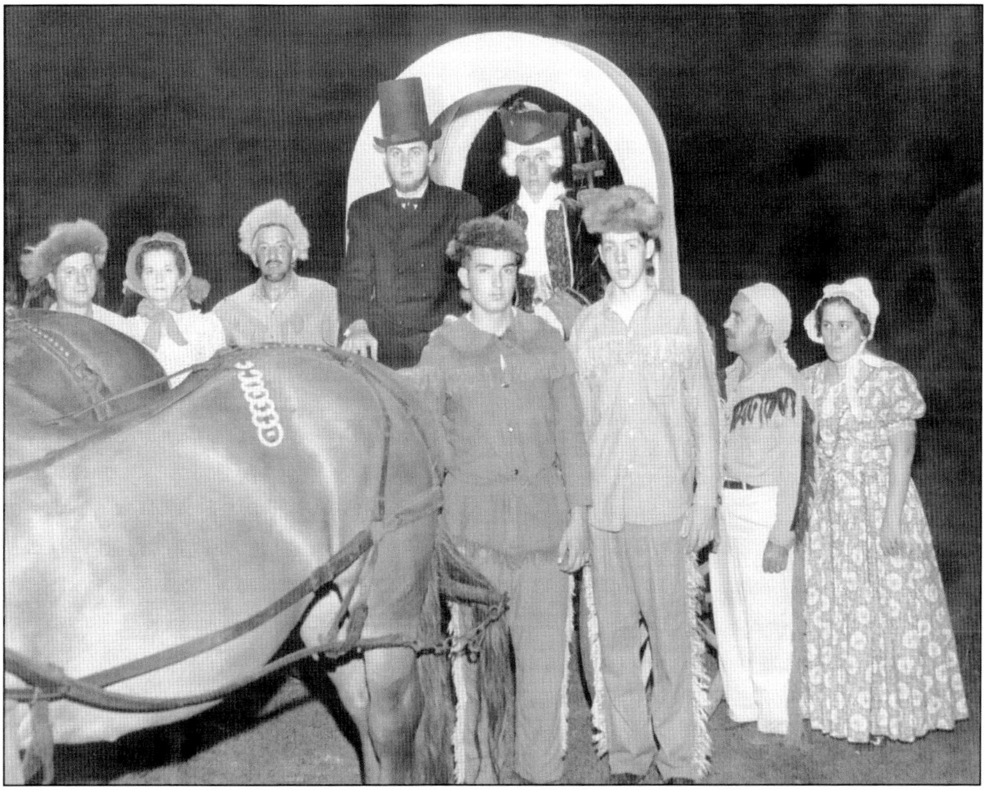

Abraham Lincoln (Roger Sparks) and Lord Dunmore (Richard Polish) are met by pioneers after arriving at the "Open Door" pageant. Pioneers were, from left to right, Leo Russin, Betty Knauer, Richard Mallas, Anthony Sarry, Brian Petrasko, Michael Arolio, and Armanda Trolio. (Courtesy of the Dunmore Historical Society.)

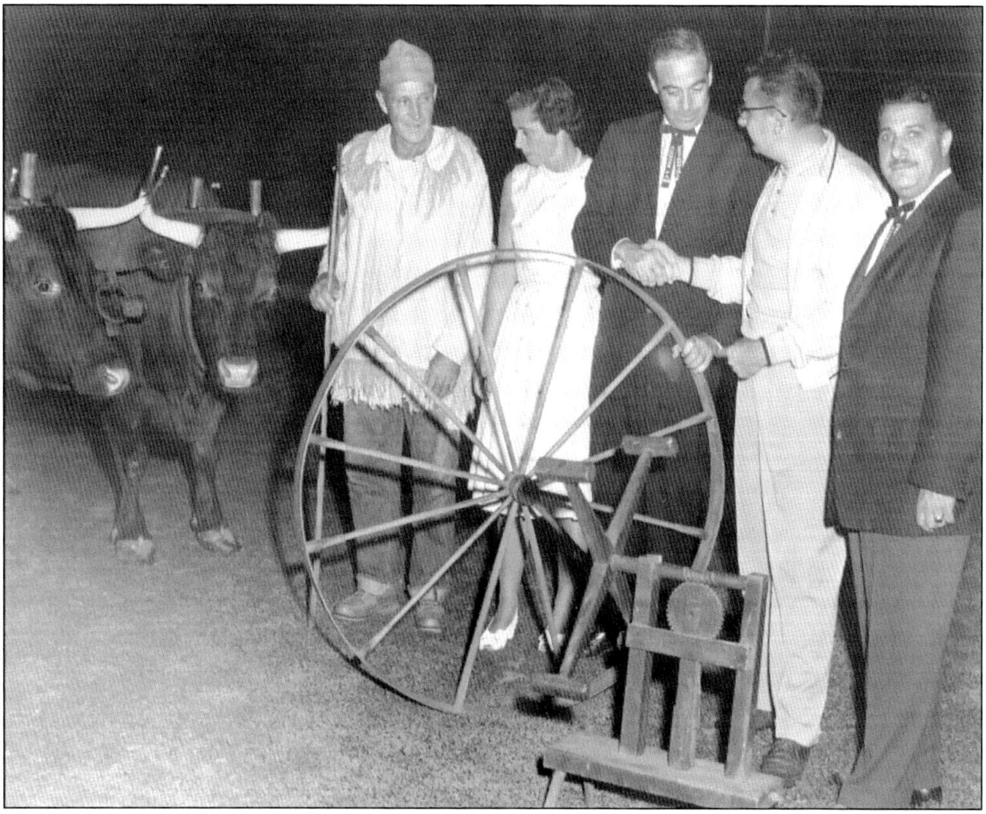

Future Pennsylvania governor William W. Scranton made a campaign stop at the "Open Door" pageant. Pictured from left to right are John Hill, Mary Scranton, William W. Scranton, William Gowden, and Sam Cali, Dunmore Republican councilman. (Courtesy of the Dunmore Historical Society.)

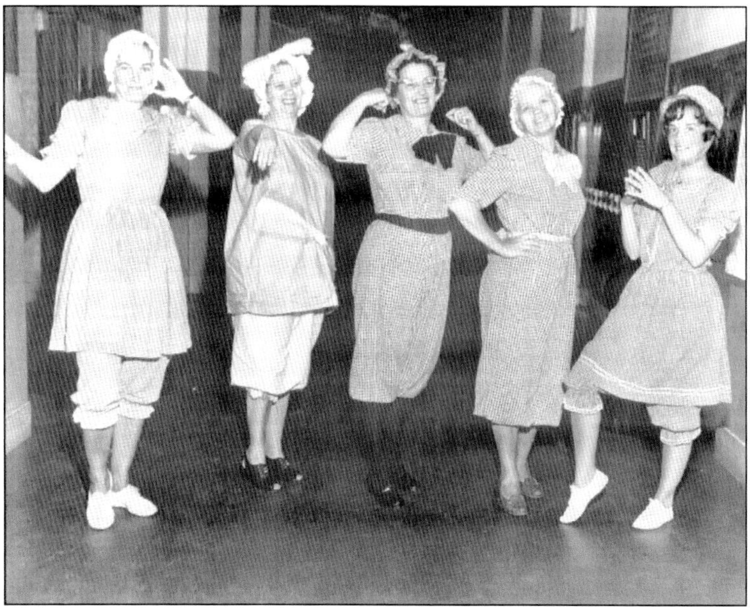

Dunmore women model their 1860s attire in the halls of Dunmore High School during the "Open Door" pageant. (Courtesy of the Dunmore Historical Society.)

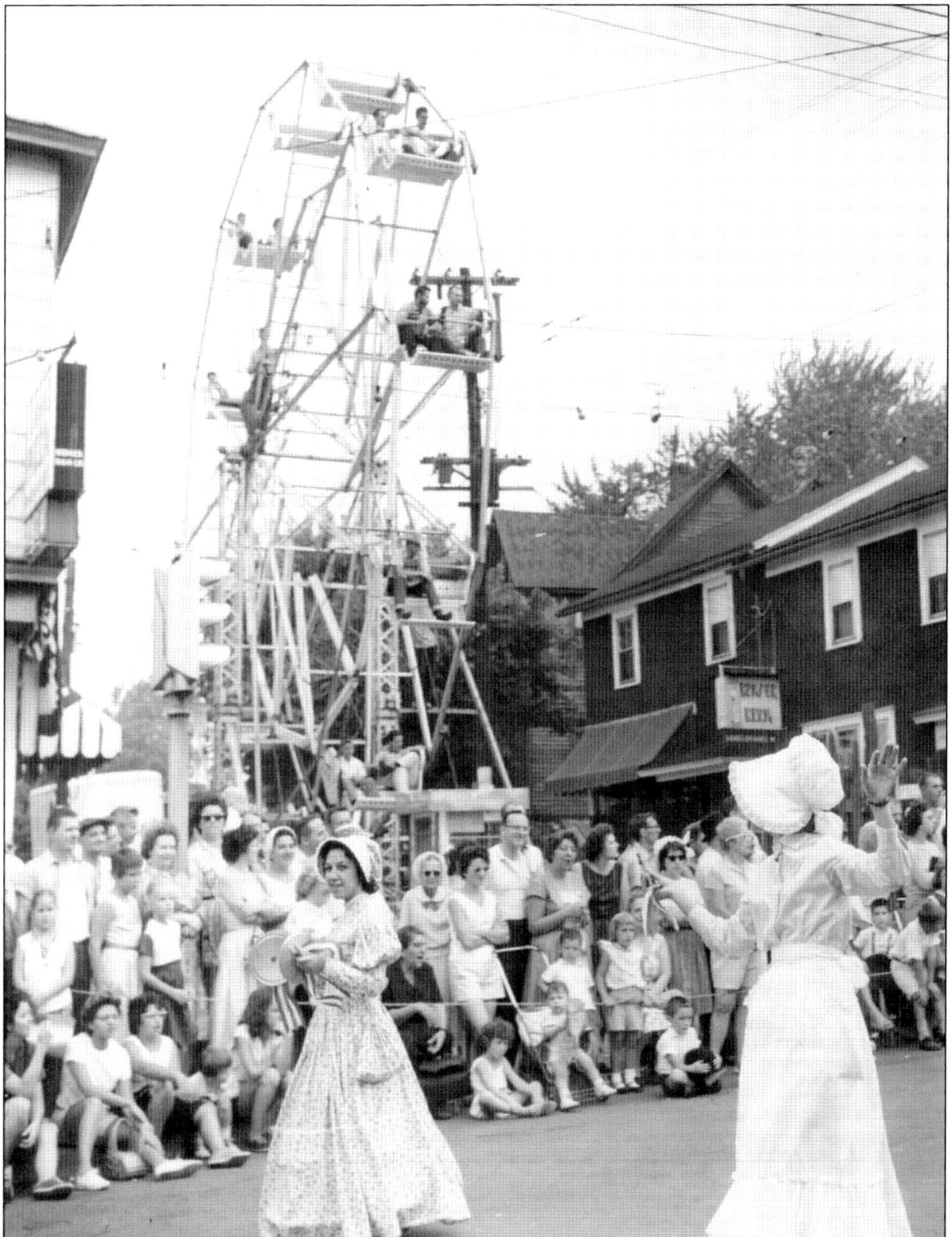

Rides, such as this Ferris wheel on Drinker Street, were part of the day's celebrations at the Dunmore Centennial Parade, held on September 1, 1962. (Courtesy of the Dunmore Historical Society.)

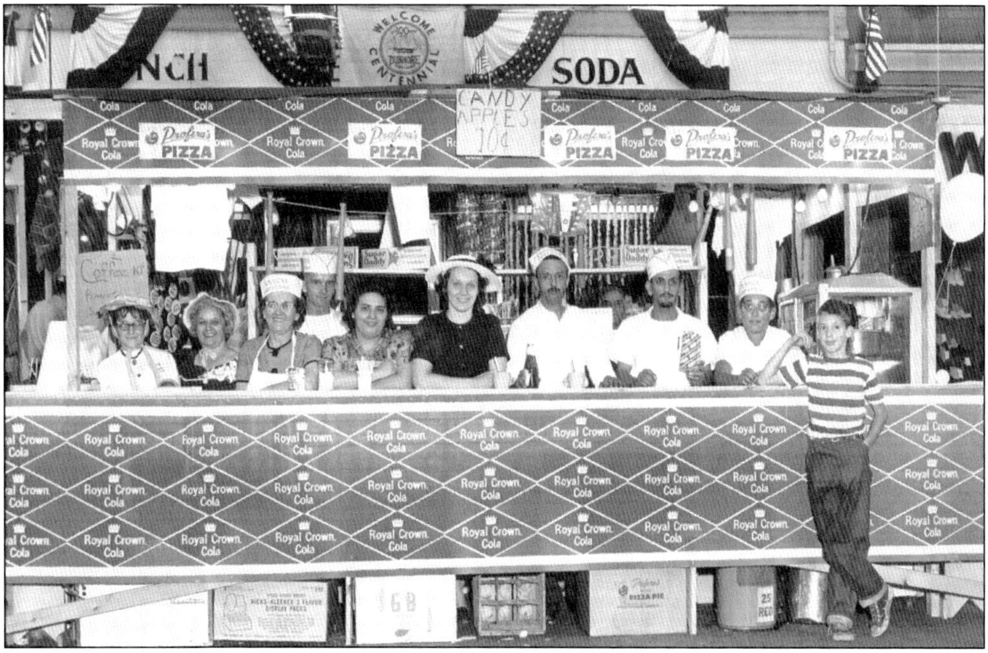

The Dunmore Candy Kitchen has been a town staple for decades. Here is the Dunmore Candy Kitchen's stand at the Dunmore Centennial Celebration in 1962. The business still operates out of its original location on Dunmore's Drinker Street near Dunmore Corners. (Courtesy of the Dunmore Historical Society.)

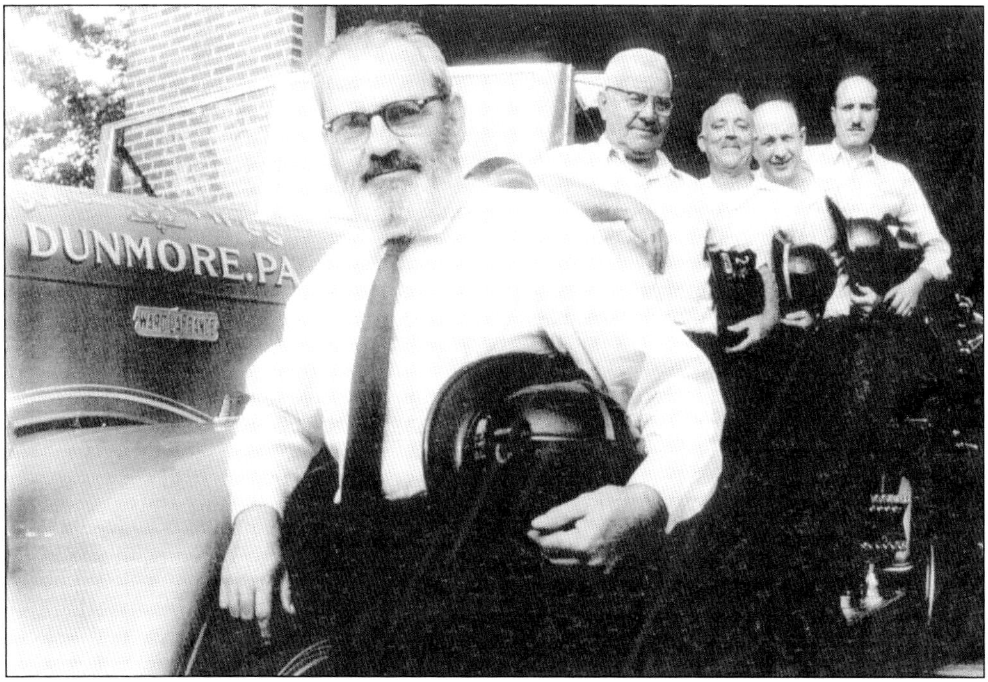

The crew of Dunmore's Engine No. 1, led by Andrew Bednar, is ready to leave for the centennial parade. Behind Bednar, from left to right are Jerry Durkin, Frank Castellano, Eugene Brady, and Frank Genett. (Courtesy of the Dunmore Historical Society.)

Pennsylvania governor David L. Lawrence crowns 19-year-old Carol Sandone as "Miss Dunmore" during a coronation ball held at Scranton's Masonic Temple, now the Scranton Cultural Center. Also seen are Carol's mother, Mrs. Anthony J. Sandone, and pageboys John Viola (left) and William Coar. (Courtesy of the Dunmore Historical Society.)

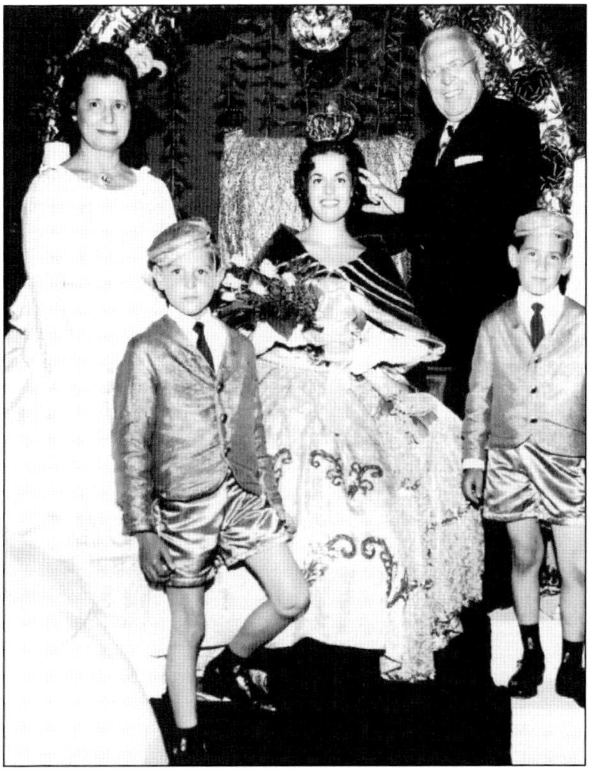

Centennial queen Carol Sandone and her court stand outside of Dunmore High School. Pictured are, from left to right, Cathy Seumenicht, Dawn Tallo, Louise Palumbo, Jeanette Bardini, Carol Sandone, Mary Dolinish, Angela Rinaldi, Jean DeMarco, and Carmel Mecca. (Courtesy of the Dunmore Historical Society.)

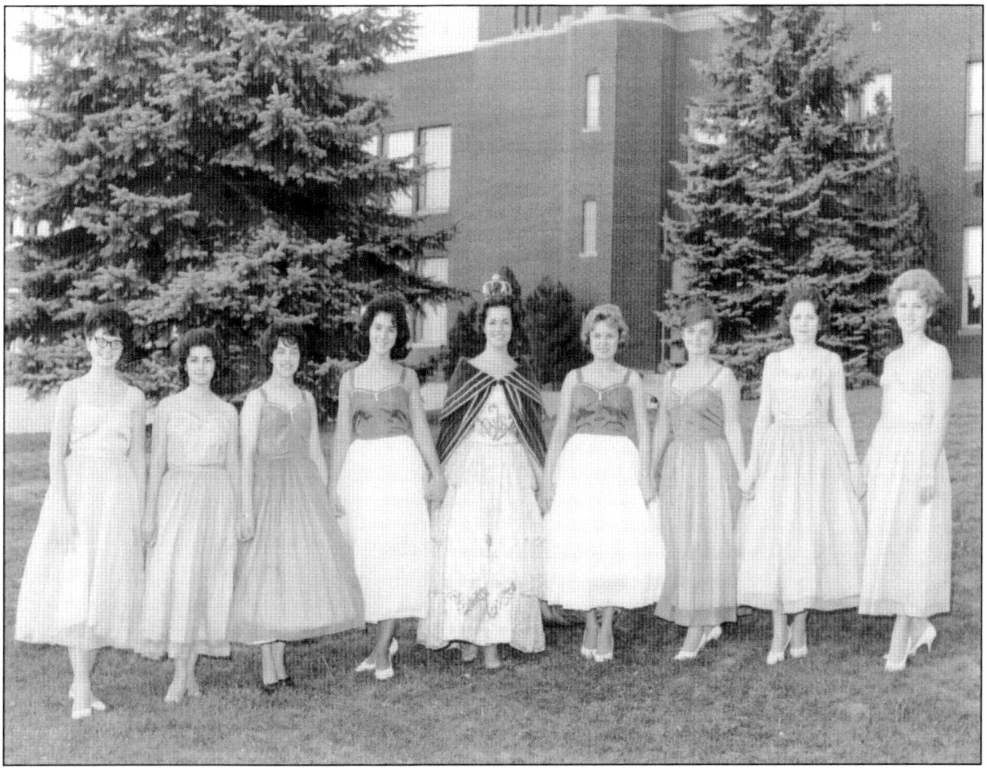

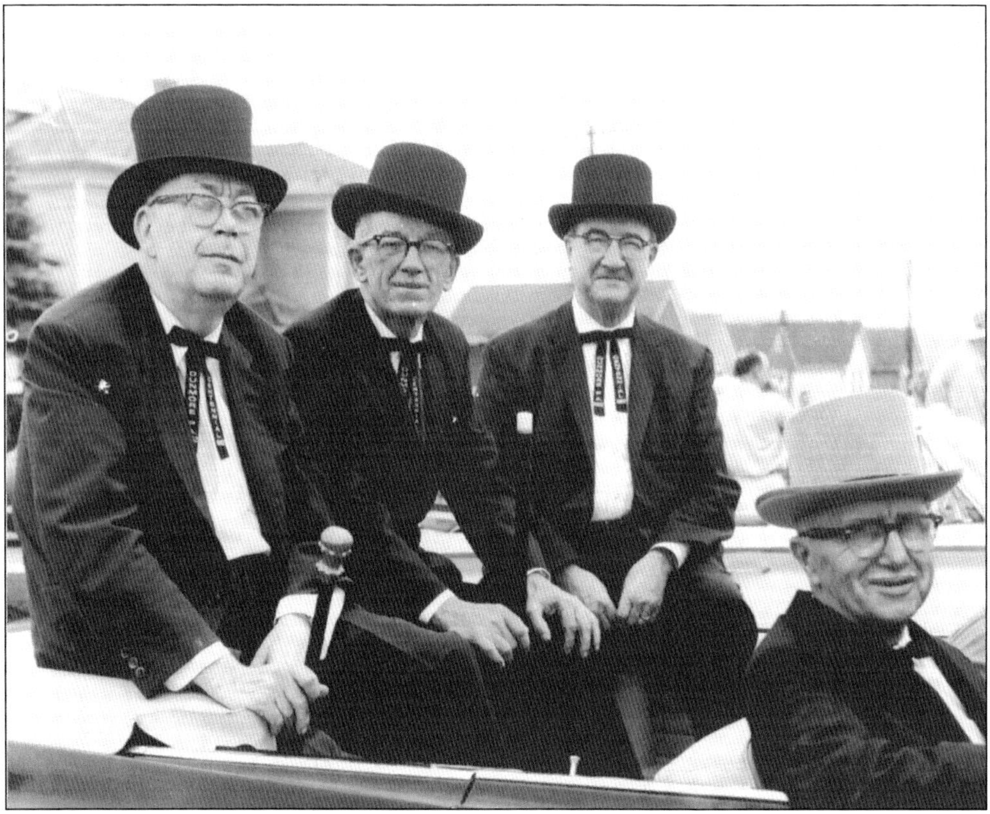

Heading the Dunmore Centennial Parade on September 1, 1962, were, from left to right, Edward J. Lynett, *Scranton Times* editor and publisher as grand marshal; Mayor Martin F. Monahan; borough tax collector M.J. "Joe" Kearney; and centennial general chairman Michael J. Cannon. (Courtesy of the Dunmore Historical Society.)

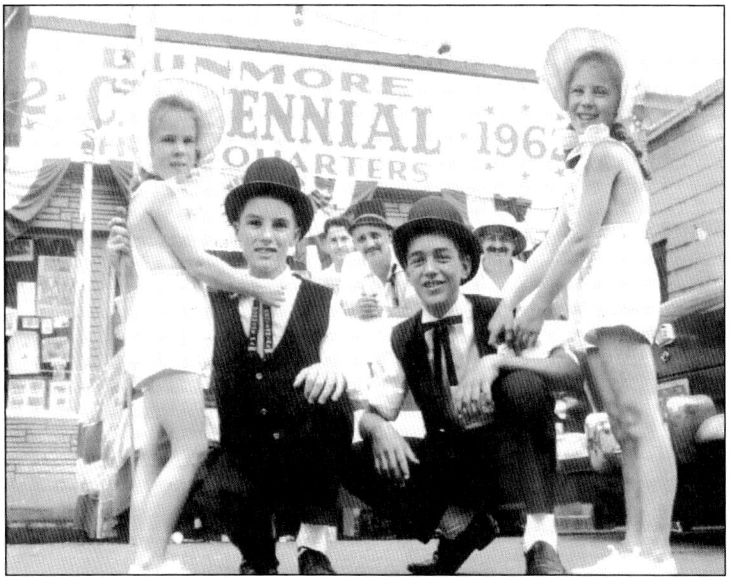

Children are seen lined up in front of the Dunmore Centennial Headquarters before the centennial parade. Pictured are, from left to right, Linda Davis, 6; David Williams, 14; Michael Incavido, 12; and Gayle Davis, 8. (Courtesy of the Dunmore Historical Society.)

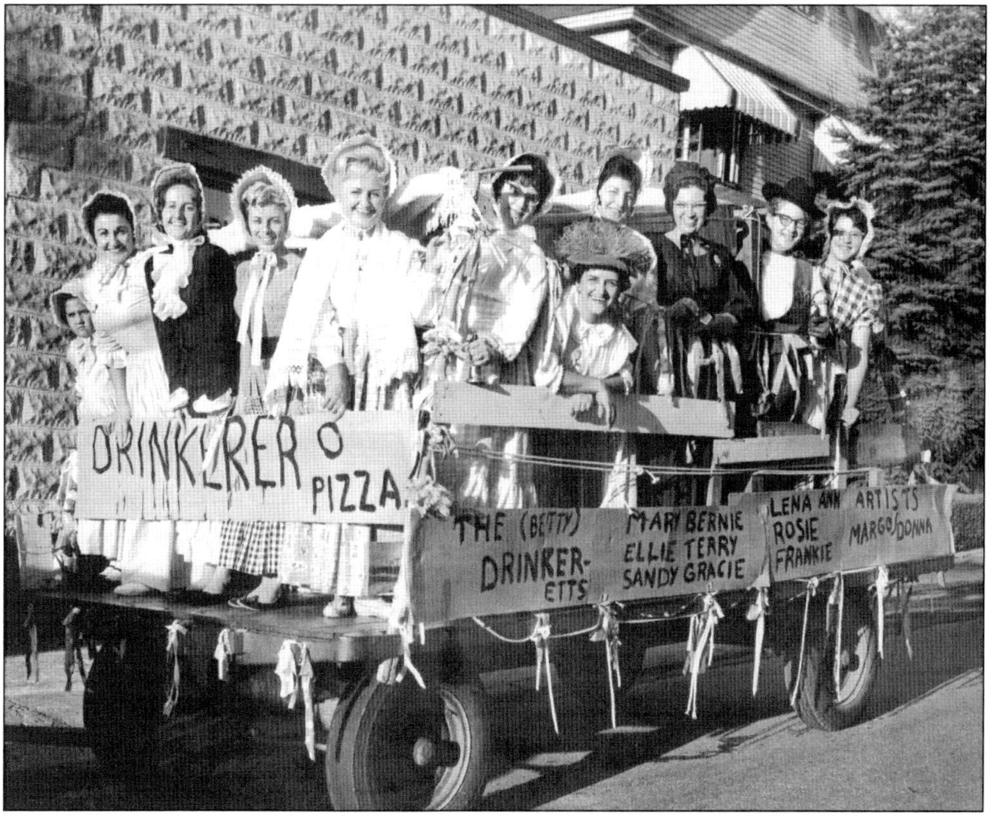

This Dunmore Centennial Parade photograph shows the "Drinkerette Belles" of Drinker Pizza during a smaller centennial parade held on August 15, 1962. Officers of the Belles were Rose Santarelli, high bustle; Rita Bio and Pat Dougherty, main stays; Eleanor Shenko, silver belle; Grace Galasso, Suzy quill; Mary Mafullo, "Calamity Jane"; and Theresa Galasso, deputy. (Courtesy of the Dunmore Historical Society.)

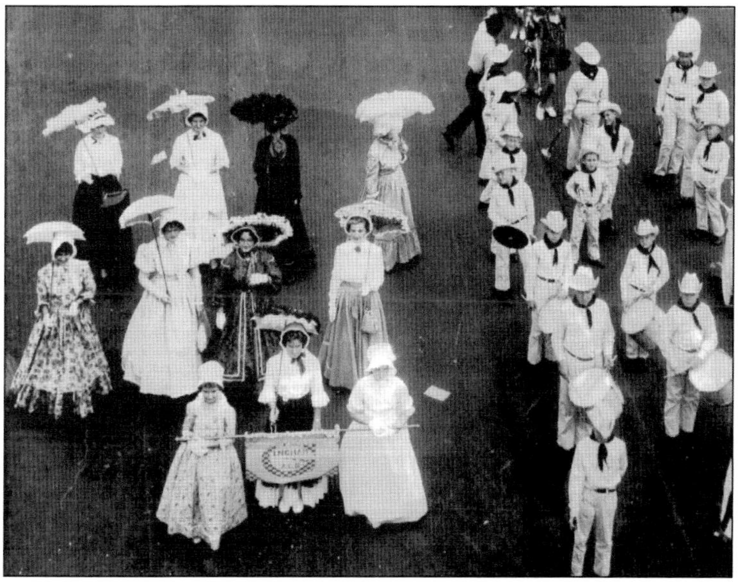

The Gingham Gals walk alongside the Boy Scout band at the Dunmore Centennial Parade on September 1, 1962. (Courtesy of the Dunmore Historical Society.)

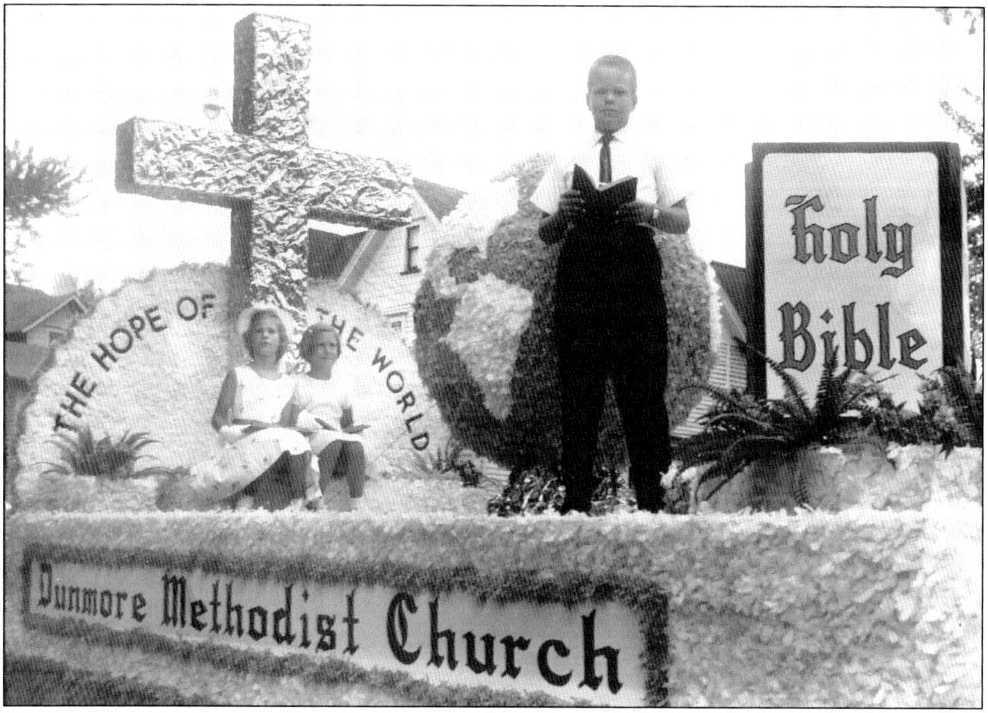

The Dunmore Methodist Church's Centennial Parade float had as its theme "The Bible: The Hope of the World." (Courtesy of the Dunmore Historical Society.)

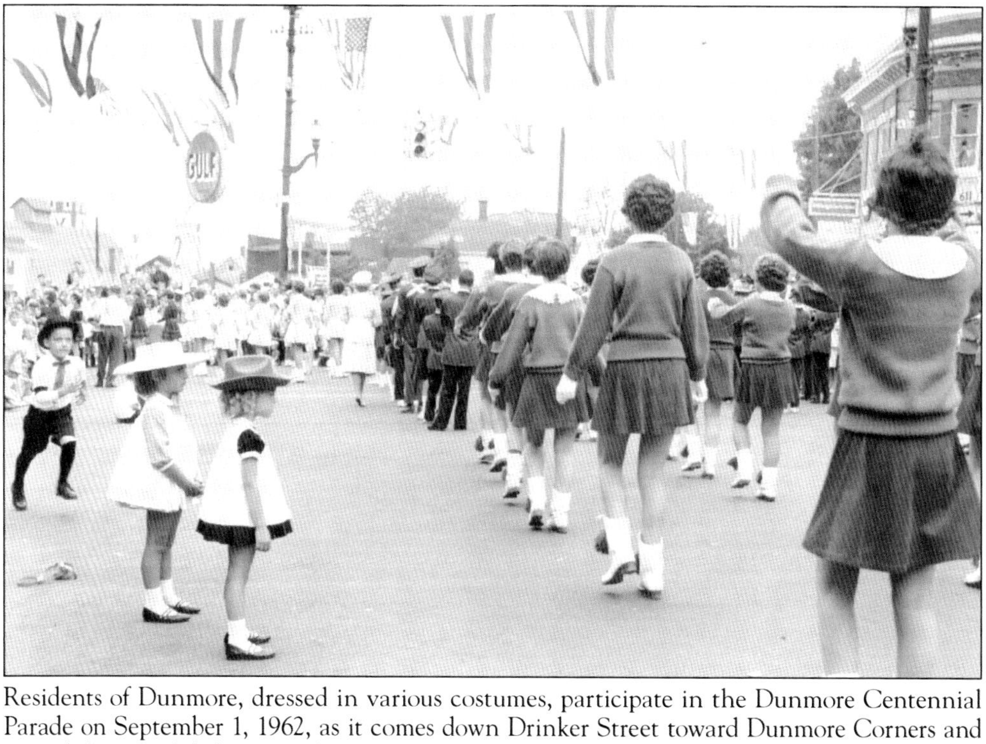

Residents of Dunmore, dressed in various costumes, participate in the Dunmore Centennial Parade on September 1, 1962, as it comes down Drinker Street toward Dunmore Corners and turns left onto Blakely Street. (Courtesy of the Dunmore Historical Society.)

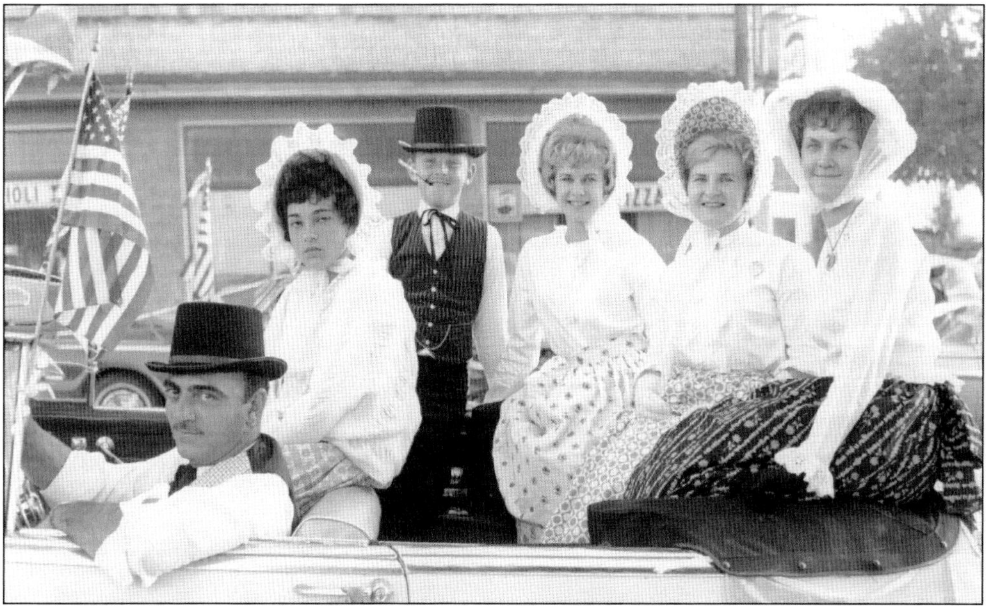

The Santarelli family rides down Drinker Street as a part of the Dunmore Centennial Parade. The driver is John Santarelli, and seated next to him is Linda Santarelli, followed by Jack Santarelli. In the back seat are, from left to right, Sandi Jacusky, Mrs. John Santarelli, and Florrie Boreshesky. (Courtesy of the Dunmore Historical Society.)

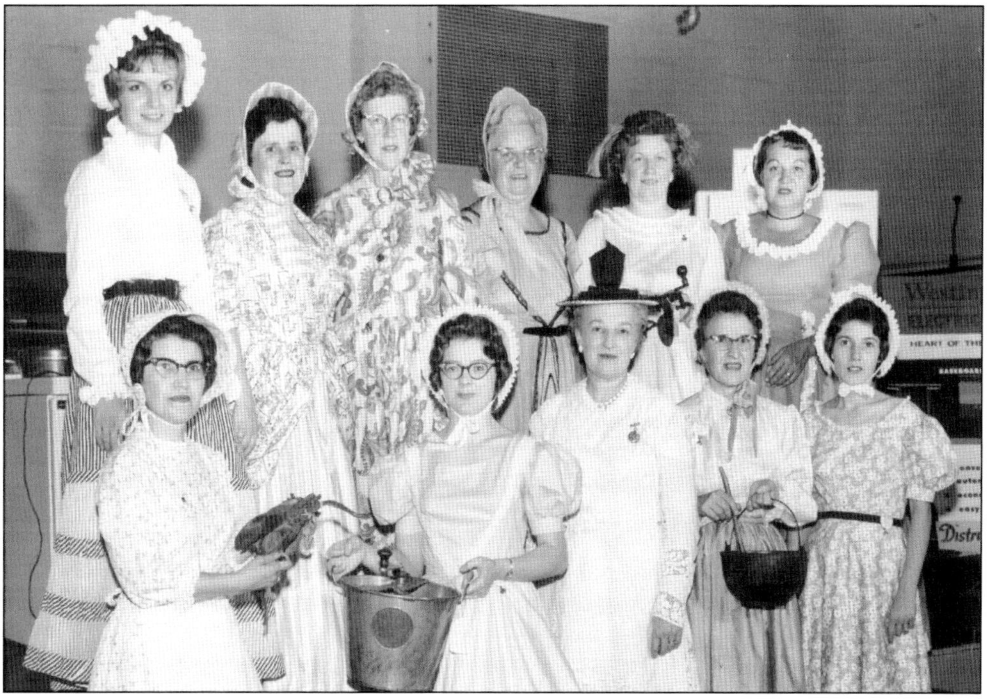

Another part of the parade-day activities was a demonstration at Dunmore High School by Ethel Gyomory, a home service economist at the Pennsylvania Power and Light Company, seen in the front row at left, comparing cooking and washing equipment of the 1860s with their 1960s counterparts. (Courtesy of the Dunmore Historical Society.)

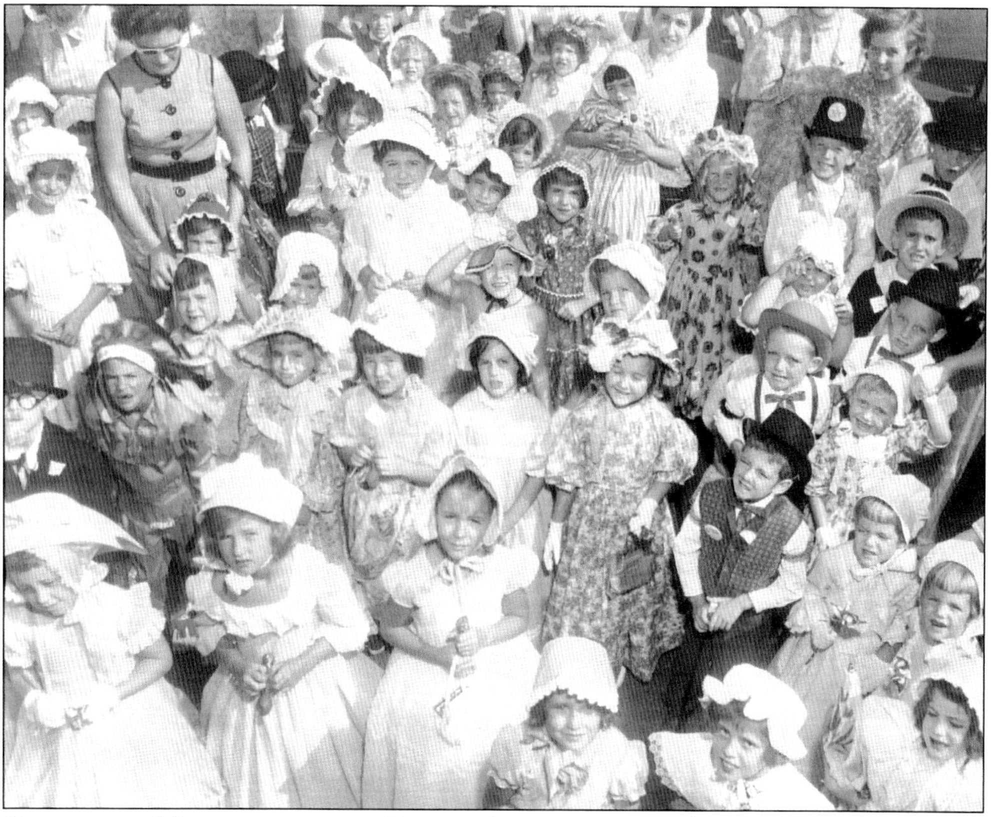

Contestants of the junior centennial king and queen contest gather at Dunmore Corners on parade day, September 1, 1962. Winners, chosen at random later that day, included John Michael Cuff as junior king and Barbara Ann Nealon as junior queen. Other winners included Mary Pat Flannelly and Paula Clemens. The contest was open to children between the ages of four and seven. (Courtesy of the Dunmore Historical Society.)

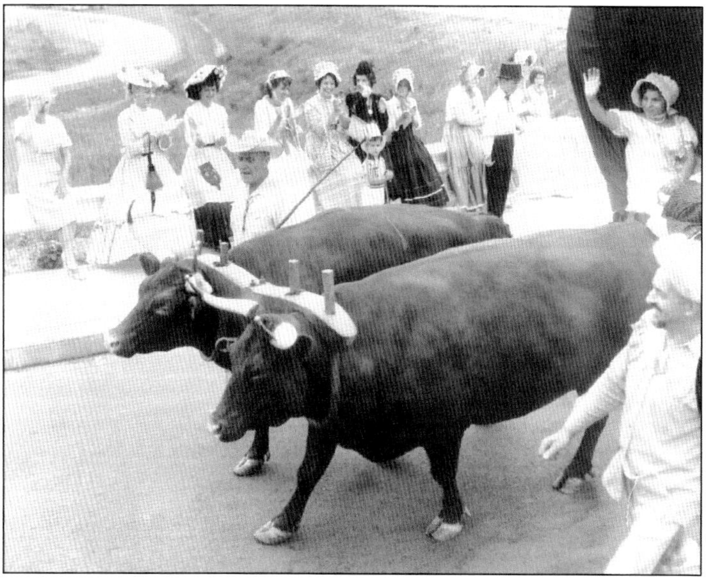

A team of oxen waits to take its turn in line in the Dunmore Centennial Parade. The parade began at the Anthracite Expressway (now part of Interstate 81) and proceeded over Drinker Street through Dunmore Corners and ended at Quincy Avenue. (Courtesy of the Dunmore Historical Society.)

Staff members of Fidelity Deposit and Discount Bank pose on the bank steps facing Drinker Street during the Dunmore Centennial Parade. Pictured are, from left to right, (first row) Frances Banick, Rosemary DelRosario Summa, Carm Demlo, Frances Fontanella, Sue Knickerbaker, Angie Rinaldi, and Carmel Ann Rinaldi (second row) Mary Ann Reinfurt, Marian Kalibah, Marie Lettieri, Pat Simrell, and Joyce Jordan. (Courtesy of Rosemary Summa.)

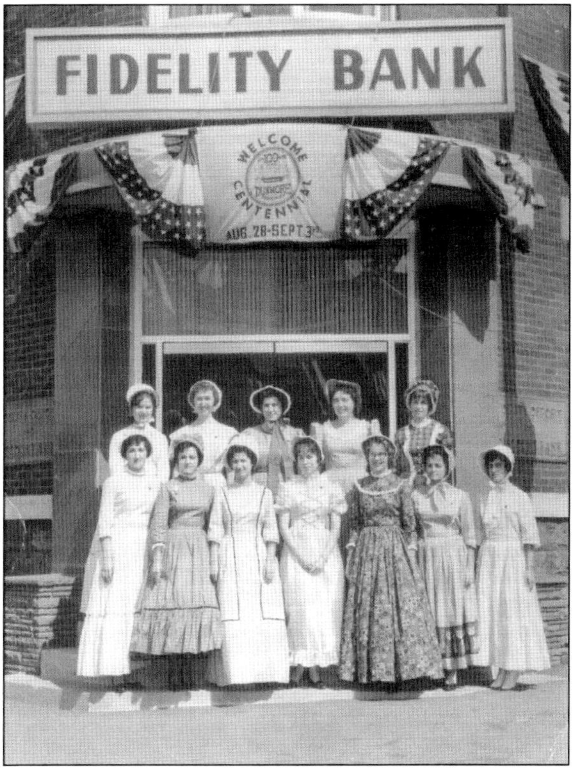

Women dressed in 1860s fashions walk down Drinker Street through Dunmore Corners during the Centennial Parade on September 1, 1962. As Dunmore plans to celebrate its 150th anniversary in 2012, it still tries to remember its proud past while looking toward its future. (Courtesy of the Dunmore Historical Society.)

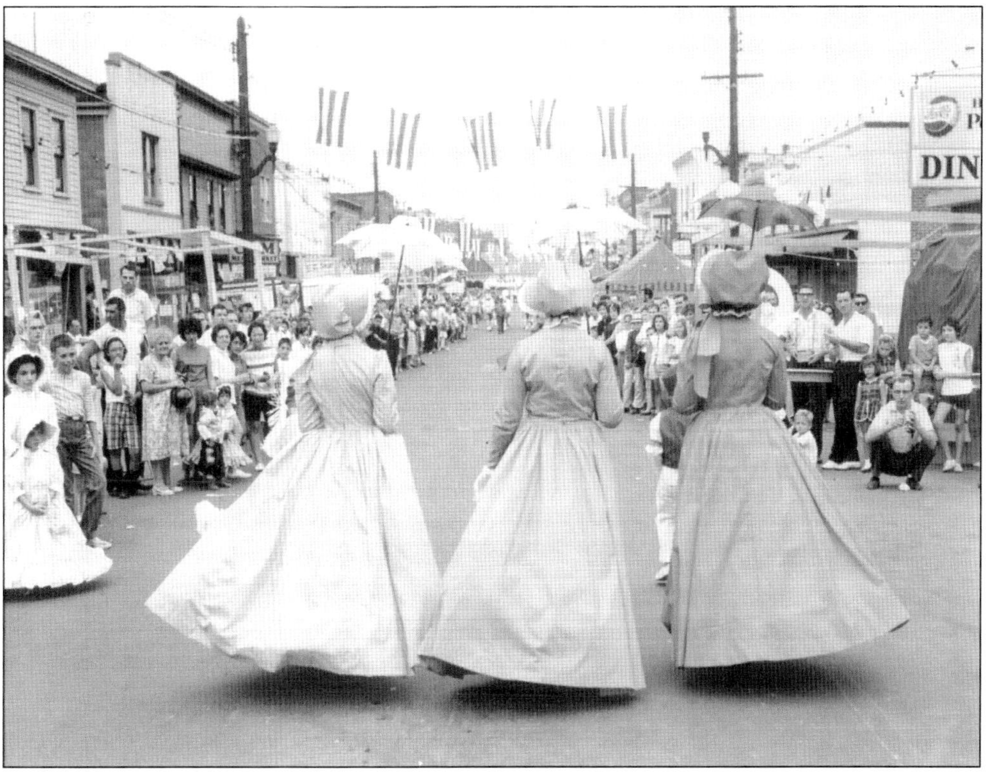

Consistent with our mission to preserve history on a local level, this book was printed in South Carolina on American-made paper and manufactured entirely in the United States. Products carrying the accredited Forest Stewardship Council (FSC) label are printed on 100 percent FSC-certified paper.

MADE IN THE USA